WE ARE
DOOMED

WE ARE
DOOMED

RECLAIMING **CONSERVATIVE** PESSIMISM

by
JOHN
DERBYSHIRE

THREE RIVERS PRESS
NEW YORK

Originally published in hardcover in the United States by Crown Forum,
an imprint of the Crown Publishing Group, a division of Random House, Inc.,
New York, in 2009.

Grateful acknowledgment is made to the following for permission to reprint
previously published material:

Black Sparrow Books: Excerpt from "Patriotic Poem" from *Emerald Ice: Selected
Poems 1962–1987* by Diane Wakoski, copyright © 1988 by Diane Wakoski.
Reprinted by permission of Black Sparrow Books, an imprint of David R. Godine,
Publisher.

The Overlook Press: Excerpt from "There are Bad Times Just Around the Corner"
from *The Lyrics of Noël Coward* by Noël Coward, copyright © 1965 by Noël
Coward. Reprinted by permission of The Overlook Press, New York, NY.

Library of Congress Cataloging-in-Publication Data is available.

ISBN 978-0-307-40959-1

Design by Lauren Dong

First Paperback Edition

146028962

FOR WALLY FEKULA

Brief is the season of man's delight.

—PINDAR, *Pythian Ode*, No.8

CONTENTS

A CALL TO PESSIMISM

The heart of the wise is in the house of mourning; but the heart of fools is in the house of mirth.

—ECCLESIASTES 7:4

THE POLITICS OF DESPAIR

This book is addressed to American conservatives. Its argument is that things are bad and getting worse for our movement, for our nation, and for our civilization. A large part of the reason they have gotten so bad is that too many of us have fallen into foolishly utopian ways of thinking.

Those ways of thinking are false because they are too optimistic about human nature and human affairs. The proper outlook of conservatives, I shall argue, is a pessimistic one, at least so far as the things of this world are concerned. We have been misled, and the conservative movement has been derailed, by legions of fools and poseurs wearing smiley-face masks. I aim to unmask them.

I have both a diagnosis and a prognosis to offer. The diagnosis is that conservatism has been fatally weakened by yielding to infantile temptations: temptations to optimism, to wishful thinking, to happy talk, to cheerily preposterous theories about human beings and the human world.

Thus weakened, conservatism can no longer provide the backbone of cold realism that every organized society needs. Hence my prognosis; hence my title. We are doomed.

By abandoning our properly pessimistic approach to the world, conservatives have helped bring about a state of affairs that thoughtful persons can only contemplate with pessimism. If we'd held on to the pessimistic outlook that's proper for our philosophy, the future might be brighter!

This looks like a paradox, but really isn't, as I'm using the word "pessimism" in two slightly different senses: to indicate low expectations of one's fellow men, and to name a belief about the probable future. If we expect too much of people, we'll be disappointed, and our schemes will fail. Heady optimism about human nature leads directly to disaster. To put it in the style of John Bunyan's *Pilgrim's Progress:* the Road of Denial leads to the Precipice of Destruction. Didn't the great utopian experiments of the twentieth century teach us that? We've repeated those experiments—in a less brazen way, to be sure, but with the same inevitable result now coming upon us.

By embracing a proper conservative pessimism, we may yet rescue something from the coming ruin. At the very least, by returning to cold reality after our recent detour into sunny fantasy, we'll put ourselves in the right frame of mind for our new life in the wilderness.

The winning candidate in the 2008 presidential election promoted something called "the politics of hope." Ladies and gentlemen of conservative inclination, I call you to our true, our proper home. I call you to the politics of despair!

THE SCOPE OF THE ARGUMENT

This book is about what we have done to ourselves, to our society and culture. It's about the hopelessness of any project to save the situation based on current conservatism, perverted as it has been by smiley-face schemes of human improvement. It's about composing ourselves to a true view of humanity and human affairs, so that we can get through our individual destinies usefully and with maximum peace of mind in the dark age to come, preserving as much as can be preserved. Who knows? Once back in touch with truth, we might even see a revival of real conservatism: self-support, patriotism, limited government, federalism . . . though of course, I don't hold out *much* hope.

Please be clear about the scope of the pessimism I urge on you. Don't mistake my thesis for any of those tabloid Chicken Little prognostications about particular economic, ecological, military, or cosmic misfortunes we may be able to science our way out of.

Have we reached Peak Oil? *I* don't know. (Neither, so far as I can gather from some extensive reading in this area, does anyone else.) Will global warming melt the polar ice caps? Sorry, I have no clue. Are suitcase nuclear weapons secreted in our cities awaiting a word of command from some terrorist mastermind or malevolent dictator? I really couldn't say. Shall we fall to some plague, some runaway particle-physics experiment, some asteroid strike or other celestial mishap? Or will human nature itself disappear into a "singularity" around the middle of this century, as futurologist Ray Kurzweil predicts? Beats my pair of jacks.

My book is not primarily about any of those things, though speaking as a constitutional pessimist, I'd lay odds that one or other of them is lurking just round the historical corner. Things are bad and getting worse, any fool can see that, but I pin my dark banner to no one particular prediction. Despair should be large and general, not petty and particular.

Nor does my scope extend beyond this human state and this earthly life. Possibly there are other states and other lives. Though no longer an adherent of any religion, I maintain an open mind on these issues. They are in any case outside the purview of this book. I'm writing about the communal arrangements of a particular social mammal on a particular planet. Believe what you like about matters beyond that; this book isn't concerned with them.

THE HAPPY PESSIMIST

That's all very well, you may say, but isn't pessimism enervating? If all is for the worst for us in this, the worst of all possible worlds, why bother? Why not sit around vegetating in a state of glum *melancholia*, like the angel in Dürer's fine engraving of that name?

That would be to misunderstand the nature of a thoughtful, considered pessimism. There is no necessary connection between a pessimistic outlook and a melancholy temperament. At most I'll allow that having a naturally glum disposition makes it easier to attain an understanding of human depravity, contrariety, mental incoherence, and imperfectibility. I myself do have such a disposition, and won't be trying to hide behind any fake jollity. Later in this book, in fact, I shall present some actual *science* suggesting that a glum melancholic is just the person you want to go to for the truth about human affairs. Yet plenty of active, convivial, and useful people have a pessimistic outlook. Some of them have done important things to improve their societies and lift up their fellow men.

Here are some of the gloomiest lines in all of English literature. They are by the poet Matthew Arnold:

> . . . *the world, which seems*
> *To lie before us like a land of dreams,*
> *So various, so beautiful, so new,*
> *Hath really neither joy, nor love, nor light,*
> *Nor certitude, nor peace, nor help for pain;*
> *And we are here as on a darkling plain*
> *Swept with confused alarms of struggle and flight,*
> *Where ignorant armies clash by night.*

Arnold was a witty and sociable man who loved sport and companionship. He worked hard at useful employment, was happily married to the same lady for thirty-seven years, and was a loving father to his six children.

Enervating? Not at all: Pessimism is *bracing*, like foul weather. (Arnold and I were both raised in England.)

It also makes you a better person. Consider the optimist Jean-Jacques Rousseau, who believed human beings to be innately good and who laid the philosophical foundations for progressive, "child-centered" methods of education. Rousseau was, by his own admission, a thief, a liar, a sexual exhibitionist, and a philanderer. He cohabited with a coarse and illiterate woman, to whom he was not faithful, and deposited the five children he gave her in orphanages because he did not want the trouble of raising them.

We pessimists, you see, are not only wiser than the smiley-face crowd; we are *better people*. This is no mere biological accident. We are better people because we know that most of the improvements that can be made in human affairs must be made by us ourselves—by individuals and small voluntary associations. Efforts at improvement by organizations much larger than that will come to naught, or even make things worse, if not based on a clear understanding of human ignorance and weakness.

That's the core of a proper conservative pessimism: the recognition that there is little hope for improvement in this world; that such small hope as there is should be directed toward the actions of one, or a few; and that most of what governments do is wicked, when not merely pointless and counterproductive.

There is work to be done; there is life to be lived; there are children to be raised, friendships to be cultivated, bills to be paid, and many pleasures to be enjoyed. You may feel, after reading my book, that there is no point in bothering with any of those things. You may even decide to head for the exit. If so, I hope you'll drop me a line, care of my publisher, before doing so, in order that I might have a chance at dissuading you. I'd be distressed to think that my book, in its modest passage through the world, had left widows and orphans in its wake.

Should you choose to stick around, I hope that you'll keep yourself busy with something useful, and try to be a good citizen. There is no reason *not* to. Jails and asylums are uncomfortable places, life on the streets is unhygienic and dangerous, and nobody will pay you a salary to sit around brooding in *melancholia*. That figure in Dürer's engraving is a symbolic personification, not an Employee of the Month.

IT'S ONLY NATURAL

I understand, of course, that many American conservatives will hesitate to accept my argument. Isn't this the country of infinite possibility, where all problems are solvable and all futures bright? Isn't optimism a part of the American creed, part of our very national essence? Yes, we can!—Can't we?

To the degree any of that is true, it is because liberals have declared it so. The original European settlers of North America were very pessimistic indeed, to a degree modern minds can hardly encompass. The Calvinist Congregationalists of New England even managed to be pessimistic about the Afterlife. Says historian David Hackett Fischer in his splendid book *Albion's Seed:*

> The fabled "Five Points" of New England's Calvinist Orthodoxy insisted that the natural condition of humanity was total depravity, that salvation was beyond mortal striving, that grace was predestined only for a few, that most mortals were condemned to suffer eternal damnation, and no earthly effort could save them.

The embreeched, powdered-wigged gentlemen of the Tidewater South were hardly any more hopeful. The corresponding section in Fischer's book has the heading "Virginia Death Ways: The Anglican Idea of Stoic Fatalism." That idea was entirely appropriate to the circumstances of the Tidewater region, whose climate and geography made for terribly high death rates—perhaps twice as high as in rural New England.

All this pessimism fit very well into the circumstances of early-colonial life. When Europeans first came to North America, it was a very wild place indeed. Those early settlers lived close to nature; and the natural world is a pitiless one. That's a fact known to few of us nowadays. I've only just recently come to appreciate it myself.

Getting acquainted with human-nature studies these past few years (see Chapter 7), I've found that the people who talk the most sense are types who have a strong interest in nature itself—or "herself," as they tend to say. Sure, you can sit in your study and introspect, or buy a shelf of philosophy courses from the Teaching Company. For sheer insight into the living world, though—including the human world—nothing can beat the kind of scientist who started out with a bug collection at age eleven and never lost his enthusiasm for the teeming, chaotic, cruel, convoluted, fantastically interconnected world of nature. Edward O. Wilson, whom I shall surely be quoting before I get through with this book, is a star example; another is of course Charles Darwin.

Annie Dillard came to nature somewhat later than that, but she struck a true note in her Pulitzer Prize–winning 1974 book about the Blue Ridge Mountains of western Virginia, *Pilgrim at Tinker Creek.*

> Evolution loves death more than it loves you or me . . . we are moral creatures, then, in an amoral world. The universe that suckled us is a monster that does not care if we live or die—does not care if it itself grinds to a halt . . . space is a beauty married to a blind man. The blind man is Freedom, or Time, and he does not go anywhere without his great dog Death.

I once took a walk with a biologist friend, Rob Woodman, in California's San Bernardino National Forest. Rob paused every few yards to show me some insect, leaf, or worm, and to tell me its story. Stories everywhere—in every fold of every leaf, in every handful of soil, in every broken-off piece from a rotting tree trunk, a story! The plots of the stories were Dillardesque: birth, struggle, mayhem, pain, death.

This all came new to me, a revelation. I'm an indoor sort of person, with no innate, unprompted interest in the natural world. My sensibility is that of Dorothy Parker: "Every year, back spring comes, with the nasty little birds yapping their fool heads off, and the ground all mucked up with arbutus." I've read enough to learn a little humility, though. If you want to get a handle on human nature, listen to the people who know *nature.*

The early settlers of North America knew it very well. They had no illusions about the gentle beneficence of the natural order. If they had, there were always bears, wolves, and crop failures to remind them of the biological facts.

If they had known more, they would have had an even darker view. If, for example, those Tidewater Anglicans had known that the diseases that swept away their loved ones in hecatombs were not signs of God's displeasure at our fallen state, but the blind actions of unthinking microbes and viruses, devoid of any personal interest in humanity, they would have reached conclusions about nature very close to Annie Dillard's.

THE RISE OF HAPPY TALK

On such noble pessimism was our republic founded. Out of such grimly low expectations for the possibility of worldly happiness was our Constitution born.

The optimistic rot set in as Calvinism gave way to Unitarianism in the later eighteenth century. The 1805 election of Henry Ware Sr., a Unitarian, to the Professorship of Divinity at Harvard University prepared the way for the great liberal-optimist flowering of the Transcendentalist movement in the 1830s and 1840s. Henry Ware Jr., the professor's son, was friend and mentor to Ralph Waldo Emerson, a key progenitor of modern smiley-face liberalism, and a person who, in my opinion, ought to be burned in effigy at the commencement of every conservative gathering.

The fine original pessimism of our nation's founders had been set aside, and the modern style of vaporous happy talk had been born.

To be fair to the happy talkers, their movement arose from a perceived need, as all intellectual and social movements do, and in the vigor of its youth it contributed to some necessary reforms. The social condition of women improved, slavery was abolished, gross and promiscuous drunkenness was abated, and a more humane attitude to our vanquished aborigines emerged.

All good ideas are of their time, though, and are liable to turn from blessings into blights if persisted in too long. The justifiable right of workers to organize in protection of their interests turned at last into featherbedding, the Teamster rackets, auto companies made uncompetitive by extravagant benefits agreements, and government-worker unions voting themselves ever-bigger shares of the public fisc. The campaign for full civil rights and racial justice turned into affirmative action, race quotas, grievance lawsuits, the Reverend Jeremiah Wright, and everlasting racial rancor.

The point of diminishing returns for American progressive optimism had long since been reached by the time Prohibition came along to demonstrate beyond any doubt that the optimists' program had turned into a war on human nature.

TWILIGHT IN AMERICA

But hold on there! (I hear you cry) What about Ronald Reagan? Wasn't he the very epitome of modern conservatism? And didn't he present a cheerful face to the world, scoff at his predecessor's diagnosis of "malaise," and proclaim Morning in America?

Again, this is to confuse a sunny disposition with a well-thought-out conviction that earthly affairs cannot be much improved by the hand of man—most certainly not by the hand of government.

Reagan, like Matthew Arnold, was a cheerful and busy fellow, but the good he did in government, he did chiefly with a pessimist's restraint. He did not follow the 1983 bombing of a U.S. barracks in Lebanon by invading and occupying that country with the dream of turning it into a constitutional democracy, as a smiley-face world-improver would have done; he pulled out. He did not, like his liberal predecessor, chide his countrymen for their "inordinate fear of communism"; he shared that gloomy fear, speaking of the Soviet Union in frank, dark terms, not as a regrettable but correctable error on the part of well-meaning reformers—Emersonian Transcendentalists who had taken a wrong turn on the road to Walden Pond—but as an "evil empire."

A very rough index of an American president's faith in plans for social or international uplift is his willingness to veto legislation. There are many variables in play here—most obviously, whether president and Congress are of the same party—but veto counts offer at least an approximate clue about presidential skepticism toward political schemes for human uplift.

Ronald Reagan's annualized rate of vetoes across his term of office was 10, the same as William Howard Taft's. This puts Reagan and Taft at ninth in the rankings. Just below them at tenth stand McKinley, Coolidge, and Hoover, with 9 vetoes per annum apiece. Above, in eighth place, are Teddy Roosevelt and Benjamin Harrison with 11. Above them stand Grant with 12 vetoes per annum, Eisenhower with 23, and fourth-ranked Gerry Ford with 27. Republicans all! Reagan noted in his diary entry for July 9, 1987: "Every pen I look at is a veto pen to me."

(It is true that the top three scorers here are all Democrats: Truman with 32, FDR with 52, and Grover Cleveland with an astounding average of 73 vetoes per annum. These were all very special cases, though—notably Cleveland, a fine classical-conservative liberal—"libertarian," we would say nowadays—and every conservative Republican's favorite Democrat. George W. Bush's score was a wretchedly hypercompassionate 1.5—12 vetoes in eight years.)

A pessimistic president knows that, as the great Calvin Coolidge told his father, "it is much more important to kill bad bills than to pass good ones." Most of what legislators legislate and executives execute is foolish, counterproductive, or downright wicked, so the less they do the better.

Coolidge is, in fact, a key figure here: a great pessimist and a great conservative, from sound New England Calvinist/Congregationalist roots—a backcountry pre-Transcendentalist in spirit, in spite of having been born shortly after Emerson's sixty-ninth birthday. Coolidge's mature philosophical outlook was formed by the charismatic Amherst teacher C. E. Garman, an orthodox New England Congregationalist: "a cheerful, happy man" according to his classmate Clarence Sargent, who nonetheless taught a stern philosophy of service and integrity.

Historian Paul Johnson, who made a close study of Coolidge, described him thus: "A constitutionally suspicious man, and not one to believe easily that permanent contentment is to be found this side of eternity."

One of Coolidge's greatest admirers was . . . Ronald Reagan. On entering the White House in 1981, Reagan had Coolidge's portrait hung in the Oval Office, replacing Harry Truman's.

WRONG BUT WROMANTIC

In any case, Reagan's "Morning in America" rhetoric needs to be discounted for a certain understandable triumphalism. By the time Reagan attained office the outcome of the Cold War was not in much doubt. America's social and economic system was obviously superior to the Soviet command-economy police state. The End of History was in plain sight, and it was clear that one pole of the bipolar world would soon melt away, leaving the United States as top dog: secure, unchallenged, and far ahead of the rest of the world in freedom and prosperity. (The negative consequences of all *that* were well out of sight over the horizon.) Under those circumstances, even pessimists could be forgiven for some lapses into happy talk.

Another great conservative pessimist—there have been so many!—the British Tory anarchist Enoch Powell, said: "All political lives . . . end in failure, because that is the nature of politics and of human affairs." I believe Ronald Reagan would have agreed with him. Here is journalist, novelist, and playwright George Packer:

According to [Patrick] Buchanan, who was the White House communications director in Reagan's second term, the President once told his barber, Milton Pitts, "You know, Milt, I came here to do five things, and four out of five ain't bad." He had succeeded in lowering taxes, raising morale, increasing defense spending, and facing down the Soviet Union; but he had failed to limit the size of government, which, besides anti-Communism, was the abiding passion of Reagan's political career and of the conservative movement. He didn't come close to achieving it and didn't try very hard, recognizing early that the public would be happy to have its taxes cut as long as its programs weren't touched.

There is a fuller exposition of this melancholy truth about the Reagan administration in Chapter 3 of David Frum's 1994 book *Dead Right.* The chapter is titled "The Failure of the Reagan Gambit."

I note in passing that the following chapter in *Dead Right* is titled "Optimists: Wrong but Wromantic." Just so. Frum took that phrase from W. C. Sellar and R. J. Yeatman's spoof British-history book *1066 and All That,* where the English Civil War of the seventeenth century is defined as a "struggle between the Cavaliers (Wrong but Wromantic) and the Roundheads (Right and Repulsive)." Now I ask you, conservative reader: Given a choice between being Wrong but Wromantic or Right and Repulsive, *are you going to hesitate for even a nanosecond?*

Ronald Reagan was far too astute a man not to have known that "the abiding passion of [his] political career and of the conservative movement" was a hopeless passion, one that the world—which in this context mainly means the U.S. electorate—would never requite; one that the conservative movement itself was soon to abjure with cheery insouciance, having convinced itself that humanity can be improved by the spending of public money.

CHILDREN OF WRATH

Back in the late 1960s, when the sectarian problems of Northern Ireland were heating up, the British home secretary (roughly equivalent to a U.S. attorney general) went over to the province to pour oil on the troubled waters.

This home secretary was a fellow named James Callaghan. A cheerful, back-slapping type, Callaghan was nicknamed "Sunny Jim." If anyone could do the oil-pouring business, Sunny Jim surely could.

As part of his tour, Callaghan had a meeting with the fiercely sectarian Unionist (which is to say, Protestant, and in fact Presbyterian-

Calvinist) politician, the Reverend Ian Paisley. Paisley launched himself into a long rant about the wickedness of the Roman Catholic Church, the perfidy of its priests, and the gullibility and treachery of its adherents.

Callaghan listened patiently until Paisley stopped to draw breath. Then he said in his best oil-pouring tones: "Come, come, Mr. Paisley. Are we not all the children of God?"

Paisley (who only ever speaks in capital letters): "NO, SIR. WE ARE THE CHILDREN OF WRATH."

Whatever you may think of Paisley's politics, sectarianism, or personality, his view of the human condition was surely a sound one. We are indeed the children of Wrath. All wisdom proceeds from this. Truly, the heart of the wise is in the house of mourning.

WIPE THAT SMILE OFF YOUR FACE

Abandon hope, then, all ye who enter here; or, if you must cling to sunny anticipations, place the objects of your hope in some place other than the one you and I currently inhabit; for this is a darkling plain, a vale of tears. Happy talk and wishful thinking are for children, fools, and leftists. We are conservatives. We know better. At any rate, we used to.

Let us then explore the badlands of current society and culture, whose soil has been turned to dust by the poisonous optimism of fools. Where to begin? Perhaps in the deepest depths of self-deceiving happy-talk folly, where dwell the smiliest smiley faces of all, those who promote the great modern ideological cult of Diversity.

2

DIVERSITY: NOTHING TO CELEBRATE

Once upon a time, Americans encountered the world's diversity with awe, anger, prejudice, erotic excitement, pity, delight—and curiosity. Then we recast ourselves as champions of tolerant diversity, became fearful of inconvenient facts, and lost interest.

—FROM PETER WOOD'S *Diversity:*
The Invention of a Concept (2002)

RODNEY KING'S QUESTION

"People, I just want to say, you know, can we all get along?" Thus Rodney King, responding to the Los Angeles riots of April 1992.

What's the answer to Rodney King's question? *Can* we all get along? Different opinions are possible, but the pessimistic answer is plainly "No." That is also, I believe, the correct answer. In this chapter I'll try to justify that belief.

Issues of race and ethnicity have been central to U.S. history. One of them helped bring about our bloodiest war. When we talk among ourselves about routine social topics—education, crime, "the culture"—they are never far from the front of our minds. We tend to default to thinking about these things in the traditional terms of black and white, but the last forty years have changed the old patterns. Massive immigration from our south has given the United States a self-consciously "Hispanic"—mainly indigenous-American or mestizo (mixed-race)—subpopulation, now actually bigger than the black one. East Asians, South Asians, Middle Easterners, and Polynesians have added to the mix. And the present-day cult of Diversity of course encompasses much more than race and ethnicity. Feminists, Muslims, homosexuals, the disabled, the obese, and a host of lesser identities also clamor for the attentions of the diversity managers.

I'm going to concentrate on the ethnic issue. If we are, as I claim, doomed, it won't be because women have asked for equal pay, or the wheelchair-bound for access ramps, or homosexuals for legal recognition of their unions.

I believe it is possible, though, that the United States might cease to exist as a nation-state because of ethnic conflicts. I think, in fact, this is more likely than not.

WILL THE UNITED STATES SURVIVE UNTIL 2022?

Back in 1969, Soviet dissident Andrei Amalrik wrote an essay with the title "Will the Soviet Union Survive Until 1984?" Some of Amalrik's predictions—notably a Soviet war with China—didn't pan out, but he was wrong by only seven years in his main thesis, and that is pretty darn good as political prognostications go. The U.S. government with all its expensive agencies, including the CIA, didn't do half as well. They overestimated Soviet economic strength to the very end, in some cases by a factor of ten times.

In 2007, having just finished reading Samuel Huntington's book *Who Are We?*, which is a gloomy look at the consequences of massive Hispanic immigration, I attempted to apply Amalrik's method to the United States in a column titled "Will the United States Survive Until 2022?" (Looking forward to fifteen years from 2007, as Amalrik had from 1969.) After discussing the possibilities for political, social, economic, cultural, intellectual, demographic, military, and spiritual failure, I ended with Huntington's remark that "a nation is a fragile thing," and with the following longer quote from his book:

The [American philosophical-Constitutional] Creed is unlikely to retain its salience if Americans abandon the Anglo-Protestant culture in which it has been rooted. A multicultural America will, in time, become a multicreedal America, with groups with different cultures espousing distinctive political values and principles rooted in their particular cultures.

I think that's right. Diversity could doom us.

That is of course the opposite of what all right-thinking Americans are encouraged to believe. Diversity is our strength!—so our politicians and educators tell us. A Google search on that phrase yielded 17,700 hits. Searching on "strength in diversity" got 33,800; "benefits of diversity," a very impressive 285,000. Happy talk, happy talk; but what does the *evidence* say?

PROFESSOR PUTNAM LAYS AN EGG

In September 2006, political scientist Robert Putnam was awarded the Johan Skytte Prize, one of the most prestigious in his field. The prize is awarded in Uppsala, Sweden, by a Scandinavian scholarly association. (Skytte was a seventeenth-century Swedish grandee.)

As usual with such events in the academic world, Putnam presented a research paper to commemorate the event. The paper is titled "*E Pluribus Unum:* Diversity and Community in the Twenty-first Century," and can easily be found on the Internet. I'll refer to it in what follows as "the Uppsala paper."

That paper has a very curious structure. After a brief introduction (two pages), there are three main sections, headed as follows:

- *The Prospects and Benefits of Immigration and Ethnic Diversity* (three pages)
- *Immigration and Diversity Foster Social Isolation* (nineteen pages)
- *Becoming Comfortable with Diversity* (seven pages)

I've had some mild amusement here at my desk trying to think up imaginary research papers similarly structured. One for publication in a health journal, perhaps, with three sections titled:

- *Health benefits of drinking green tea*
- *Green tea causes intestinal cancer*
- *Making the switch to green tea*

Social science research in our universities cries out for a modern Jonathan Swift to lampoon its absurdities.

DIVERSITY BITES

Putnam, who is a professor at Harvard University, is best known for his work on the concept of *social capital.* The argument behind this concept is that a society is better off and more stable if it has many social networks—civic groups, friendly societies, PTAs, church groups, amateur sports clubs, common-interest associations, car pools, and ordinary one-to-one friendships. The aggregate of these social networks forms a society's social capital. As Putnam says in the Uppsala paper: "Like tools (physical capital) and training (human capital), social networks have value."

That's not a new idea: Think of Edmund Burke's praise for the "little platoons" of civil society—those same social networks, clubs, and groups. No doubt the idea of social capital can, like most ideas in political science, be traced back in some form all the way to Aristotle.

So far as the general public is concerned Putnam made his name with a book titled *Bowling Alone*, published in 2000, and based on an article with the same title that Putnam had published five years earlier in a scholarly journal. The thrust of both the book and the paper was that social capital had declined drastically in the United States through the later twentieth century.

What were the causes of that decline, though? Any thoughtful person can come up with half a dozen candidate explanations.

Putnam fingered several in his book: the increased variety and so-phistication of home entertainments; the rise of the working woman leading to less aggregate free time for the doing of domestic tasks; suburbanization placing home life far from work life, and so on.

And then perhaps ethnic diversity has had something to do with it. If you compare the lives of Americans at the middle of the twenti-eth century with their lives at the beginning of the twenty-first, you can't avoid noticing that people were more *mixed* at the later date.

For one thing, there were simply more kinds of people in America—more races, religions, nationalities, mother tongues—in 2000 than there were in 1950, due to the mass immigration from all over the world that began after the 1965 Immigration Act. For another, peo-ple were more prosperous and mobile—better able to buy a house they wanted, in a district they liked.

People also became more open-minded, more *willing* to mix, after race prejudice had been shamed out of polite society by the civil rights movement of the 1960s. Many kinds of separation and exclu-sion were made illegal, too, especially in the arenas of business and employment, so that people had no choice but to mix more, whether willing or not.

In the year 2000, Putnam set himself the task of finding out whether, and how much, all this diversity contributed to the loss of social capital he had recorded in *Bowling Alone*. He undertook a major study, involving thirty thousand Americans in forty-one loca-tions, to see if he could find a relationship between increased diver-sity and loss of social capital. The locations varied from the very diverse (San Francisco, which was 30–40 percent white) to the hardly-at-all diverse (a South Dakota county that was 95 percent white, and where Putnam observes drily that "celebrating 'diversity' means inviting a few Norwegians to the annual Swedish picnic").

The results of the study are quite conclusive, and are summarized in the Uppsala paper. Diversity correlates negatively with social cap-ital. The more you have of the one, the less you have of the other. The study showed clearly that "out-group trust"—how much you trust people who are different from yourself—is lower in places with lots of diversity. More surprising, "in-group trust"—the degree to which you trust people *like* yourself—is depressed by the same amount (around 50 percent) when your neighborhood is diverse.

Diversity seems to affect every kind of social connection. In places with more ethnic diversity, people have fewer friends, watch more TV, are less inclined to vote, trust local government less, and rate their personal happiness lower. As a conscientious social scientist, Putnam of course controlled for income, home ownership, crime rates, and so on. Same results.

Putnam, a mild-mannered and unimaginative midwesterner of conventionally liberal opinions, was surprised and perplexed by the results staring back at him from his worksheets. Having spent his entire professional life in the warm, perfumed soak-bath of political correctness that is the modern American university, he had completely internalized the notion that diversity is a *good* thing, from which nothing negative could possibly come.

Putnam's convictions were exactly in line with those spelled out by anthropologist Peter Wood in the book I went to for this chapter's epigraph.

Here is another quote from Wood's book. Ahead of it I need to explain a quirk of the book's typography. Wood distinguished carefully between "diversity" as an ordinary English word with a dictionary meaning ("the condition of being different or having differences"—*Webster's Third New International Dictionary*) and *diversity* as the name of an ideological cult. When using the word in its latter sense, Wood prints it in italics, as I just did. When the ordinary dictionary meaning is intended, he leaves it in plain text. Now here is the quote.

> The ideal of *diversity* is that once individuals of diverse backgrounds are brought together, a transformation will take place in people's attitudes—primarily within the members of the formerly exclusive group, who will discover the richness of the newcomers' cultural backgrounds. Diversity will breed tolerance and respect, and, because it increases the pool of skills, will enhance the effectiveness of work groups and contribute to economic prosperity. In the more extended flights of the diversiphile's

imagination, *diversity* creates good will and social betterment in every direction. The African-American manager, the gay white secretary and the Latino consultant learn from each other's distinctive cultural experience and become better workers, better citizens, better persons.

That was not what Professor Putnam's results were telling him. What they were telling him was, as he put it in the Uppsala paper, that "people living in ethnically diverse settings appear to 'hunker down'—that is, to pull in like a turtle."

This downside of ethnic diversity will keep cropping up throughout my book. Like Peter Wood, I want to emphasize the difference between mere diversity—a neutral condition that might be present in any society, and reacted to in all sorts of ways—and the *cult* of Diversity, the particular way we, present-day Americans, have chosen to deal with our diversity. I'm freer with italics in my writing than Wood is, though; so for clarity I shall write "diversity" when I mean the mere thing, "Diversity" for the ideological cult, capitalizing the "D." Ideological cults are important enough to deserve a capital letter. I believe this one is, anyway.

SIX YEARS OF AGONIZING

The attentive reader may have noticed a rather long gap between Putnam's study, done in 2000, and the publication of the results in summary form in the 2006 Uppsala paper (which actually became publicly available in 2007). What was Professor Putnam doing with the data for six years?

In the fall of 2006 he incautiously gave an answer to that question while being interviewed by reporter John Lloyd of the *Financial Times*. Putnam had, Lloyd reported, "delayed publishing his research until he could develop proposals to compensate for the negative effects of diversity, saying it 'would have been irresponsible to publish without that.' "

The *Financial Times* report caused a minor stir among people who pay attention to these things. Social scientists, like scientists in general, are supposed to be, well, *scientific*. That is to say, they are supposed to conduct open-ended inquiries—answers not known in advance!—into the world of nature, in their case human nature, and publish what they find, whether or not it agrees with something they might have *expected* to find or *wanted* to find.

In fact it's possible to sympathize with Putnam. After all, nontrivial questions of social responsibility arise even in the physical sciences. What if my open-ended physical-science inquiry leads to a method by which a nuclear bomb could be built by anyone with a well-equipped garage workshop? Or a smallpox virus by anyone with access to a high-school biology lab?

But then, why would Professor Putnam think that the results of his study were dangerous at the garage-nuke or school-lab-smallpox level? Those results did not, after all, show ethnic groups in diverse areas setting about each other with axes and pitchforks. People just watched TV a lot, went out less, mixed less, carpooled less, and trusted each other and their politicians less. Why the distress? Why the six years' agonizing?

THE DIVERSITY THEOREM

The surprising thing about that story is Professor Putnam's having been surprised. As columnist Ilana Mercer noted when remarking on the Putnam study: "When an academic 'discovers' what ordinary mortals have known for eons, it's called science."

I'm sure Ilana meant to write "*social* science." The physical sciences *do* come up with quite startling and unexpected results. The social sciences much more often only verify the wisdom of the ages, as chronicled in literature and folklore.

This is just what you'd expect. We've only been acquainted with protons, galaxies, chromosomes, tectonic plates, neurotransmitters, and superconductors for a few decades. We've been acquainted with our fellow human beings, and observing each other with careful attention, since *Homo sapiens* first showed up around two hundred thousand years ago. *Of course* there are few surprises in the social sciences!

Unless, that is, you have allowed yourself to be confused by a false ideology. The good professor was so surprised and disturbed by the results of his inquiry because he had completely absorbed and thoroughly internalized all the precepts of the Diversity cult, as spelled out above in the extract from Peter Wood's book: "Diversity will breed tolerance and respect . . ." etc. And that cult *is* a false ideology, rooted, like all false ideologies, in wishful thinking and optimistic happy talk about human nature.

The central theorem of the Diversity cult—its mission statement, you might say—can be stated more briefly than in my extract from Peter Wood's book. Here's my own formulation:

The Diversity Theorem

Different populations, of different races, customs, religions, and preferences, can be mixed together *in any numbers or proportions at all*, with harmonious result. Not only will the result be harmonious, it will be *beneficial* to all the people thus mixed. They will be better and happier than if they had been left to stagnate in dull homogeneity.

A corollary to the Diversity Theorem states that if the experiment were to be carried out on a nation—a territory under independent self-government—then the nation would be made stronger and better by an increase in diversity, so long as the system was controlled by properly approved and trained Diversity managers. It would be more peaceful, more prosperous, better educated, more cultivated, better able to defend itself against its enemies. Diversity is our strength!

Diversity ideologues will concede that there may be some initial frictions arising from mutual unfamiliarity among the groups being mixed. There may, too, be antidiversity agitation by individuals who are angry that their own group's culture, once dominant, is now only one among many (*unum inter plures*, if you like). These matters can easily be dealt with by education and propaganda, and by the silencing, through social ostracism or police action, of the small, scattered number of angry diversiphobes.

Soon, we are promised, when absurd old prejudices and attachments have been shamed or legislated out of existence, the mingled millions will live in harmony, celebrating their diversity and happily acknowledging what the wise shepherds of the Diversity cult knew all along: that diversity is a great boon to all, a source of strength and wealth.

The blessings of diversity are said to apply at all levels of society, from the national to the local and particular.

- A company that is diverse is more creative, better placed to sell into a diverse marketplace.
- A school with a diverse teaching staff and student body will better equip those who pass through it with the skills and attitudes appropriate to an interconnected world, as well as making them morally better just for having encountered diversity.
- A government department should of course be diverse, the better to serve the diverse nature of the population.
- The people in movies, TV shows, and sports teams should be diverse, to enlighten spectators about the benefits of diversity while entertaining them.
- Diverse military units help to cement diversity in the larger society by showing diverse citizens cooperating under the extraordinary stress of combat.

. . . and so on.

Thus Diversity monitors are needed everywhere in society. Every large company or institution must have a vice president for diversity—if not, as is increasingly the case, a chief diversity officer. (The CDO at Washington State University has an annual budget of $3 million and a full-time staff of fifty-five.)

It follows that Diversity, as well as being healthful and morally uplifting, is a great source of employment. In the United States today, hundreds of thousands of people are employed in the Diversity industry—teaching, propagandizing, monitoring, lawyering. Diversity is a major sector of the national economy.

The money is good. Michelle Obama, when she was vice president for community relations—which is to say, Diversity enforcer—at the University of Chicago Medical Center, had an annual salary of $316,962. That's more than most doctors earn after three years in practice. The average base salary for ob-gyns, for example, is listed as $248,294 on the PhysiciansSearch website. But hey, how can delivering babies compare in importance with Diversity?

Diversity, Inc. is a monthly magazine devoted to diversity in the corporate world, nationally distributed and packed with upmarket advertising. Each year the magazine publishes a list of the top fifty companies in the United States for diversity. (Ranked one, two, and three on the 2007 list were Bank of America, Pepsi, and AT&T.)

It should be noted that Diversicrats are not, or not often, stone-faced commissars in shiny suits enforcing a reign of terror on a cowering populace. Most of them are bland, cheerful, middle-class careerists. Go to the website of any office concerned with Diversity indoctrination or enforcement—the University of Delaware's "Residence Life" department, for instance. The Diversicrats smile out at you—well-groomed citizens with sheaves of paper qualifications and good salaries. *See how happy we are!* they seem to say. *Come join us! Help us to celebrate Diversity!*

Are these really the foot soldiers of a false ideology? Are these really pod people, their minds taken over by nonhuman forces? Yes they are.

It might occur to the more compassionate reader to wonder what will happen to all these smiley-face yuppies employed in the Diversity industry when Diversity has done its work—when the last traces of anti-Diversity poison have been flushed from the national metabolism, the last Diversiphobe has been hustled off to a reeducation camp, and the vibrant, harmonious society promised to us by Diversity propagandists has arrived. Will not all the Diversity consultants, Diversity trainers, Diversity assessors, Diversity lawyers, writers of Diverse school textbooks, distributors of grants for Diversity workshops, vice presidents for community relations, staff of magazines like *Diversity, Inc.* (it is by no means the only Diversity-interest publication), chief diversity officers, and all the rest—will they not be unemployed?

My advice would be not to worry too much about this. Diversity will be with us for a long time. Perhaps its work will never be done.

A MASS DELUSION

I'm sorry to have made such fun of Robert Putnam's paper. He's an earnest academic professional (and by all accounts a very nice man). The social-science "meat" in his three-layer Uppsala sandwich is elegantly and rigorously done—he's not a Harvard professor for nothing.

The happy-talk arm-waving at front and back of that "meat" is, though, perfectly and irresistibly illustrative of the point I'm making: The cult of Diversity is so powerful and so attractive, it has corroded even first-rate minds like Robert Putnam's, not to mention the minds of all too many conservatives. And yet it is demonstrably—*easily* demonstrably—false.

The remarkable thing about the Diversity cult is that all the circumstances of the actual human world refute its tenets, wherever we look. I don't think it is an exaggeration to say that there has never been an ideology so heartily and jealously embraced by all the main institutions of a society, that was at the same time so obviously at odds with the evidence of our senses. It is as if the entire Western world had committed itself to the belief that human beings can fly by flapping their arms.

Diversity-the-ideology is in fact a very pure example of the kind of magical, counterfactual thinking that has led conservatives astray. By letting this ideology triumph unchallenged—even, in some deplorable cases, *embracing* it—we have surrendered key political positions: equal treatment under the law, allegiance to one nation, freedom of association, public education in one language . . . By holding firmly to a pessimistic, realistic view of what is and is not possible in a society of different ethnicities, we might have maintained the principles of a free republic, and saved ourselves much trouble and expense.

In the world at large, diversity causes nothing but problems.

Open your newspaper, or scan a news website like news.bbc.co.uk or Drudgereport.com. At random from the past two years' international news:

- Tribal fighting in Kenya, once considered the most promising African nation, claimed more than a thousand lives in early 2008. Hundreds of thousands were displaced as a result of ethnic cleansing. Political and economic life are at a standstill. From the *London Times:* "Chaos reigned in and around [Nakuru], Kenya's fourth largest [town], as tribal gangs fought with knives, pangas, stones and poisoned arrows. After more than 60 people had died, the police imposed a dusk-to-dawn curfew. The tourists left and have not come back."

- Belgium's main political parties have begun discussions on constitutional reform. "The aim is to resolve long-standing differences between parties from Belgium's richer Dutch-speaking Flanders region and those from poorer francophone Wallonia, who are battling over Flemish demands for larger regional autonomy."

- Mid-2008 saw Lebanon in its worst political crisis since the end of the 1975–90 civil war. Parliament was deadlocked for months over the election of a new president, divided between the government of Prime Minister Fouad Siniora (a Sunni Muslim allied with Christians) and the opposition, led by the Shiite militant group Hezbollah.

- The racial spoils system that has kept Malaysia peaceful since the race riots of the late 1960s is running into trouble, as the Indian minority demonstrates for greater representation. "Ethnic Anger on the Rise in Malaysia" was the headline on a January 2008 story from the *International Herald Tribune.* Malaysia's population is Malay-Chinese-Indian in percentages 65-27-8. Malays dominate politics and public-sector work; Chinese dominate business and the professions. The rate of Chinese-Malay intermarriage is close to zero.

- Four of Bolivia's nine departments, all in the northern and eastern regions of the country, whose populations are European and mestizo (mixed race) have passed legislation demanding autonomy for themselves. This is in defiance of President Evo Morales, who is an indigene and a socialist, and is trying to impose a new constitution that favors the four-sevenths of the population that is indigenous.

- The preschools of New South Wales (a province of Australia) have begun a program to educate infants in "tolerance and multiculturalism." From a January 2008 newspaper report: "The Menindee Children's Centre . . . has just received a $4000 grant to launch the first State Government–funded program of its kind. The focus on racism follows the 2005 Cronulla Riots [between immigrant Lebanese and white Australians] . . . the centrepiece of the program would be regular discussions about racism . . . race-fuelled events such as the Cronulla Riots . . . were discussed with the children, who range from newborns [sic] to school age."

- In Lhasa, the capital city of Chinese-occupied Tibet, there were demonstrations in March 2008. The Chinese authorities responded clumsily, and Tibetans reacted with riots and the torching of Chinese stores. It was all a great embarrassment to the Chinese government, which was trying to show its best face to the world in the run-up to the Beijing Olympics.

- In the city of Malmö, Sweden, young Muslims rampaged during the Christmas 2008 holiday following the closing of an Islamic center. A school was burned. Police riot squads were met with rocks and Molotov cocktails. A quarter of Malmö's population is Middle Eastern Muslims. Ninety percent are unemployed.

- In February 2009, racial tensions gripped the French Caribbean island of Martinique as two thousand mostly black protesters backing a wage strike chanted slogans against the island's white elite. The protesters marched Friday through the capital, chanting slogans against "bekes"—the descendants of colonists and slave holders. "Martinique is ours, not theirs!" they yelled.

- Fiji, an archipelago nation in the South Pacific, has two big demographic groups: native Melanesians (58 percent) and descendants of contract laborers from India, brought to the islands by the British in the nineteenth century (37 percent). Fijian politics is dominated by conflict between these two groups. There have been four coups since 1987, the most recent in 2006. The Fijian constitution was suspended in April 2009.

Africa, Europe, the Middle East, Asia, Latin America, Australia, the Caribbean, and Oceania—everywhere you look, diversity is a source of discord. How does this square with the claims of the Diversity ideologues? Are the Kenyans, Belgians, Lebanese, Malaysians, Bolivians, Australians, Chinese, Swedes, Martiniquaises, and Fijians just not trying hard enough? (The Australians, at least, are plainly trying very hard indeed, with their Diversity-indoctrination programs for *newborns.*)

Here in the United States, too, ethnic diversity, far from being a boon, is the source of endless trouble. The reader hardly needs reminding; or, if he does, he need only open his newspaper or switch on his TV. Race-based gangs are rioting in prisons and schools (and infiltrating the U.S. armed forces); there are endless lawsuits by people who believe they have been discriminated against; and we have school programs like this one:

California's Byron Union School District requires their seventh-grade children to participate in a three-week "be a Muslim" class activity. The children must wear traditional Muslim attire, adopt Muslim names, recite a portion of a Muslim prayer, observe the "five pillars" of the Islamic faith, and even stage their own "jihad" or "holy war." Several parents sued to stop the program, but without success. An appeal is under way.

The happy talkers tell us that diversity is a boon, making our society stronger and better. Our own lying eyes tell us that it is the source of continual trouble; not merely the solitary "hunkering down" that Robert Putnam discovered, but rancor, disorder, litigation, and violence.

Professor Putnam tells us in his Uppsala paper that "this article is but a prolegomenon to a larger project on how to manage the challenge that immigration and diversity pose to social capital and solidarity."

Oh, so it's a *challenge*. Well, there's no avoiding the challenge of diversity. It's been with us from the start (next section). It is, though, hard to see why a sane people would be so intent on making the challenge *bigger*. As Putnam says, mass Third World immigration has added enormously to our diversity, so that today's challenge is hugely bigger than the one we faced forty years ago, which mainly involved bringing African Americans and Native Americans fully into the national life. Why would a nation strive to *increase* the challenge it faces? Was the original challenge so contemptibly small that we needed to double and triple it, to give our moral fiber a workout?

Perhaps the idea is that by enlarging and then defeating this challenge, we shall be a better nation. In that case, if challenges are so good for us, why not create a few more? I suggest flooding some low-lying cities; causing landslides on inhabited hillsides with well-placed explosive charges; letting loose a few dangerous pathogens . . . Or why not set off a nuclear weapon or two in populated areas to see how well we meet the challenge of swamped hospitals and mass evacuation?

It seems to me that the human world presents enough challenges, without our needing to concoct more, or multiply the ones we have. Resource depletion, climate instability, economic stagnation, demography, and international terrorism all seem likely to present us with severe challenges in the years to come. Why should the United

States add more challenges to the menu? What happened to the old adage about not troubling Trouble until Trouble troubles you? Why are we putting ourselves through this ever-swelling diversity challenge?

But I am wandering into the immigration issue, which deserves a chapter to itself. Let's take a look at our nation's original diversity, the one we might have had a shot at solving if unbridled optimism hadn't run away with our senses.

DIVERSE FROM THE START

There are many styles of American diversity, and always have been. In earlier days the most salient kind of diversity was religious. That is to say, it manifested itself in friction among different styles of Christian worship and belief. Quakers were hanged in Massachusetts; Roman Catholics were resisted by the Know-Nothings; Mormons were chased across the country.

(Intra-Christian conflict in the United States has mostly died down now, but it is still going strong elsewhere. Consider, for example, the Church of the Holy Sepulcher in Jerusalem, supposed to be built on the spot where Christ rose from the dead. The church is managed by six different Christian sects under a complex set of protocols dating from the Ottoman Empire. Each sect guards its rights very jealously, and there are frequent petty conflicts. The keys to the main entrance of the church have been held by a Muslim family since the twelfth century because the Christians do not trust one another. In 2002 a Coptic monk placed his chair in a section of the church claimed by Ethiopians; the resulting fracas put eleven monks in the hospital. In November 2008 things got nasty yet again, when a rumble between Greek Orthodox and Armenian monks had to be broken up by Israeli police. One of the Greeks, having perhaps been a tad too slow at turning the other cheek, had a nasty gash on his forehead. But really: if diversity is a chronic, ongoing failure in the Church of the Holy Sepulcher, among people all of whom have dedicated their lives in service to the same loving God, *where can we expect it to be a success?*)

And then, also from the earliest days, there was racial diversity in the United States. By the time of Independence, the territory of the present-day forty-eight contiguous states contained Europeans, indigenes, and Africans (or African-white and African-indigene mixtures, both counted as "black"), in percentages roughly 62, 22, and 16, respectively. The United States was *born* racially diverse—three of the great old prehistoric inbred human populations sharing the same territory.

The sharing was never very harmonious. There were wars: not only the Civil War, but also the Indian Wars—which, it is often forgotten, began far back, the earliest New England colonists fighting savage wars against local tribes, with exterminatory intent on both sides. There were slave rebellions and massacres. There were the humiliations of Jim Crow and grinding poverty on barren Indian reservations.

The nineteenth- and early-twentieth-century waves of immigration mainly had the effect of making the United States whiter. The 1950 census recorded the population as slightly less than 90 percent white and 10 percent black, with other races making up the difference.* The near-moratorium on immigration imposed by the 1924 Immigration Act had lasted for a generation. The Great Wave immigrants had assimilated. Ethnic diversity was now a matter of whites and blacks, with the ratio about nine to one. How was it to be managed?

The developments of the next few years are well known. Segregation was outlawed and true equality under the law for African Americans established. Hopes at the time were high. I am old enough to remember having shared them in my high school and college years, though vicariously, from a different part of the Anglosphere. All thoughtful white people supposed that with legal segregation eliminated and race prejudice shamed out of existence, functional equality between black and white in the United States would soon follow.

Some eminent participants in the revolution put a date on their hope. Thurgood Marshall, who argued for the plaintiffs in the classic

---

* The precise numbers were: 89.54 percent white, 9.98 percent African American, 0.23 percent Native American, and 0.25 percent "other."

desegregation case *Brown v. Board of Education of Topeka* in 1954, said it would take five years to attain full school integration nationwide. Others were less optimistic. Arnold Rose, coauthor with Swedish sociologist Gunnar Myrdal of the tremendously influential 1944 book *An American Dilemma*, offered the opinion in 1962 that black-white friction would be inconsequential—"in the minor order of Catholic-Protestant prejudice"—by 1992. Which was, as if in willful mockery of Rose's prediction, the year of the Rodney King riots.

AN EDUCATION IN RESIDENTIAL SEGREGATION

That year, 1992, was also, as it happens, the year my wife and I decided to buy a home in New York's Long Island suburbs, in order to start a family. Knowing next to nothing about the region, we took to riding out on the Long Island Railroad at weekends, getting off at random stops, looking around for Realtors, and asking about house prices and the quality of local schools. This gave us a brisk education in residential diversity.

The single major factor determining house prices in the suburbs, we quickly discovered, was proximity to a good school; and "good school" was universally understood—by friends, colleagues, and Realtors (though the Realtors speak in careful code for fear of undercover Diversity cops)—to mean "school with not too many black students." Nowadays the meaning has changed slightly, to "not too many black and Hispanic students"; but Hispanics were not a big factor on Long Island in 1992.

We ended up buying a house in Huntington, where the mean price of a detached house in 2007 was $777,772 according to the City-Data.com website. The racial breakdown for Huntington shows NAMs ("Non-Asian Minorities," which means African Americans plus Hispanics) at 5.7 percent. In the tonier village of Cold Spring Harbor next door, which my wife and I liked the look of but could not afford, the mean house price is up at $1,089,622; NAMs are 2.0 percent. A few miles away in Hempstead, median house price is a measly $345,655 while NAMs are 84.3 percent. Am I telling you something you don't know?

This illustrates the emerging demographic split in the United States: whites and East Asians on one side, African Americans and Hispanics on the other. African Americans and Hispanics—NAMs—"travel together" when you scrutinize U.S. demographics. East Asians, with some fringe exceptions like the Hmong, "travel" with whites.

I haven't so far seen any term as snappy as "NAMs" for whites-plus-East-Asians. I've tried to float the term "Arctics," which seems sound to me on paleoanthropological grounds, but my coinage hasn't met with any acceptance. Looking around for an alternative, I think I've found what I need.

Leonard Jeffries, professor of black studies at City College, New York, has suggested the terms "Ice People" for whites and East Asians, "Sun People" for blacks and Hispanics. This is just the ticket. For the purposes of this book, and by way of tribute to a distinguished local scholar, I shall henceforth follow this usage.

THE MENDACITY OF HOPE

The great hopes of the 1950s and 1960s largely fell flat. Able and talented African Americans rose into the upper-middle classes, where they mix easily with high-achieving whites, Asians, and Hispanics. Anywhere much below those levels, the races keep to themselves except when forbidden by law from doing so. African Americans, most particularly, keep themselves separate from other citizens. They watch different movies and TV programs, listen to different music, give their children different names, live in different places.

There is even an Internet Web browser for African Americans: Blackbird, built using the Mozilla Foundation open-source code. This makes Blackbird basically just Mozilla's Firefox browser in blackface. It comes with preset bookmarks to black college fraternities and sororities, black news ("Bush Exit Strategy: Damage America"—

it's taken for granted that black news is left-wing), bling vendors like Sicka Than Average, and links to some of the innumerable black-only professional organizations like the National Society of Black Engineers.

"One nation . . . indivisible." Well, that was a pleasant dream, wasn't it? Brief, but pleasant. Racial integration has had some small successes, but overall it's been a bust below the high-elite levels, who always have, and always will, live by their own rules.

Following the race riots of the mid-1960s, President Lyndon Johnson set up a commission to inquire into the causes. That commission, commonly called the Kerner Commission, warned: "Our nation is moving toward two societies, one black, one white—separate and unequal." Today, forty years later, that prediction has come true over large areas of the national life, though the terms "black" and "white" need some slight modification: Sun People, Ice People.

DIVERSITY VERSUS MODERNITY

It's a curious thing that in the world at large, traditional kinds of ethnic diversity declined throughout the twentieth century, at least in the advanced nations. Anyone born in the middle of that century has seen this with his own eyes.

In my own student days forty years ago, I traveled through Transylvania, a region occupying the northwestern part of the modern nation of Romania. I couldn't speak Romanian, but didn't need to. Every town and village in Transylvania had a German-speaking population as a consequence of Saxon migrations in the High Middle Ages. Since I knew German, language was no problem.

The German-speaking population of Transylvania was 360,000 when I passed through. It is now less than 60,000 and still dwindling, the rest having migrated to Germany, where they have the right to immediate citizenship on ethnic grounds. Why live among strangers when there is an ethnic homeland you can move to? Once the Iron

Curtain came down, Transylvania's ethnic Germans were out of there. But why had they not returned to the ethnic homelands in any numbers during the preceding eight hundred years? Something about modernity caused their migration; something about modernity makes us less willing to live among strangers.

The first person to comment on this, so far as I know, was political scientist Walker Connor, in his 1994 book *Ethnonationalism.* Prior to the nineteenth century, Connor tells us, "there was no keen competition for group allegiance." Today, however, peoples all over the world are keen to identify themselves with some group, some culture of customs and beliefs, in order to

> permit the typical individual to answer intuitively and unequivocally the question, "What are you?" The spontaneous response, "I am Luo" rather than Kenyan, or "Bengali" rather than Pakistani, does not bode well for the architect of a nation-state.

The topic was taken up again more recently in a striking essay by historian Jerry Z. Muller in the March/April 2008 issue of *Foreign Affairs.* The essay is titled "Us and Them: The Enduring Power of Ethnic Nationalism." After noting the discomfort that Americans feel toward ethnic nationalism, Muller states bluntly that a peaceful system of neighboring nations is usually the result of violent ethnic separation (think of modern Europe). Where that separation hasn't taken place, politics is liable to be crude and vicious (Kenya, Lebanon, post-Tito Yugoslavia, etc.).

Muller repeatedly links ethnic nationalism to key features of the modern world.

> The rise of ethnonationalism . . . was not some strange historical mistake; rather, it was propelled by some of the deepest currents of modernity.

Most of his discussion concerns twentieth-century Europe, where a long period of "ethnic disaggregation" (and yes, of course Muller is aware of the mountain of human suffering behind that phrase) created a stable and peaceful system of nation-states at last—a system, indeed, that was strong and confident enough to contain or subdue remaining pockets of severe ethnic discord: Cyprus, Northern Ireland.

Muller's paper is very audacious in the United States of today, under the reigning Diversity ideology. For example: "Liberal democracy and ethnic homogeneity are not only compatible; they can be complementary." It is a short step from there—though a step Muller does not take—to the thought that ethnic homogeneity may be *necessary* for a stable, modern, liberal democracy.

Why, after all (Muller asks), has Europe been so harmonious since World War II? Cowed by the horrors of the war? Then why was the place so sensationally *un*harmonious after World War I, whose horrors were surely instructive enough? The harmony, Muller tells us, was a result of ethnic disaggregation, "which removed some of the greatest sources of conflict both within and between countries."

Muller sees ethnonationalism as a key consequence of modernization. In those parts of the world still modernizing, it will grow, and if we want a world system of stable nation-states, we should welcome and encourage it.

> Ethnonationalism was not a chance detour in European history: it corresponds to some enduring propensities of the human spirit that are heightened by the process of modern state creation, it is a crucial source of both solidarity and enmity, and in one form or another, it will remain for many generations to come.

Does any of this have relevance to the United States? Isn't our country a very particular and exceptional place, where immigrants shed their ethnicity—if not immediately, at any rate after a generation or two—to blend into our "proposition nation"? Or might Professor Muller's "enduring propensities of the human spirit" show themselves here, too?

THE FUTURE OF DIVERSITY

At the end of their 2004 book *Race: The Reality of Human Differences*, Vincent Sarich and Frank Miele offer three possible scenarios for the near future of ethnic diversity. They take it as a given that differences in custom, aptitude, and talents among ethnic groups are likely to remain as intractable as they have shown themselves to be this past forty years—not an unreasonable assumption, given the great efforts we have invested in erasing those differences, with such meager results.

Here are Sarich and Miele's three scenarios:

- *Meritocracy in the Global Marketplace.* Let the group-difference chips fall where they may, and try to manage resentment toward high-performance groups.
- *Affirmative Action, Race Norming, and Quotas.* State-enforced leveling down "at the expense of individual freedom and, ultimately, the total level of accomplishment."
- *Rising Resegregation and the Emergence of Ethnopolitics.* Polarization and separation, with more danger, both domestic and international, from groups who see themselves as "victimized and shut out by the global marketplace."

Which is a more probable future for the United States? For the world at large? Sarich and Miele declare their preference for meritocracy in their own country. It "resonates quite well with a major tradition in American history," they say, and: "the United States is probably better positioned to choose this option than any other."

Ah, if wishes were horses! Probably most people like Sarich (emeritus professor of anthropology at the University of California, Berkeley) and Miele (senior editor at *Skeptic* magazine) share that preference for meritocracy. Probably you do too, gentle reader. However, if the preferences of First World high-achieving intellectuals and readers of books about the prospects for conservatism were great forces in human affairs, our societies would be very different from what they are. What are we most likely *actually to get?*

The trend lines, it seems to me, are all currently in the direction of the third scenario. Meritocracy has sharpened, made more visible, both individual and group differences. For "market-dominant minorities" like the Chinese of Southeast Asia, the Indians of East Africa, the Jews of most Western nations, and the tall, pale-skinned European-ancestry elites of South America, globalization and meritocracy have been great blessings, but they have widened the gaps between the more and the less successful population groups.

Amy Chua's fine 2003 book about this, *World on Fire*, is wonderfully descriptive of the gap-widening process. The book begins with the story of the author's aunt, a member of the prosperous Chinese minority in the Philippines, who was murdered by her Filipino chauffeur. The murderer got away, and the local police—poor ethnic Filipinos themselves—made no effort to catch him. The police report listed his motive as "Revenge."

The world is chock-full of such ethnic envy and resentment, wherever diversity can be found. Americans were treated to the sight of some of them in the 2008 election season, courtesy of three (unless I missed others) different preachers at Barack Obama's former church, Trinity United in Chicago.

Meritocracy only makes matters worse. "He's better off than me because he was born with a silver spoon in his mouth" is a more palatable thought than "He's better off than me because he's more capable than I am." It's so much more palatable that the second opinion is always pulled gravitationally toward the first. People rationalize high achievement as being the result of unfair advantage even when it's not.

Even *without* diversity, meritocracy may generate deep social problems. At the end of Michael Young's 1958 classic *The Rise of the Meritocracy*, set in a future Britain that is utterly *un*-diverse ethnically, we learn that the (fictional) sociologist who narrated the story has been stomped to death by a low-IQ mob.

Diversity, especially the acute *consciousness* of diversity cultivated and encouraged by the Diversity cult, adds the even more disturbing suspicion that "his people are more capable than my people," leading to the kinds of consequences suffered by Amy Chua's aunt. Ms. Chua really has no solutions to offer but philanthropy and "enhanced social awareness." That's because there *is* nothing else.

Sarich and Miele's second scenario—managing group differences by social engineering—demands, as does all social engineering, a permanent and constant effort of will on the part of government to apply the appropriate pressure at all points, untiringly. America's forty-year experiment with affirmative action suggests that society does, in fact, sooner or later tire of the effort, and that the fundamental unfairness of it is eventually too offensive to too many.

That leaves us with ethnic disaggregation—more precisely, continuing ethnic disaggregation, since, as I have described, the process is well under way, both at home and abroad. (I'll bring up more evidence of the domestic situation in my education chapter.)

At some point we shall be forced to face the fact that the Diversity Theorem is false, and the answer to Rodney King's question is "No." Whether, past that point, we can maintain ourselves as one nation under one set of laws, is an open question. If conservatives had had the sense—and the moral courage—to throw up some effective resistance against this woolly-headed idiocy at its outset, we might have headed off a demographic disaster.

3

POLITICS: SHOW BUSINESS FOR UGLY PEOPLE

All those men have their price.
— SIR ROBERT WALPOLE, ABOUT 1740

It is . . . a just political maxim, that every man must be supposed a knave.
— DAVID HUME, 1742

There is danger from all men. The only maxim of a free government ought to be to trust no man living with power to endanger the public liberty.
— JOHN ADAMS, 1772

The greatest part of men are gross.
— SAMUEL JOHNSON, 1778

Experience [has] shown that, even under the best forms [of government], those entrusted with power have, in time and by slow operations, perverted it into tyranny.
— THOMAS JEFFERSON, 1779

Few men have virtue to withstand the highest bidder.
— GEORGE WASHINGTON, ABOUT 1780

A POLITICAL DUST BOWL

Just look at those quotes! All that splendid pessimism! All that fine dark loam of minimal expectations in which our nation was planted!

What's happened to it? It's gone, bleached and parched by the false sun of optimism, then blown away by the cold winds of reality, leaving all the roots of our liberty exposed to the colorless, feature-less glare of infantile cheeriness, to wither and die.

Our noble republic, founded by free men with a cold-eyed appre-ciation of human weakness, has fallen to smiley-face happy talkers bleating sentimental cant, assuring us that if we hand over ever more of our property and our freedoms to *them*, the wise and virtuous ones, we shall be secure and happy, able to fulfill the infinite poten-tials of our noble natures. Idiots!

All this has come upon us quite quickly, in just a couple of gener-ations. Overnight, as historical processes go, we have lost our repub-lican virtue, and shall lose our republic, unless we return to the unillusioned view of human nature subscribed to by the Founders. That view was the common one of their century, a far wiser century than ours. Perhaps never in human history did civilized men expect less of each other.

THE FRAGILITY OF NATIONS

In the previous chapter I quoted Samuel Huntington's comment that "a nation is a fragile thing." It's in the realm of politics that you see this most clearly.

A couple of years ago I got an e-mail from a reader concerning one of my monthly "Straggler" columns in *National Review*. The col-umn had actually been about American football, to which I'm a new-comer, my son having joined a youth league team that previous fall. In my column I had said the following thing: "If a foreigner should tell you that a nation as young as this one has had no time to develop a unique culture, take him to a college football game."

What my e-mailer objected to was my referring to this country as "young." He actually said: "Politically speaking, of the 190-odd nations that clutter up this planet of ours, the United States is the fourth oldest ranking right behind Denmark, Sweden, and Britain."

That's rather a striking observation. At any rate, it's striking to a person from the Old World. The people of, say, France, or Hungary, or Turkey, or Thailand, or Iran, feel their nations to be very old indeed. A Chinese person, if you ask him how old his country is, will reply reflexively: five thousand years. That's a bit of an exaggeration, but if he were to say four thousand years, he'd have a pretty good case. All these people would laugh at the idea that the United States is an older nation than theirs.

Yet of course my correspondent has a point. He did, after all, preface his remarks with the phrase "Politically speaking." Something recognizable as a Chinese nation may indeed have been around since the Bronze Age, but China's present constitution dates only from 1982, and that superseded three former constitutions in the previous thirty years. *Politically* speaking, China is a very new country.

From my correspondent's perspective, then, the United States looks like a very robust creation, at least politically. Is it, though? Is our political system stable? Will it survive another 220 years? Will it survive the current century? Will it survive until 2022?

PRESIDENT AND CONGRESS—THE BALANCE OF POWER

The federal government, as every schoolchild learns, has three branches: the executive, the legislature, and the judiciary. The tensions among these three are a principal theme of American political history. In practice, for most of that history, those tensions have taken the form of a tug-of-war between president and Congress, with the judiciary sometimes called in as referee. The thumbnail descriptors here are "Hamiltonian" and "Madisonian," indicating a preference for, respectively, the executive or the legislative power, as expressed by Founders Alexander Hamilton and James Madison.

Thoughtful commentators have always acknowledged that both executive and legislature have characteristic inbuilt temptations. For the executive, there is the plebiscitary conceit: "I alone represent the whole nation (or at any rate a majority of its electoral-college voters)! I alone have truly *national* legitimacy!" For the legislature there is the inclination to ducking and fence-sitting that always comes with collective responsibility.

Further down the moral scale, megalomania might drive a president to abuse the powers of the agencies he controls—strictly for the good of the nation, of course—while opportunities for corruption in the home district, far from the eyes of one's congressional colleagues, beckon the morally challenged legislator, along with everything encompassed by the word "pork."

The search for a point of balance between the two main power centers forms the largest part of American political theory. It's generated countless books and essays from the very beginning of the republic. As Western philosophy has been called a series of footnotes to Plato, American political science has been a long commentary on the *Federalist Papers* of 1787–88 and, in regard to foreign affairs, the further Hamilton-Madison "Pacificus-Helvidius" debates of 1793–94.

In broadest outline, the usual narrative is as follows:

- The Constitution somewhat modified the Revolutionary mistrust of executive power, but . . .
- The Madisonian preference for legislative over executive authority nonetheless predominated through the nineteenth century, until . . .
- First Theodore Roosevelt, then (after the Taft hiatus) Woodrow Wilson infused the presidency with new vigor, the latter especially taking the opportunity offered by war to aggrandize his office. However . . .
- The peace and prosperity of the 1920s allowed a retreat to nineteenth-century norms, until . . .
- The Great Depression and World War II swung the balance of power back to the executive, where . . .

- It has remained ever since, with only occasional and short-lived reassertions of legislative authority, as after the crippling of Nixon's presidency by the Watergate crisis.

The modern conservative movement was at first Madisonian, but as the Cold War ground on through the 1960s and 1970s, conservatives came to believe that the presidency was a more reliable guarantor of eventual victory over communism . . . so long, of course, as the president was a conservative.

Liberals, in reaction to what they perceived as Richard Nixon's excesses, were simultaneously traveling in the opposite direction, carrying in their backpacks Arthur M. Schlesinger Jr.'s 1973 book *The Imperial Presidency*. The two factions passed each other, going in opposite directions, sometime during the Ford administration, though it took until 1988 for a book titled *The Imperial Congress* to appear. (Its foreword was written by Newt Gingrich.)

Supporters of the president's party are of course always inclined to look favorably on presidential dominance, while supporters of the other party are inclined to dislike it; but these inclinations, and others related to particular issues of the moment, are imposed on the deeper trend, like harmonics on a pure musical note. The conservative Willmoore Kendall wrote his great Madisonian essay *Two Majorities* during the Eisenhower administration. Contrariwise, when Newt Gingrich told his fellow Republicans that "I want to strengthen the current . . . President because he is President of the United States," the date was 1995 and the president was Bill Clinton.

COMPREHENSIVE DOOM

Prophecies of political doom, like all other considered thoughts about U.S. politics, generally lean to one side or the other: a Hamiltonian doom of presidential Bonapartism, or a Madisonian one of "legislative usurpation" (*Federalist* 48).

My own eschatology will naturally be more comprehensive. I take no sides. We'll likely get both, and be comprehensively damned.

"There is danger from all men," presidents and congressmen both, if we yield up too much of our wealth and liberty to them. Which we have.

For clues as to the fate of our federal system, permit me a brief detour into the sphere of political *sensibility*. Prior to thought, there is feeling.

Psychologist Paul Ekman, who in the 1960s made a pioneering study of human facial expressions, identified six primary emotions: sadness, anger, fear, joy, surprise, and disgust.

There is little joy to be had from contemplating the current U.S. political scene, and few surprises (this is being written after a year-long presidential election campaign in which, to the best of my recollection, neither major candidate said anything interesting about any important topic), but there is sadness, anger, and fear aplenty. And then, there is disgust.

DISGUSTING SPECTACLES—PRESIDENTIAL DEIFICATION

To anyone of a republican (small "r" please, Mr. Editor) sensibility, American politics frequently throws up disgusting spectacles. It throws up one most years in January: the State of the Union speech.

You know how it goes. We're shown the House chamber, where the nation's highest civilian and military officials wait in gathering expectation. The sergeant at arms announces the president's arrival. The great man appears at last. In his progress through the chamber, legislators jostle and maneuver to catch his eye and receive the favor of a presidential greeting.

On the podium at last, the president offers up preposterously grandiose assurances of protection, provision, and moral guidance from his government, these declarations of benevolent omnipotence punctuated by standing ovations and cheers from legislators of his own party, and often from the others too, after every declarative clause.

Included in the audience in recent years have been citizens, or foreign visitors, who represent some quality the president will call on us to admire and emulate—selflessness, achievement, or support for U.S. ideals abroad. (The model citizens in these displays are known collectively as "Lenny Skutniks" after the first of them, showcased during President Reagan's 1982 address. Skutnik had performed a heroic rescue in January that year when a plane crashed in the Potomac River. You even hear political wonks use this as a verb: "Karzai's going to be Lenny Skutniked this year . . .")

This Stalinesque extravaganza has sprouted from a tiny seed: the requirement in Article II, Section 3 of the Constitution that the president "shall from time to time give to Congress information of the State of the Union and recommend to their Consideration such measures as he shall judge necessary and expedient."

Practically all of the development from acorn to mighty oak occurred during the twentieth century, with the most objectionable trends accelerating during the last quarter of that century.

The "annual message" (as it was called until 1945) was not in fact a speech at all for most of the republic's history. Washington and John Adams made a speech of it, but Jefferson—correctly, of course—thought this too monarchical. The annual message was thereafter delivered in writing to Congress until Woodrow Wilson reverted to speech mode in 1913. There was partial re-reversion to the written presentation by the more modest presidents of the immediate post-Wilson era (Harding, Coolidge, Hoover), and then occasionally since (Truman's first and last, Eisenhower's last, Carter's last, and Nixon's fourth), but for most of this past three-quarters of a century the president has delivered a speech.

This whole historical development was mapped in fine detail by political scientist Elvin T. Lim in a 2002 paper titled *Five Trends in Presidential Rhetoric: An Analysis of Rhetoric from George Washington to Bill Clinton*. Lim carried out a careful semantic study of 53 inaugural addresses and 211 State of the Union messages. Among his conclusions, he noted the steady inflation of the presidential office by comparison with the other branches. By scrutinizing their words, he tested the theory that modern presidents have had less concern for the other branches of government—"a concern that is the hallmark of idealized republican government." He found that they had indeed.

Lim also saw a trend away from "prose" to "poetry" in presidential speechifying. The Founders used some high-flown rhetoric, of course, but their main technique for swaying public opinion was substantive argument. Lim shows that the proportion of poetry to prose—or, to be less kind about it, of hot air to cold water—increased across the later twentieth century.

And there is the other movement from argument and exhortation to show-and-tell Lenny Skutniking. Says Lim:

> My data reveal that presidential rhetoric has become more anecdotal in recent decades. . . . Clinton's seventh State of the Union message . . . made specific references to nine political figures and shared the story of five American citizens . . . Several indicators reveal this movement toward anecdotalism, with number of words for say and tell—the kind of words a storyteller regularly employs—and descriptive verbs of an action increasing exponentially from Jimmy Carter.

Lim offers many illustrative comparisons between the presidential rhetoric of past and present times. William Henry Harrison, in his fatal inaugural address, likened liberty to "the sovereign balm for every injury which our institutions may receive." George H. W. Bush, in *his* inaugural address, likened it to a kite. "Freedom is like a beautiful kite that can go higher and higher with the breeze," he proclaimed. We may only be a president or two away from hearing liberty compared to a chocolate fudge sundae.

Both in style and in substance the presidency has drifted far from the Founders' intentions. As the State of the Union speeches show, the president is no longer merely chief administrator of one of the three branches of our federal government. He is a pontiff, in touch with Divinity, to be addressed like the Almighty in Robert Grant's fine old hymn.

> *Our Shield and Defender,*
> *The Ancient of days,*
> *Pavilion'd in splendour,*
> *And girded with praise.*

Interestingly—though not, by this point I hope, counterintuitively—Elvin T. Lim notes that "references to religious-words, which followed a downward trend for most of the nineteenth century, have increased in the twentieth. For example, the invocation of God has become very popular in the twentieth century, and particularly during the Reagan years."

DISGUSTING SPECTACLES—CONGRESSIONAL STAGNATION

It is not only the elevation of the presidency to the aspect of an omnipotent pharaonic priest-king that inspires disgust. The legislative branch also offers many repulsive spectacles. We witnessed one in May 2008.

The news had just come out that Senator Edward Kennedy, the chamber's second-longest-serving member with forty-five and a half years in office, had been diagnosed with a malignant brain tumor. In these circumstances, civilized standards—which I wholeheartedly endorse—dictate that both political enemies and political allies offer expressions of sympathy and support, with a somewhat greater degree of emotion naturally permitted to the latter.

There is a right measure in all things, though. The U.S. Senate's longest-serving member, Robert Byrd, with forty-eight and a half years in the chamber, far exceeded that measure, crossing well over into the zone of embarrassment and disgust.

As the Senate embarked on deliberations for an appropriations bill, Senator Byrd asked to be recognized. His request granted, the doddering ninety-year-old legislator delivered a mawkish, barely coherent tribute to his afflicted colleague.

Before we begin consideration of this important spending bill, I want to take a moment to say how distraught and terribly shaken I am over the news of my dear friend . . . my dear, dear friend . . . dear friend Ted Kennedy. My thoughts and my humble prayers [snuffling] are with Senator Kennedy [voice cracking] my dear friend

Ted [sob] with his wife Vicky [snuffling] and with the members of the Kennedy family [snuffling and sobbing]. I hope and pray that an all-caring . . . omnipotent God will watch over Ted . . . and keep Ted here [sob] for us . . . and for America. Ted . . . Ted . . . my dear friend . . . I love you, and I miss you . . . and . . . [unintelligible] . . . my darlin' wife [unintelligible] . . . want to say: Thank God for you, Ted [snuffling] thank God for you . . . [blows nose] . . . [slurred speech] Mister President, Mister President . . .

How could any constitutional republican watching this deplorable spectacle not find himself thinking the thought I was thinking: *What on earth is this decrepit, sniveling old fool doing in the world's greatest deliberative body?*

What he is doing is showing us, in a particularly repulsive way, the worm at the heart of the congressional apple: the stagnation and self-indulgence brought on by long incumbency.

To grasp the scale of the problem, let me first list the longest-serving members of the U.S. Senate at mid-July 2009:

Senator	Affiliation	Age	Years in office	No. of U.S. presiden-cies while in office
Robert Byrd	D-WV	91.6	50.4	11
Ted Kennedy	D-MA	77.4	46.7	10
Daniel Inouye	D-HI	84.8	46.5	10
Patrick Leahy	D-VT	69.3	34.5	7
Richard Lugar	R-IN	77.3	32.5	7
Orrin Hatch	R-UT	75.3	32.5	7

By comparison, here are the longest-serving of the world's national leaders, hereditary monarchs excluded:

Leader	Country	Age	Years in office	No. of U.S. presidencies while in office
Muammar al-Gaddafi	Libya	67.1	39.9	8
Ali Abdullah Saleh	Yemen	67.3	31.0	6
Teodoro Obiang Nguema Mbasogo	Equatorial Guinea	67.1	30.0	6
Robert Mugabe	Zimbabwe	85.4	29.4	6
Hosni Mubarek	Egypt	81.2	27.8	5
Paul Biya	Cameroon	76.4	26.7	5

As can be seen, the presidents-for-life of Third World sinkholes cannot compare with our senators for longevity in office.

This situation won't get better. According to current trend-lines, in fact, it seems sure to get worse. The House of Representatives actually illustrates this more clearly.

REPRESENTATIVE DEMOCRACY, RIP

On January 6, 2009, when the 111th Congress convened, 381 of the 435 members of the House of Representatives were returnees, having sat in the previous Congress. (Of the other 54, 31 had retired and 23 were defeated in either primary or general elections.)

This signifies a "reelected incumbent prevalence" (RIP in poli-sci jargon) rate of 88 percent, a tad on the low side for recent years. The corresponding rates for the previous five Congresses, the 106th through 110th, were 91, 91, 88, 91, and 87.

If we go back fifty years, to the 80th through 84th Congresses, the rates were 76, 73, 83, 81, and 87.

Back another fifty years, to the 55th through 59th: 59, 69, 74, 66, and 78.

Back yet another fifty years (we are now in the mid-nineteenth century): 44, 42, 42, 36, and 38.

Fifty more, to the 5th through 9th Congresses: 55, 57, 49, 45, and 67.

Notice anything? The averages for those five-session spans were, in order as above, going backward through time: 89, 80, 69, 40, and 55. So our RIP rate bottomed out at around 40 percent in the middle of the nineteenth century and has been rising pretty steadily ever since, now frequently exceeding 90 percent.

The causes of congressional stagnation are much debated by political scientists. Popular culprits are:

- Gerrymandering of congressional districts, assisted by clever software operating on census databases to draw optimal (from the point of view of incumbents, that is) boundaries for House districts. Once an approximate art, gerrymandering is now a precise science.
- Campaign finance rules favoring incumbents.
- The draining away of social capital described in the previous chapter, leading to citizens identifying less with their "little platoons," including their local party chapters.

These trends feed each other. In a district drawn to be maximally safe for one party, why waste money contributing to the other? With declining public participation, career politicians are freer to manipulate district boundaries . . . and so on. (Voter participation in U.S. elections has been declining since 1960: in percentage terms, from the low 60s to the low 50s.)

TWO CHRISTMAS TREES

The aggrandizement of the presidency, the stagnation of Congress—the trends I'm identifying here have been under way for decades. There is no force in sight that might halt or reverse them. And underneath both trends, raising them ever upward like kids on an inflating play castle, is the inexorable growth of the federal government under the general optimistic agreement, shared by all too many conservatives, that it can solve problems and improve the lives of citizens.

Wise Americans have always grumbled about the federal power. "No man's life or property is safe when Congress is in session"—that saying seems to go back at least a hundred years. A hundred years ago, however, the U.S. government and its laws occupied a far smaller zone of the national life than they do today. And there are signs that government wealth and power may have reached some kind of critical mass.

If you graph various proxies for state power—the number of pages of federal tax law and regulations (66,498 in 2006—I can't find a later figure, but you may be sure the number hasn't decreased), annual federal spending per household ($23,494 in 2007—higher, in inflation-adjusted dollars, than in World War II, and up 15 percent since 2000), federal employment (up nearly 80,000 under George W. Bush *in non-defense-related positions alone*), and so on—if you graph these proxies across time, the curves are turning sharply upward.

And yet the constituency for smaller government is weaker now than it has been for thirty years. "Self-government means self-support," said Calvin Coolidge. Well, guess what: People aren't all that keen on self-support. Welfare statism has caught the United States in its suffocating embrace, and it is not going to let go. It never has, anywhere.

The natural opposition to these statist tendencies is the conservative movement. The conservative movement, however, is in its death throes. My *National Review* colleague Ramesh Ponnuru wrote an article titled "Conservatives on the Couch" for a recent issue of the magazine. In that article Ramesh noted that ever since the Gingrich debacle of 1995–96, when parts of the federal government were shut down by a revolt of congressional Republicans, conservatives have been trying to reinvent their party without any of that scary talk about smaller government.

Pat Buchanan tried to throw out the free traders to bring in socially conservative union members. George W. Bush offered a "compassionate" (read: more statist) conservatism. John McCain and his fans had a "national greatness conservatism."

Conservatism has rejected each ideological novelty like a body rejecting a transplant.

As a result, the conservative movement has turned inward, away from being the promoter of smaller government, toward being the promoter of traditional values. It has always been both, of course; only the components of the mix change. With the antistatist cause apparently lost, American conservatives have little to occupy their time but right-to-life issues, squabbling over Middle East policy, and some v—e—r—y cautious, halfhearted, Diversity-whipped support for "national question" issues—immigration, citizenship, border security, visa integrity, multiculturalism, assimilation. And the state keeps on growing.

Yet can the federal government really run the United States? It's not obvious. Next to India, which I don't think is a very happy model, we are the biggest—the most extensive, most populous—free nation in the world. Centralized government, of the top-heavy European kind that is being imposed on us, may not work. We don't know. We have never tried it.

Certainly our federal government inspires little confidence. I have a sheaf of credit cards in my wallet, any one of which my local merchants can validate with a quick swipe. Why can't a person's social security card similarly be validated, to assure prospective employers or welfare agencies that he is a legal resident of the country? Because private corporations are approximately 100,000 times better—more efficient, more capable—of doing anything than is the U.S. government, that's why.

Federal capabilities in this area were demonstrated unforgettably on March 11, 2002, when the Huffman Aviation flight school of Venice, Florida, received notification from the Immigration and Naturalization Service that student visas had been approved for Mohamed Atta and Marwan al-Shehhi, six months to the day after those applicants had flown planes into the World Trade Center.

I, at least, wasn't surprised by any of that. In the 1990s, I had a job that required me to make occasional phone calls to banks and investment houses, and also to the offices of federal regulatory agencies like the FDIC in Washington, D.C.

To call a private company with a request, then to call a government agency, was to step through a horological time warp. A business would deal with me more or less well—sometimes less so, to be sure, but usually in a single call. To get the equivalent response from a government agency in Washington needed a whole week of calls. If anyone picked up the phone at all, I would hear a slow, indifferent voice, irked at having had its game of Solitaire interrupted, saying: "She ain't here today. . . . Oh, he left early . . ." Would my contact be in the office next day? "Hard to say . . . I guess . . ."

The old quip about Washington, D.C.—"Northern charm combined with Southern efficiency"—still describes the place.

And while the actual capabilities of the federal government stagnate, its size and wealth and power over our lives grow remorselessly. Centralized government is now a great fatted beast, swallowing up land, property, and wealth. Here is commentator Peggy Noonan, writing in the *Wall Street Journal* just before Christmas 2008:

> To drive through the suburbs of Northern Virginia is to marvel still at the widespread wealth, the mansions and minimansions that did not exist a quarter-century ago and that now thicken the woods and hills. It used to be sleepy here; it used to be horse farms . . . The other night, the big houses were strung with glittering white Christmas lights . . . heading toward Great Falls, we saw a house with a big glass-walled living room that faced the street, and below it a glass-walled entrance room, and each had its own brightly decorated tree. "Two Christmas trees," murmured a companion, and it captured the air of prosperity and solid well-being of the area. It reminded me: Government is our most reliable current and future growth industry, and the near suburbs of the capital are where those who run it, work it, lobby it, feed off it and finagle it live. "You have to go farther out to see the foreclosure signs," said a friend.

WEALTH AND POWER

Our republic began with the Cincinnatus ideal. Government office, even the highest government office, was a service and a sacrifice, not a path to personal enrichment. Until the Former Presidents Act of 1958 established a presidential pension (originally $25,000, now $191,300), it was the rule for presidents to leave office poorer than when they arrived. (See Chapter 12.)

We've come a long way very quickly. The founding ideal of the federal power was that it should be restrained and modest. It remained so until well within living memory. The president was not expected to do much, and the vice president was expected to do well nigh nothing at all. Of Benjamin Harrison, in office 1889–93, White House usher Ike Hoover recorded in his memoirs that "very seldom did [the President] work after lunch." Harding played golf in the afternoons, while Coolidge invariably took a nap "lasting from two to four hours" after lunch.

The District of Columbia was a drowsy backwater until the 1930s. Wiliam Howard Taft kept a cow in the White House stables (which had been empty since the coming of the automobile in the previous administration). At the time of Harding's inauguration, the District contained over two hundred working farms. Harding's vice president was Coolidge, of whom Claude M. Fuess's mesmerizing biography says the following:

> As Vice President of the United States, Coolidge occupied a position which paid him a salary of $12,000 a year. In addition to this, he was allowed his own automobile and chauffeur, his own secretary, page, and clerk, and his private telegraph operator. His chief duty was to preside over the Senate; and he was entitled to a room in the Senate office building but also to one in the Capitol, directly behind the Senate chamber. In the Senate proceedings he had no vote except in case of a tie. He was also *ex officio* President of the Smithsonian Institution. His actual duties, beyond these, were not numerous, and he had plenty of time to himself.

The vice presidency is a good index of the vast flabby sprawl of federal power. Memorably described by FDR's first vice president (i.e., the next but one after Coolidge) as "a bucket of warm piss," the office was a poor stepchild of the federal-legislative apparatus until very recently. Presidential biographies fill in the details. When Richard Nixon moved from the Senate to the vice presidency in 1953, for example, his staffing allowance dropped from $70,000 as a senator to less than $48,000 as veep. Nixon seems to have held on to all thirteen of his senatorial staff members somehow, but he was an exceptionally skillful player at bureaucratic games.

From Coolidge's five helpers to Nixon's thirteen took thirty years. What are we up to now? Try finding out. I did, at the time of the flap over Scooter Libby in 2007. Libby was chief of staff to Vice President Dick Cheney. How many Indians was he chief of? I went looking. It was like wading into quicksand.

I still have some scattered notes from my inquiries. The United States Government Manual for 2007/08, published by the Office of the Federal Register, lists seventeen names under "Office of the Vice President," with titles from chief of staff to executive assistant. That's by no means the whole story, though. Only three of those names have titles containing the phrase "national security"—four if you include "homeland security"—yet we know that in 2004 Dick Cheney had fourteen staff members dealing with national security. The Legistorm.com website, a good source for this kind of thing, listed forty names, but only six matched those in the U.S. Government Manual, so other names were presumably lurking in the shadows beyond the overlap. I *think* the answer to my question, if you add in both full-time staffers and regular consultants, is about two hundred. Even the vice president's *wife* has a chief of staff!

It's that way all over. Today's District of Columbia is a vast hive of federal power. Great towering ziggurats house the worker bees who supervise government's innumerable functions. Clustered nearby, like peasant huts beneath a medieval cathedral, are the offices of lobbyists, lawyers, journalists, consultants, and financiers, all parasitic on the federal leviathan.

And as in the great imperial-despotic systems of old, power

generates wealth. Bill and Hillary Clinton, neither of whom have ever done anything that ordinary citizens would recognize as a job, and who lived mainly in government-supplied accommodations until late middle age, have attained stupendous wealth through what is coyly referred to around the District as "public service." Countless others have followed their example on a more modest scale. Big government is big business.

And big government is *big*. Federal spending grows by leaps and bounds. The first few years of the twenty-first century have seen massive expansion of federal power over education (the No Child Left Behind Act, 2001), the biggest new entitlement program since Lyndon Johnson's administration (the Medicare Prescription Drug Act of 2003), and the biggest program of public works in U.S. history (the 2005 highway bill). And all this, from a conservative president!

The legislative process sucks up ever more of the national wealth, delivers ever more favors to noisy interest groups, with ever less oversight. As part of my journalistic duties in the spring of 2008, I watched the progress of the Iraq Supplemental Spending Bill, a $108 billion measure designed to keep our troops in Iraq and Afghanistan supplied through September of that year. By the time it reached the Senate floor, the bill had acquired amendments costing $36 billion for spending on NASA, Medicaid, Planned Parenthood, public works in Louisiana, and a host of other items utterly irrelevant to war funding. Most obnoxious of all was an amendment proposing to grant permanent residency to 1.35 million illegal-alien farm workers. Since their families would be eligible, too, this would have created three million new citizens, increasing the U.S. population by 1 percent at a stroke. (This particular amendment was killed after massive public protests.)

All that was written before the vast "bailout" and "stimulus" packages of 2008–9 when, quite suddenly it seemed, the word "trillion" became normal in speaking of single government initiatives.

Here is H. L. Mencken in 1935, describing how Harry Hopkins and three of his aides thought up the New Deal:

Four preposterous nonentities, all of them professional up-lifters, returning from a junket at the taxpayer's expense, sit in a smoking car munching peanuts and talking shop. Their sole business in life is spending other people's money. In the past they have always had to put in four-fifths of their time cadging it, but now the New Deal has admitted them to the vast vaults of the public treasury, and just beyond the public treasury, shackled in a gigantic lemon-squeezer worked by steam, groans the taxpayer.

Hopkins and his "uplifters" had a mere billion dollars to work with—equivalent to $16 billion in today's money. One wonders how Mencken would have summoned up enough scorn to cope with the multitrillion-dollar government spend-a-thons that fill today's news stories. And if $16 billion is "uplift," what's a trillion? Celestial optimism, perhaps.

LORDS AND PEASANTS

Along with all this swelling government power and largesse has come ever greater distance between the political classes and the public they "serve." A congressman is videotaped by the FBI receiving $100,000 in bribes. A raid on his home turns up $90,000 stashed in frozen-food containers in the refrigerator. He is reelected the following year, and three years after the FBI sting is still sitting in Congress. A senator is arrested after trying to procure sex partners in an airport restroom. He remains active in the Senate—was in fact cosponsor of that farm-worker amnesty amendment I just mentioned.

Our congressional overlords find it increasingly difficult to hide their contempt for us, the Great Unwashed.

They seem to take that last phrase literally, in fact. In December 2008, Senate Majority Leader Harry Reid said the following thing at the opening of the new, air-conditioned, $621 million Capitol Visitor Center: "My staff tells me not to say this, but I'm going to say it anyway. In the summer because of the heat and high humidity, you could literally smell the tourists coming into the Capitol. It may be descriptive but it's true." Pity our poor legislators, obliged to put up with the noise and stink of—ugh!—*voters* traipsing through their palace. But then, since we keep reelecting the swine (see above), perhaps their contempt for us is justified.

Meanwhile, in the White House, a proper republican respect for the office of the president has morphed into a style of groveling adulation more appropriate to the court of Heliogabalus. Gene Healy offers a particularly stomach-turning example in his 2008 book *The Cult of the Presidency*.

> Robert Draper, a journalist granted unique access to [George W.] Bush in 2006 and 2007 to write the president's biography, notes that in every cabinet meeting since White House Chief of Staff Josh Bolten took over for Andy Card in 2006, Bolten has begun by looking at Bush and saying, "Thank you for the privilege of serving today." At no point, it seems, did Bush thank Bolten for his deference and then tell him to *cut it out.* [*Emphasis in original*]

I have not so far heard that White House functionaries walk backward away from the presidential presence, as is done in the royal courts of Britain and Japan, or get down on their knees and knock their heads on the floor in a full formal kowtow, as was the rule in imperial China, but surely such protocols cannot be many years away. To be ready for their implementation, you might like to note that a full kowtow requires three kneelings from a standing position, the forehead striking the carpet three times at each kneeling, for a total of nine head-carpet contacts.

THE LOSS OF REPUBLICAN VIRTUE

We have, I repeat, lost our republican virtue, traded it in for a passel of gassy rhetoric, imperial grandeur, and promises of managerial competence from rooted incumbents like Senator Robert Byrd and Representative John Dingell (longest-serving member of the House at 53.6 years and counting). The practical, provincial farmers and merchants of the founding era have given way to a professional political class. Here are the announced members of Barack Obama's cabinet as of April 2009:

Position	Name	Résumé
Attorney General	Eric Holder	Government lawyering
Secretary of Agriculture	Tom Vilsack	Lawyering, politics
Secretary of Commerce	Gary Locke	Lawyering, politics
Secretary of Defense	Robert Gates	CIA, Mil-Int
Secretary of Education	Arne Duncan	Education bureaucracy (never taught)
Secretary of Energy	Steven Chu	Research physicist, academic
Secretary of Health and Human Services	Kathleen Sebelius	Politics
Secretary of Homeland Security	Janet Napolitano	Lawyering, politics
Secretary of Housing and Urban Development	Shaun Donovan	Bureaucracy
Secretary of the Interior	Ken Salazar	Lawyering, politics
Secretary of Labor	Hilda Solis	Racial lobbying
Secretary of State	Hillary Clinton	Politics
Secretary of Transportation	Ray LaHood	High school teaching, politics
Secretary of the Treasury	Timothy Geithner	Lobbying, bureaucracy, diplomacy, tax "forgetfulness"
Secretary of Veterans' Affairs	Eric Shinseki	Military

Military service, scientific research, and high school teaching are certainly honorable and praiseworthy occupations. The other lines of work listed in the table on page 60 are essentially parasitic. Not one name in the table, *not one*, has ever created a dime of wealth. So far as the gross national product is concerned, and even including those three honorable and necessary professions, these are, to a man and a woman, subtracters, not adders.

To be fair, I should note that President Obama did once work for about a year at Business International Corporation, called by the *New York Times* "a small newsletter-publishing and research firm" in New York City. In his autobiography, Obama described this one experience of private-sector work as making him feel "like a spy behind enemy lines."

These are our masters: lawyers, bureaucrats, and race hustlers who regard creators of wealth as the enemy. By looking for too much from politics, by putting our optimistic faith in their bogus stories about expertise and competence, in their promises to "fix" things and "improve" things, in their vapid talk of bringing us "hope" and "change," we have sold our birthright to hacks, frauds, and cynical time-servers—"public servants" who don't even pay their income taxes. Feugh!

4

CULTURE: POOPED OUT

Is It Just Me or Is Everything Shit?
— Title of a 2005 book by Steve Lowe
and Alan McArthur

Pop culture is filth.
— Section heading in an article by this author on
National Review Online, 8/2/02

NO, WE CAN'T

To deal first with the arresting title of Lowe and McArthur's book: No, not everything is shit. *Some* things are shit, though—including some of the artifacts of modern Western high culture. Consider, for example, a work by Italian artist Piero Manzoni.

Signor Manzoni died tragically young in 1963 at age twenty-nine, from a heart attack. He was, however, vouchsafed enough time on earth to complete his creative masterpiece: *Merda d'artista* ("Artist's Shit"). This consists of 90 one-ounce portions of Manzoni's own solid waste, each portion neatly canned and each can numbered. When he had recovered from the aesthetic exhaustion that must have been brought on by creating so much art, Manzoni headed for the auction houses. His asking price was based on the value of a quantity of gold of weight equivalent to the substance in the cans. He got it, of course.

These treasures continue to fetch high prices, in spite of a tendency to explode. (Manzoni *deliberately* left tiny faults in the sealing of the cans. How would you like to be in the Restoration Department when one of those suckers comes in?) *Can #4* was sold to London's Tate Gallery in 2002 for $61,000, a sum nearly two hundred times the equivalent weight of gold at the then spot price of $318 per ounce. Questioned by reporters, the Tate extruded the following explanation:

> The Manzoni was a very important purchase for an extremely small amount of money: nobody can deny that. . . . He was an incredibly important international artist. What he was doing with this work was looking at a lot of issues that are pertinent to 20th-century art, like authorship and the production of art. It was a seminal work.

(It seems to me there is an element of physiological confusion in that last sentence . . . but let's pass right along, shall we?) The most recent of Manzoni's cans to be auctioned, *#19*, sold for $80,000 in February 2007 to an American collector.

So while not everything in our culture is shit, some things indisputably *are*.

Should you be tempted to buy Lowe and McArthur's book, I had better say that the authors are British, and the book itself is largely incomprehensible to a non-British reader. Even to those of us acquainted with BritCult, in fact, the thing is a bit lame. Sample, at random from the book's precise center:

Kabbalah

Back when people imagined The Future on [TV] programmes like *Tomorrow's World*, the 21st century was full of jet-packs and robots doing your ironing. None of the so-called "experts" predicted that everyone would be getting into a weird sect vaguely related to an ancient Jewish tradition that sells bits of red string to its followers at £18.50 a pop. Dr Heinz Wolff? You're a fucking charlatan.

(I have no clue what Dr. Wolff, a popularizer of science on British TV, is doing in there.)

IIƒMOIES is also, insofar as it has any political "line"—which, to be fair, is not really very far—a critique from the Left, with snarky comments about George W. Bush, oil companies, and so on. This puts Lowe and McArthur, for all their laddish frivolity, in a respectable line of cultural critics, including some very deep brows like Morris Berman (*The Twilight of American Culture*, 2000) and the late Jane Jacobs (*Dark Age Ahead*, 2005).

Cultural critiques from the Right either attack the science-envious intellectual fads of college humanities departments, like Roger Kimball's classic *Tenured Radicals* (1990, but reissued in 2008 in an updated version) or else offer traditionalist diatribes, usually from a religious angle, against, to quote from one of them (Bill O'Reilly's *Culture Warrior*, 2006), "secular-progressive values."

As a conservative by temperament, I hate to say this, but I think the Left has the better of the argument here. Western culture *is* in its twilight; there *is* a dark age ahead; and while college-humanities fads and "secular-progressive values" have certainly done much damage, they are symptoms, not causes—fragments of junk sucked into a vacuum. The fundamental reason why so much of our culture is shit— either literally, like Signor Manzoni's masterwork, or figuratively— is exhaustion, cultural exhaustion. We are pooped out.

Listen to one of the greatest educators of the twentieth century, Kenneth Clark, in his book *Civilisation:*

> Civilisation requires a modicum of material prosperity—enough to provide a little leisure. But, far more, it requires confidence— confidence in the society in which one lives, belief in its philosophy, belief in its laws, and confidence in one's own mental powers. . . . So if one asks why the civilisation of Greece and Rome collapsed, the real answer is that it was exhausted.

We, too, are exhausted, not because we have run out of things to say, but because we took a wrong turn in the twentieth century.

Art and entertainment rest on assumptions about human nature and human capabilities, and we have been working from wrong assumptions.

The modernist composer Anton Webern predicted back in the 1930s that mailmen on their rounds would one day whistle his atonal nonmelodies. People like melody and harmony? Webern would make us like his modernistic "tone rows." Why not? Human nature and human tastes are infinitely adjustable, infinitely adaptable, infinitely plastic, aren't they?

This is a sort of grand theme running through all of modernity. Infinite possibility! Infinite changeability! Infinite hope! Yes, we can! The whole Modern Movement in the arts and literature drew from this infinite-possibilities dogma. I doubt it's a coincidence that these ideas came up at the same time as the "Culturist" anthropology of Franz Boas—much more on that in Chapter 7.

The obvious, true, and conservative response to "Yes, we can!" is "No, we can't." We *can't* like tone rows as much as we like melodies. We *can't* like free verse as much as we like rhyme and meter. We *can't* like numbered cans of shit as much as we like landscapes, portraits, and still lifes. We can't. We are human. We have limits. That's not even really pessimism, just *reality*.

LOW CULTURE, HIGH CULTURE

What kind of culture are we talking about, though? Signor Manzoni's work, being traded among oak-paneled auction houses and tony art galleries, obviously belongs to the realm of high culture. It's probably more logical to start a discussion of culture from the other end, though (oh, you know what I mean); so let's take a look at *popular* culture. I'll return to the heavy-duty stuff later.

At the beginning of this chapter, I have quoted myself—look, I don't get *that* many opportunities—saying that pop culture is filth. So it is. Take, for example, TV.

To be perfectly frank, I watch very little TV. I'm not a snob about this—not the more obnoxious kind of snob, anyway. It's mostly just generational. I was a radio kid; we didn't have a TV till I was thirteen, which is too late to really acquire a habit. I'll sit and watch one of the TV talking-head programs: I like O'Reilly, and I used to watch *The McLaughlin Group* pretty regularly, until Eleanor Clift just got too grating. There were sitcoms I liked, too: *Married with Children* was a favorite: I still sometimes sing the "Psycho Dad" song in hopes—vain, of course—of terrorizing my children. Way back before that, I enjoyed the great 1970s Saturday night lineup with Mary Tyler Moore, Bob Newhart, and Carol Burnett.

Second childhood is setting in, though, with regression to my pre-TV days. I can less and less be bothered with the thing. I sit and watch O'Reilly or Lou Dobbs for twenty minutes, then start to fidget, and have to go put up a shelf or tidy the basement.

Fortunately, there are people willing to watch TV for me. There is, for example, Adam Buckman, TV critic of the *New York Post*. Here he is on September 21, 2008, talking about a drama series called *Sons of Anarchy* on the FX channel. The series concerns "outlaw bikers in California":

> It's not so much the show's violence that gets to me; I expect these people to be violent. Instead, it's portions of the dialogue that are so gratuitously shocking . . . The dialogue in question has to do with certain male bodily fluids from which DNA can be extracted (and I'm not talking about blood or saliva either).
>
> In "Sons of Anarchy," the ingestion of said fluids is described in graphic language that is so extreme that I doubt even the sociopathic ex-cons depicted in this show would talk this way.

He moves on to a cop show titled *The Shield*, also on FX.

> The actors on "The Shield" are tossing off some of the filthiest lines of dialogue in the show's history, also with a pornographic emphasis on sex and other bodily functions, such as a reference in an upcoming episode about federal agents metaphorically urinating in someone's mouth.

Hmm. My minimal-TV decision is looking better and better. But perhaps FX is the filth channel, or perhaps this is just a general cable-TV phenomenon. Nope:

> In the premiere episode of "The Ex List," an upcoming CBS series about a woman trying desperately to land a husband, I counted six separate conversations about one female character's pubic hair.

That female character is at least alive. Though I don't watch much TV myself, my wife and kids have the thing on a lot, and I catch stuff as I pass through the living room. Some fleeting impressions:

- *Dead whore shows.* There is a whole clutch of shows called *CSI Something* in which plainclothes police types and pathologists in lab coats converse in a sort of portentous murmur over the mutilated corpses of street ladies. Wikipedia: "The most-watched program on American television by 2002, with 30 to 40 million viewers a week . . . As of the Fall of 2008, *CSI* commands an average cost of $262,200 for a 30-second commercial . . ." There is no background music in these shows, just that continuous heavy murmuring and an occasional cop-car siren. You get lingering close-ups of entry wounds, exit wounds, contusions, abrasions, lacerations, dismemberments, decapitations, eviscerations, exsanguinations, etc.

- *Amateur hour shows.* People who can't sing, sing; or guys in pirate blouses and women with superhigh-reflectivity lip gloss dance for a couple of minutes. The performers then submit to humiliating critiques from a panel of judges, one of whom, by some kind of cosmic law applying to these shows in general, has to be a caustic Brit. (The dance show is actually called *Dancing with the Stars.* I never heard of any of the stars, but that's probably just me.)

- *Toon shows.* No end of them. *Family Guy,* with the wisecracking baby; *SpongeBob SquarePants,* which I have watched just enough of to understand why my kids address me as Squidward; *Jimmy Neutron*, whose writers once used an entire paragraph *verbatim* from my book about the Riemann Hypothesis. (I got into an e-correspondence with one of them about it—nice guy, very science-savvy); *The Simpsons*, which has some kind of cult status among very smart and clued-in people of the generation below mine, for reasons I don't understand, never having stayed awake through an entire episode; *South Park*, which people sometimes send me funny clips from, and with whose name Brian Anderson tagged an entire political cohort in his 2005 book *South Park Conservatives*, but which, when I've tried to sit and watch a whole episode, always disappoints.

- *Girly shows.* It is, I believe, a fact that women watch much more TV than men. I suppose that accounts for all the girly shows. The striking thing about these shows is how very, very girly they are. Estrogen is practically oozing out of the TV screen and dripping down onto my carpet. I warn my son sternly that if he watches one of these shows all the way through he'll start menstruating. Some of them are "relationship" dramedies in which thirtysomething women talk competitively and tirelessly about men *(Sex and the City)*; some are from the Amateur Hour border zone, women judging other women's looks *(America's Top Model)* after a few shots of the competitors sitting around primping while shrieking "Oh my God!" at each other; some are more traditional sitcom formats in which clever women outwit slow, dumb men *(Friends)*; some are teen-oriented, dealing with pond-life status-struggles among the young offspring of people with more money than sense *(Gossip Girl)*.

Now, I don't claim that is a statistically representative sample of current TV, it's just what I see on the way from my study to the liquor cabinet and back.

Newton N. Minow's 1961 speech to the National Association of Broadcasters, in which he called the TV programming of his time "a vast wasteland," is number twenty-two on the DVD titled *Twenty-five Speeches That Changed the World.*

"Changed the world"? What changed?

ALL DOWNHILL SINCE *SATURDAY NIGHT FEVER*

It's not so much the filth aspect of pop culture as the impression that *there's nothing there.* It's contentless. Most pop culture productions are just struggling to fill airtime.

This hasn't always been the case with pop culture, even in its lowest manifestations. The vaudeville songs of a hundred years ago were often funny and clever. Some of them consisted of really good poems set to music. (Kipling was a favorite.) Even the "vast wasteland" of TV in 1961 had some gems. There were real TV dramas still; and *The Twilight Zone,* often very imaginative; and really ingenious comedies like *The Phil Silvers Show.*

I know, the contrary case has been made—for example, by Steven Johnson in his 2003 book *Everything Bad Is Good for You.* The technological complexity of the modern world—video games, gadgets—is making us smarter, Johnson argues, and that is reflected in the much greater complexity of today's TV shows.

> Compare the way comedy unfolds in recent classics like *Seinfeld* and *The Simpsons . . .* to earlier sitcoms like *All in the Family* or *Mary Tyler Moore.* The most telling way to measure these shows' complexity is to consider how much external information the viewer must draw upon to "get" the jokes in their entirety.

But having more things to know is not the same as knowing more, unless the depth of knowledge you bring to each thing is the same as it was in past times. Recall the old quip about the increasing specialization of higher education: We come to know more and more about less and less, until at last we know everything about nothing. It may be that in a world of ever-increasing complexity and variety, we just end up knowing next to nothing about an enormous number of things. My kids can swiftly and deftly program gadgets for which I can't even locate the controls. That this is a worthwhile form of knowing, I am not convinced.

I'm a bit better acquainted with movies than I am with TV. I have even done a few movie reviews. A year or so ago, fishing around for a topic for a column, I noticed that the thirtieth anniversary of the movie *Saturday Night Fever* was coming up. This was the 1977 John Travolta disco movie, with all those plaintive songs by the Bee Gees on the soundtrack. I rented a DVD and sat down to watch it, sure I could get twelve hundred words out of the thing if I tried hard.

The piece I eventually published ran to thirty-seven hundred words, and I sent it off thinking I'd barely cleared my throat. I was astonished at, to quote the first section heading in my piece, "the richness of the movie."

> The first thing that struck me, watching *SNF* again after a lapse of years, was the *richness* of it. There is so much going on. How did they get it all into 118 minutes? [Here I gave a three-paragraph summary of the plot and subplots.] All this in 118 minutes! *Hamlet* doesn't get so much more into four hours.

> There is plenty to dislike about *SNF*: coarse sex, foul language, some technical cinematographic lapses. Narratively and musically, though, it is wonderfully nourishing.

Thus encouraged, I thought I'd try some more movie reviewing, but taking on current movies rather than ones from thirty years ago. I had a go at the movie *300*, director Zack Snyder's superhit about ancient Sparta, which was well reviewed at all levels (and which was later ranked number five on the "Best Conservative Movies" list in the February 23, 2009, issue of *National Review*). I couldn't find anything to say about the thing, and at last gave up on my review. Nothing there. I tried a few more: still nothing there. Possibly I'm missing some point. Can we really have gone downhill from disco? Downhill? From *disco?*

I would add something here about pop music, except that I haven't voluntarily listened to any for a couple of decades. The main story seems to be one of fragmentation. The last time I really paid much attention, there was rock, R&B, soft rock, folk, jazz, and lounge singers. Nowadays, well . . . What are "Techno," "Electro," "Chillout," and "House"? What's the difference between "Emo" and "Screamo"? I remember Reggae, but what's "Ragga"? How do "Nu Metal," "Black Metal," "Alternative Metal," and "Death Metal" differ? Does anybody know? Would having a degree in metallurgy help? Is this like having forty-five different kinds of breakfast cereal that all taste pretty much the same?

I don't know. Don't want to know. Don't care. I have bigger fish to fry. Let's get back to *high* culture.

NO BOOKS, NO GLORY

If pop culture has emptied out and fragmented, high culture has just *stopped.*

This is a thing that sometimes happens. Stage drama in the West pretty much stopped after the Roman dramatists of the second century B.C. Even they were working slavishly from Greek models. Some classicists would tell you ancient stage drama really stopped with Sophocles and Euripides, who both died in 406 B.C. Things got going again in sixteenth-century England, but that's after a pause of *two thousand years.*

It's the same all over. Ask any educated Chinese person to quote some lines from a favorite poem. It's very unlikely his choice will be from any poet later than the Song Dynasty (thirteenth century). Or try Chinese philosophy. Here is Chai Ch'u's *The Story of Chinese Philosophy*, which I received as a gift from the author's brother some years ago. It's a useful little handbook. Professor Chai takes you through all the main schools: Confucius, Mencius, Taoists, Legalists. The last philosopher he discusses in detail is Han Fei Tzu, *floruit* middle third century B.C. This chapter ends on page 223. We turn the page and find ourselves looking at a chapter named "Conclusion." Ten pages later the book ends.

Sometimes entire aspects of culture just *stop.* They may start again, like Western drama; or, like Chinese poetry and philosophy, they may not. (There have, of course, been Chinese poets since the Song Dynasty, and Chinese philosophers since Han Fei Tzu, just as there were mumming plays and traveling acrobatic troupes in the Middle Ages; but only specialist scholars know or care.)

That's how it is with high culture. I hang out with well-educated people, who sometimes drop a line of poetry into their talk. The poem quoted is rarely less than a hundred years old. I am sure that entire days go by when nobody in the United States quotes, for purposes other than pedagogical, any poem later than Robert Frost's "Stopping by Woods" (1922). The exceptions are memorable for being so exceptional: for example, Ronald Reagan quoting John Gillespie Magee's "High Flight" (1941) at the 1986 commemoration of the *Challenger* astronauts.

"The chief glory of every people arises from its authors," opined Samuel Johnson. Not anymore it doesn't. But let me play the good social scientist; let me *quantify*.

An approximate measure of glory in our culture is getting your picture on the cover of *Time* magazine. How are authors doing on that?

CLEAR OUT OF GLORY

This is easy, if a bit time- (not to mention *Time*-) consuming, to check, as *Time* has put all their covers on the Internet. I just spent a happy couple of hours trawling back through them. I need to make some qualifications here. First, only live authors count; the July 14, 2008, cover story on Mark Twain, for example, doesn't. Second, I'm going to restrict myself to novelists, the novel being the premier form of high-culture book-writing in our age. Third, I've only tallied authors who get a *Time* cover to themselves. Showing up in one of those "100 Most Influential" cover stories doesn't count. Finally, I'm only tallying people whose fame comes from their novels, not people like the late William F. Buckley Jr., who wrote novels but were mainly famous for something else. Okay, whadda we got?

As of early 2009, it has been *over ten years* since *Time* did a cover story on an author. That was Tom Wolfe (November 2, 1998). Two other authors showed up in the 1990s: Toni Morrison (January 19, 1998) and Michael Crichton (September 25, 1995). So that's three for the 1990s, *none* to date for the 2000s.

The 1980s also had three: Garrison Keillor (heck, I'll count him), John Updike, and John Irving.

In the 1970s there were five: John Le Carré, Alex Haley, Gore Vidal, Alexander Solzhenitsyn, and Günter Grass.

The 1960s featured six authors: Vladimir Nabokov, Solzhenitsyn again, Updike again, John Cheever, James Baldwin, and J. D. Salinger. There were even three living poets on *Time* covers in the 1960s: Robert Lowell, Phyllis McGinley, and Yevgeny Yevtushenko. *Poets!* (More on that below.)

For the 1950s, I count seven: Boris Pasternak, James Cozzens (another fine conservative pessimist, now well-nigh forgotten), Herman Wouk, André Malraux, Ernest Hemingway, Joyce Cary, and Graham Greene. Poets again, too: Robert Frost and T. S. Eliot.

Time covers for the 1940s were crowded up with dictators and military men, quite excusably. They managed to find cover space for five authors, though: John Marquand, Rebecca West, Craig Rice, Sinclair Lewis, and Kenneth Roberts. We might allow C. S. Lewis for six, though it was his Christian apologetics that got *Time*'s interest, not his fantasy novels.

The 1930s were exceptionally author rich. Ten cover stories featured authors: James Joyce, Malraux again, Hemingway again, Virginia Woolf, John Dos Passos, John Buchan, Upton Sinclair, Thomas Mann, Joyce again, and Willa Cather. Three poets got in there, too: Carl Sandburg, Gertrude Stein (I'm allowing a generous definition of "poet"), and Robinson Jeffers.

For the 1920s, I need to do a little scaling, as *Time* only started publishing on March 3, 1923. That loses us 1,157 of the 3,653 days in the 1920s, so I have to scale by a factor of 1.4635. Doing that for the eight authors with *Time* covers in the 1920s (Joseph Conrad, Israel Zangwill, Booth Tarkington, H. G. Wells, Sinclair Lewis again, Michael Arlen, E. Phillips Oppenheimer, and Edgar Wallace) gives me nearly *twelve* for the decade. There are three poets, too: Rudyard Kipling, Paul Claudel, and Robert Bridges—scaling up to 4.4.

Ignoring the poets and scaling where necessary, I have for the past nine decades (present to past), the following numbers of authors with *Time* cover stories to their glory:

> 2000s: 0
> 1990s: 3
> 1980s: 3
> 1970s: 5
> 1960s: 6
> 1950s: 7
> 1940s: 5
> 1930s: 10
> 1920s: 12

If you add in the poets:

> 2000s: 0
> 1990s: 3
> 1980s: 3
> 1970s: 5
> 1960s: 9
> 1950s: 9
> 1940s: 5
> 1930s: 13
> 1920s: 16

Allowing the 1940s as a pardonable lapse, the trend is all too plain. If "the chief glory of every people arises from its authors," we have clear run out of glory.

SPRAWL, EQUIVOCATE, MYSTIFY

Not that literature is extinct, even if *Time* can't be bothered with it. Novelists we have aplenty, and each has his little cheering section.

Here, though, we are back with those forty-five varieties of breakfast cereal. It is hard to believe that any of the names of today's novelists will be known to my grandchildren's generation.

Even the middlebrow novel is slipping away from us. The last one I can recall that you could reliably bring up in a group of educated Americans, in the reasonable certainty that enough of them had read it to keep a conversation going, is Tom Wolfe's *Bonfire of the Vanities* (1987).

The less said about the highbrow novel, the better—though if you want to see all that needs to be said, I recommend B. R. Myers's 2002 diatribe *A Reader's Manifesto*, subtitled: "An Attack on the Growing Pretentiousness of American Literary Prose." In an appendix, Myers offers ten spoof rules for "serious" writers. The first is:

I. Be writerly
  Read aloud what you have written. If it sounds clear and natural, strike it out. This is the whole of the law; the rest is gloss.

(Myers's other nine headings are: *Sprawl, Equivocate, Mystify, Keep Sentences Long, Repeat Yourself, Pile on the Imagery, Archaize, Bore,* and *Play the Part.*)

SING, HEAVENLY MUSE!

Poetry, the other big wing of the House of Literature, presents an even sadder spectacle. After a spell of employment with the stuffily Establishment BBC of the 1940s, broadcasting literary programs to India, George Orwell observed: "Poetry on the air sounds like the Muses in striped trousers."

He should have worried. To get the Muses into striped trousers nowadays, you'd first have to find them. They have fled, and the poetry Muses (there were three) have fled further than the others. They don't seem to want to have anything to do with the human race anymore. You can see their point, but it's a grave loss nonetheless.

It's hard to blame the poets. I happen to believe that the Modern Movement was all a ghastly mistake, like communism, and that, as with communism, it will take a century or so to clean up the mess. Now, in art and literature new things must be tried, old habits challenged, eggs broken in the hope of making omelets. It is just our bad luck that none of the things tried in the twentieth century worked very well, that the omelets were all inedible. We took a wrong turn, and ended up in this cultural Death Valley.

In particular, of course, free verse—poetry without rhyme or regular rhythm—didn't work very well. I'm not a purist about free verse, as were Robert Frost ("playing tennis without a net") and G. K. Chesterton ("Free verse? You may as well call sleeping in a ditch 'free architecture'!") Free verse can occasionally be very striking. The trouble is that there is far too much of it about, and people have been led to believe that fundamental poetic skills are not very important, or even that they are altogether unnecessary; or even— see below—that to use them is fascistic.

In the early 1980s, I taught a college course in poetry, using the second edition (1965) of C. F. Main and Peter Seng's *Wadsworth Handbook and Anthology*, an excellent text for that purpose. I lost the book somewhere on my subsequent travels, but three or four years later decided to buy another copy, and duly did so. By this time the book had advanced to a fourth edition (1978), and I was dismayed to see that the lessons on scansion—patterns of regular rhythm—which in the second edition were part of the main text, in the fourth had been hustled off to an appendix! Probably they have been dropped altogether by now.

Here are some lines from a collection titled *The George Washington Poems*, by Diane Wakoski, published in 1967:

> *George Washington, your name is on my lips.*
> *You had a lot of slaves.*
> *I don't like the idea of slaves. I know I am*
> *a slave to*
> *too many masters, already*

If this is poetry, what's *not* poetry? One thinks of Doctor Johnson's reply when asked if he thought many men could have written

Macpherson's bogus epic poem *Ossian:* "Yes, Sir, many men, many women, and many children."

When an impressionable young person is told that this is poetry, and that the kind of gassy drivel extruded by Maya Angelou at the first Clinton inauguration, or by Elizabeth Alexander at Obama's, is also poetry; and when that young person furthermore learns that Diane Wakoski is actually a full-time professional poet, who makes a decent middle-class living at it, and that Ms. Angelou has even got modestly rich from her vaporings, and that Ms. Alexander is a professor at Yale, then that young person's attitude to poetry has been corrupted.

Free verse is not the whole of the problem, though. Even in the coldest depths of the free-verse nuclear winter, around 1970, plenty of dedicated poets were still writing formal, structured verse. Elizabeth Bishop's perfect little villanelle "One Art," for example—sufficiently well known, at any rate among literary types, to have generated at least one good parody—was written in 1975. Richard Wilbur, John Hollander, and many others produced, and are still producing, verse in traditional forms.

The late 1970s in fact saw the birth of the so-called "New Formalism," in which a whole tribe of younger poets committed themselves to working with rhyme, meter, and traditional structures. That got a ferocious counterblast from the modernists. The aforementioned Diane Wakoski published a broadside titled "The New Conservatism in American Poetry," in *American Book Review*, May–June 1986. She pretty much said that anyone who writes formal poetry is a fascist. With Hollander she went further, calling him "Satan."

The current (early 2009) poetry bestseller in the United States is Camille Paglia's anthology *Break, Blow, Burn*. It took the lady five years to put it together, she tells us. An editor gave me it for review. Here is the conclusion of my review (which wasn't published):

> Reading this book was like flipping through one of those pretentious, absurd catalogs you get when visiting an exhibition of the sillier kind of fashionable art. I even had a fleeting suspicion that the whole thing might be a spoof—a send-up of ponderous

academic over-interpretation. No, the author is in earnest. Paglia has opened a window into the precious, self-referential little world of literary theorizing.

For this poetry lover, it was a glimpse of Hell. And what is burning in that hell is our poetry, for a thousand years the greatest glory of the English-speaking people, but now dead, smothered under the horrid rotten mass of literary academicism. We must have done something very terrible to have our birthright taken from us, to see it suffocated in dust like this.

As quality has declined, quantity has increased. In modern poetry circles, indeed, the bitter little joke is that there are more people writing the stuff than reading it, which may very well be true. Here is an excerpt from the January–February 2009 issue of *Poets & Writers* magazine, house journal of the M.F.A. set—I'll explain about that a little later. *P&W* mentions the proliferation of small poetry presses and self-publishing options, then:

> It's no wonder that more and more poets are publishing books and getting them into the marketplace. Last year at the Poets House Showcase—an annual event for which new poetry books published in the last year or so are put on display—the nonprofit poetry library received nearly 2,200 books, at least 20 percent of which were debuts.

Twenty-two hundred books of poetry in one year! You'd have to read six of them every day to get through them all.

I recommend, for the sake of your sanity, that you not try it. A high proportion of current poetry is solipsistic twaddle, with victimological (race-conscious or feminist) whining much favored.

THE DEATH OF CREATIVITY

Surveying culture both high and low, the striking thing is the lack of anything original. I sometimes wonder if perhaps we have said everything that can be said about the human condition. In poetry, certainly, it's rare to hear anything that prompts you to think, "Gee, I never looked at it that way before."

This sad truth was demonstrated to the whole nation at the inauguration of Barack Obama in January 2009. The incoming president decided to revive the custom of having a poet read something from the inaugural dais. The poet he chose was Elizabeth Alexander.

I had never heard of this lady before the president-elect tapped her for the inauguration spot. Taking a wild shot in the dark, I guessed her to be a whiny left-wing black feminist, as most female poets nowadays are.

Sure enough. I looked up her website. What topics excite this poet? Well, there's the Middle Passage:

> *The slave-ship empty, its cargo landed*
> *And sold for twelve ounces of gold a-piece.*

And then there's the "Hottentot Venus," a steatopygous (that is, having massive deposits of fat on thighs and buttocks) African woman exhibited in early-nineteenth-century Europe:

> *Monsieur Cuvier investigates*
> *between my legs, poking, prodding . . .*

Not forgetting childbirth, of course, which is kind of like jazz.

> *Giving birth is like jazz, something from silence . . .*

. . . And kind of like the Middle Passage.

> *. . . Long, elegant boats,*
> *blood-boiling sunshine, human cargo . . .*

On the evidence of the poems Ms. Alexander has put on her website, you could sum up her thematic range as "I'm black! Black black

black! And I have a vagina!" Pretty much all current "establishment" poetry—the kind of poetry that will get you picked to read at a presidential inauguration—traipses around and around a narrow track of victimization, racism, sexism, and the rest of the dreary catalog of modern grievance culture.

Elizabeth Alexander writes essays, too, which are about—what else?—black poets . . . including herself, natch. Of her own poem "Amistad," which is about, uh, the Middle Passage, she tells us on her website:

> I . . . wanted to explore the past in the face of the aggressive ahistoricity that plagues and misnames this nation and is a tool for misleading the people.

In what way is our nation misnamed? Which part of the name does Ms. Alexander object to: the "United," the "States," or the "America"? Or is it perhaps the "of," or the "the"? Hard to figure.

All this dismal solipsism and picking at historical scabs might be easier to take if it was delivered with any art or wit. No, there is nothing here but formless stream-of-consciousness driveling, padded out with feeble imagery and nonsensical similes. It was all on display at the inauguration, as a rapt nation heard Ms. Alexander tell us about

> *Love beyond marital, filial, national,*
> *love that casts a widening pool of light,*
> *love with no need to preempt grievance.*

The verb "preempt" means, according to *Webster's Third*, "to seize upon to the exclusion of others: take for oneself." So this kind of love, which I'd guess Ms. Alexander wants us all to feel for each other, has no need to take all of some grievance for itself, leaving none for anyone else. What kind of love *would* do that? What's the grievance, anyway? The poem offers no clue.

It goes without saying that nothing rhymes or scans here. I suppose that would be "acting white." Nor is there any familiar form to rest the eye on—a sonnet, straightforward quatrains, a villanelle. (In one of the interviews on her website, Ms. Alexander refers to having written formal verse, but I couldn't find any examples.) Nothing worth remembering, nothing striking, nothing amusing, nothing of universal appeal, nothing that owes anything to the magnificent centuries-long tradition of English verse; only the monotonous, structureless, subliterate whining of nursed and petted victimhood.

And with all that victimology, what is Ms. Alexander a victim of? She had a very comfortable upper-middle-class upbringing, a deal more comfortable than my working-class one, I'd guess—her father was secretary of the Army! Born in 1962, she went to Yale, did "a one-year stint as a reporter for the *Washington Post*," and has spent the rest of her life since in academia, teaching bogus subjects like "African American studies," of which she is currently a professor.

M.F.A.—MAKING A LITERARY LIVING

The modern college and Diversity rackets have provided a cozy home for whole legions of parasitic subintellectuals like Ms. Alexander. You go to college; you graduate; you do a year or two of some kind of marginally useful desk work, probably editing or lawyering; then you get yourself back into the academy for life teaching some fluff nonsubject, or go run one of the Diversity shakedown scams under some such title as "community organizer" or "community affairs adviser." There must be other prominent examples of this career path, though none comes to mind just at the moment.

Once this was a nation of farmers, builders, inventors, creators, explorers, and thinkers. Now we are a nation of bubblehead academic poseurs, race-guilt hucksters, and keening middle-class "victims" of imaginary wrongs. Pah!

Perhaps I shouldn't be *too* unkind to poets in general. Conservative magazines like *The New Criterion, Chronicles,* and *National Review* publish thoughtful and nonsolipsistic, nonvictimological poetry, more often than not in traditional forms with detectable rhyme and scansion. There's an underground of decent poetry, if you know where to look. That's the point, though: It's an underground.

That daunting pile of twenty-two hundred new books in one year shows the difficulty of looking, unless you are really determined. In any case, the high ground of current poetry is occupied by the likes of Elizabeth Alexander and the M.F.A. set.

M.F.A. stands for Master of Fine Arts, a two-year postgraduate qualification you can get, for a fee (annual tuition is comparable to undergraduate programs), at numerous colleges and graduate schools.

The M.F.A. programs are the engine of modern literary livelihood. A lot of people you never heard of are making a modest middle-class living at poetry. You get a couple of books into that pile of twenty-two hundred. You have a poem or two published in one of the tiny-circulation literary magazines. You pick up an award or two—there are dozens—and soon you can sink happily into a slot as instructor in an M.F.A. program, though you will most likely have gotten an M.F.A. yourself somewhere along the way. From then on, you work to feed more condemned souls into the M.F.A. furnace. Hey, it's a living.

FLED IS THAT MUSIC

It's the same with music. The last opera that anyone but a fanatic wants to see was *Turandot* (1926). Flip on your radio and tune to the classical music station. I just did, to 96.3 FM, my local one. They're playing something Baroque. There was a skimpy chance I might have got a late Shostakovich symphony (early 1950s) or something of Benjamin Britten's (same date or slightly later), but 99 percent of "serious" music on radio, as in concert, dates from before 1920.

(The Baroque composer was Telemann, the radio just informed me. He died in 1767.)

People have, of course, been composing music since 1926. Have they ever!—just look at the "List of Compositions" for American modernist composer Milton Babbitt on his Wikipedia page. I counted 122.

As a longtime, and pretty regular, listener to stations like the aforementioned 96.3 FM, why can't I recall ever hearing one of Babbitt's pieces? The guy's a musical big shot, for sure. Wikipedia: "In 1973, Babbitt became a member of the faculty at the Juilliard School. In 1982, the Pulitzer Prize board awarded a 'special citation to Milton Babbitt for his life's work as a distinguished and seminal American composer.' Since 1985 he has served as the Chairman of the BMI Student Composer Awards, the international competition for young classical composers. In 1986, he was awarded a MacArthur Foundation Fellowship . . . He is also a member of the Academy of Arts and Letters. Babbitt's notable students include [long list]."

I suspect the answer to my last question is: because Babbitt's music is no good. I thought I would get an *informed* opinion, though, so I asked my *National Review* colleague Jay Nordlinger, who knows everything there is to know about music, and then some. Jay: "Babbitt's music is difficult and not very often listener friendly. Terribly bright guy, though." Hngh. Isn't music *supposed* to be listener friendly?

I'm inclined to translate "not very often listener friendly" as having no appeal to human nature, which is predisposed to like some kinds of music (melody) and not others (atonal experiments). We are now eighty years on from Webern's prediction that mailmen on their rounds would one day whistle his atonal, melody-free ditties. If my acquaintance with mailmen is representative, Webern's prediction has not yet come to pass.

Human nature is a large enough subject to need a chapter of its own, though, so I shall defer further discussion.

ROTTING FISH FOR FUN AND PROFIT

Pictorial art? Let's see. *Art* is an old word for "skill." The first meaning given in the *Oxford English Dictionary* under "art" is "Skill in doing anything as the result of knowledge and practice." Doctor Johnson's dictionary gives "Science, skill, dexterity, cunning."

Cunning has pretty much taken over the pictorial arts, while science, skill, and dexterity have gone by the board (or canvas). The tale of Piero Manzoni's fecal exhibits, which I told above, illustrates the state of affairs. It would be comforting if I could tell you that that was the furthest extreme of bogus-art folly, and that since the 1960s there has been a road back to real art—to skill in making beautiful things that appeal to us as we are, not as the artist wishes us to be, or as some intellectual cult has told him we can be. Alas, I can't tell you that.

The art event of 2008 was a two-day September auction in London of works by Damien Hirst. The 223 items on auction earned *$200 million* for Hirst and the auctioneer (Sotheby's), with an average of $900,000 per item.

Hirst made his name with "installations." These were mainly large animals preserved in glass tanks filled with formaldehyde. His 1991 work *The Physical Impossibility of Death in the Mind of Someone Living* was a fourteen-foot tiger shark thus preserved. It sold in 2004 for $8 million, though not before it had had to be replaced, as the original was visibly rotting. Perhaps Hirst could have used some science, skill, and dexterity. Or just possibly the shark's deterioration was a "statement" of some kind: Hirst's earlier work, *A Thousand Years*, consisted of a large glass case containing maggots and flies feeding off a rotting cow's head.

At this 2008 auction, the biggest sale was of *The Golden Calf*, a white bullock pickled in formaldehyde, with hooves and horns made of 18-carat gold and a gold disc crowning the head. This item went for $19 million after some ferocious bidding. Not everybody was happy about the artistic validity of the thing, and the word "bull" was bandied about in a rather disrespectful way by many commentators. Noted the *New York Times:*

> The reaction to the auction and its contents has run the gamut from doomsday end-of-civilization laments and serves-you-right righteousness directed at the art world, to the crowning of Mr. Hirst as superartist and speaker of deep truths.

Here, you understand, I'm on board with the doomsday end-of-civilization lamenters.

Art has come to an end, all right—a rear end, in the late Signor Manzoni's case. What has happened to "skill in doing anything as the result of knowledge and practice"? What do you think? Art historian Paul Johnson:

> The most worrying aspect of art at the beginning of the twenty-first century was . . . the decline, and in some cases the disappearance, of effective training in art skills . . . Many art schools do not actually teach pupils how to draw or paint. Teaching of sculpture in its traditional forms, as opposed to unskilled constructions, is even harder to obtain . . . The studio chain, stretching back to the early Middle Ages, along which knowledge was passed from master to assistant or apprentice over countless generations, has been broken. At the heart of the process whereby beautiful objects are produced there is an abyss.
>
> —*Art: A New History* (2003)

Hermann Göring is said to have been fond of declaring, "When I hear the word 'culture,' I reach for my gun." (A sentiment he borrowed from a German playwright.) Surveying the current state of our culture, it's hard not to think the old junkie has a point.

THE LONG EXHAUSTION

That's our culture. That's the end point of three thousand years' development: Homer to Elizabeth Alexander, the lyre to the synthesizer, Nefertiti's bust to Signor Manzoni's poop. I'd like to tell you there's a road back, but I don't see one. Modernism, after all, has been with us awhile now—a lifetime and some. Things aren't getting better, they're getting worse.

Back in 1916, two American poets, Witter Bynner and Arthur Davison Ficke, decided they'd had enough of the multiplying schools of poetry that were springing up all around them—Vorticists, Imagists, Futurists, Chorists . . . Hiding behind the pen names "Emanuel Morgan" and "Anne Knish" (kosher delicacies weren't widely known in the United States in 1916), they brought out a book titled *Spectra*, announced as the founding work of a new school, the Spectrists.

It was all a hoax. The two of them wrote the poems straight down without thought or plan, in a spirit of frivolity. Bynner: "It was a sort of runaway poetry, the poet seated in the wagon but the reins flung aside." Several big literary names were taken in, most notably (though she tried to deny it) Imagist queen Amy Lowell, who never forgave the hoaxers.

The awful, depressing thing is that the *Spectra* poems read quite well now. Here's a sample, by "Anne Knish":

OPUS 118

If bathing were a virtue, not a lust,
I would be dirtiest.

To some, housecleaning is a holy rite.
For myself, houses would be empty
But for the golden motes dancing in sunbeams.

Tax-assessors frequently overlook valuables.
Today they noted my jade.
But my memory of you escaped them.

That is as good as some of the stuff in Camille Paglia's poetry bestseller, which is *not* a hoax.

At least, I don't *think* it is. How does one tell nowadays?

5

SEX: SURPLUS TO REQUIREMENTS

No one attached to the traditional image of authoritarian patriarchy could imagine the consternation men endure. They have suffered an unexpected blow to the emotional quality of their lives. Its gravity has not been calculated. They have far fewer reliable links than women to the classic currents of family life. They are alienated not only, as Marx said, from the means of production but also from the means of reproduction.

—Lionel Tiger, *The Decline of Males*

THE CASE AGAINST FEMALE SUFFRAGE

I mean no offense here—well, not *much* offense—to ladies. There are of course female conservatives, even bestselling female conservative authors. There aren't many, though.

I have attended approximately a million conservative gatherings. If you subtract out the dragged-along wives and girlfriends from these events, the normal male-female ratio of the remainder is around ten to one. In the collage of twenty-five head shots decorating the dust jacket of George H. Nash's *The Conservative Intellectual Movement in America Since 1945*, there is not a single gyno-con. (Though admittedly my edition of the book is from 1976.)

The "gender gap" in political attitudes has been remarked on since at least 391 B.C. That was the year Aristophanes staged his play *The Assemblywomen (Ecclesiazusae)*. In the play the women of Athens, disguised as men, take over the assembly and vote themselves into power. Once in charge, they institute a program of pure socialism.

> Everyone is to have an equal share in everything and live on that; we won't have one man rich while another lives in penury, one man farming hundreds of acres while another hasn't got enough land to get buried in . . . No one will be motivated by need: everybody will have everything . . . the children will regard all older men as fathers. . . .
> —from Alan Sommerstein's translation for Penguin Classics

Aristophanes' intent was ribald comedy. The wrinkled old hags of the city are soon demanding equal sexual access to the handsome young men, a thing that even a modern American liberal—a male one, at any rate—might regard as taking the doctrine of universal entitlement a bit too far. The playwright grasped the essential point, though: Women incline to socialism much more naturally than do men.

George Orwell, whose insights into these matters were very deep, also noticed this. He has Winston Smith, the protagonist of *1984*, observe:

> It was always the women, and above all the young ones, who were the most bigoted adherents of the Party, the swallowers of slogans, the amateur spies and nosers-out of orthodoxy.

I saw the same thing myself when living in communist China in the years just after Mao. If you wanted to hear a total-credulity, utterly unreflective parroting of the Party line, a woman was always your best bet.

Given that feminization is going to mean socialization, the feminization of our society must be bad news for conservatives. Is feminization in fact happening? Oh yeah.

CONSIDER HER WAYS

Back in 1956 the British science-fiction writer John Wyndham published a short story with the title "Consider Her Ways." A woman of that time, Jane Waterleigh, volunteers to test a hallucinogenic drug. She wakes in the body of another woman some generations in the future. That future is a woman's world. All men had been killed off by a rogue virus, which also prevented the birth of any more male babies. After a spell of disorder, the women got civilization going again, and erected a society modeled on those of the ants (hence the story's title, from Proverbs 6:6).

Bloated, obese "mothers" are dedicated full-time to childbearing. It is in the body of one of these monsters that Jane's personality has lodged itself. The "mothers" are attended by midget, sterile "servitors." Society's heavy lifting is done by muscular Amazon types, also sterile, and the whole thing is presided over by a wise "Doctorate" of normal-looking women who can give birth if they wish to. The medical specifics are left unclear, but some sort of parthenogenesis seems to be involved.

Wyndham's purpose was to set a fictional frame for some 1950s-ish arguments about "romance" and the place of women in a consumer society. In years to come, though, he may be hailed as a prophet. There are ample signs that the world we're heading into, with its unprecedented demographic changes and momentous advances in the biological sciences, will be a woman's world. Those qualities we're used to thinking of as "masculine," which have been brought forward more or less intact from our origins as hunter-gatherers in the Paleolithic, are now surplus to requirements. Masculinity, as it has been understood from the beginning of our species, is now at last obsolete.

The signs are everywhere. In postindustrial society, men just don't do very well. As everyone knows, we don't live as long as the other sex. (Or "gender," as we are supposed to say nowadays. Well, the hell with that.) A woman aged twenty can expect to live 4.9 years longer than a man; at age sixty the gap is still 2.2 years. I note in passing P. J. O'Rourke's comment on this: "Women live longer than us. That's our revenge."

It's less well-known that this is a recent phenomenon. Until the early twentieth century, American men lived longer than women. Nowadays men are less healthy than women, and get more of most diseases. The culprit here is testosterone, which weakens the body's resistance, and causes it to age more rapidly. Eunuchs have a longer life expectancy than intact men.

It's notorious that men misbehave much more than women. Ninety percent of U.S. jail inmates are men, as are 90 percent of murderers and 80 percent of drunk drivers. Men are also of declining economic importance: Male participation in the civilian labor force has dropped from 86 to 75 percent since 1950, while the female rate has risen from 34 to over 60 percent.

When men do have jobs, those jobs are less secure than women's. As the great recession of early 2009 got seriously under way, the *New York Times* reported that "a full 82 percent of the job losses have befallen men, who are heavily represented in distressed industries like manufacturing and construction. Women tend to be employed in areas like education and health care, which are less sensitive to economic ups and downs."

As Western society moves ever closer toward pure meritocracy, it's becoming clear that women are not only healthier and better behaved than men, but also smarter—or, at any rate, more willing to sit still and be educated. More women than men pass straight from high school to college (this has been true since the early 1970s) and more women than men now earn degrees.

The National Center for Education Statistics tells us that "since 1984, the number of females in graduate schools has exceeded the number of males. Between 1995 and 2005, the number of male full-time graduate students increased by 27 percent, compared to a 65 percent increase for female graduate students." The education business is, in fact, being colonized by women at all levels, including the administrative: In late 2008, four of the eight Ivy League colleges had female presidents.

Even more striking results come from England, where single-sex secondary schools are still common and the Department of Education publishes "league tables" of schools nationwide based on results in standard examinations. For "advanced" and "scholarship" examination results, the highest levels taken in English secondary schools, the seven top-ranked schools for 2007 were all either mixed or girls-only. Only four of the top twenty were boys-only schools (ranks eight, nine, twelve, and eighteen). Eleven were girls-only, five mixed.

GIRLS, MEN, GIRLY-MEN

As men slip further behind in the meritocratic rat race, the culture sends out more and more signals that traditional masculinity is passé. Clark Gable arrived on the set of *Gone With the Wind* two days before his thirty-eighth birthday, a milestone that Tom Cruise reached in July 2000, Brad Pitt in December 2001, and Matt Damon in October 2008. The difference is, of course, that Gable was unapologetically and unambiguously a man, while Cruise, Pitt, and Damon are, in their screen personae, essentially boys, acting out schoolyard cops-and-robbers games.

The trend line is heading off even further into pretty childishness, too—think of Leonardo DiCaprio (who will hit the Gable mark in November 2012). Peter Whittle of the *Los Angeles Times*, on the centenary of Clark Gable's birth:

> In my interviews with countless fans, it became clear that for teenage girls, the boyish but androgynous look was the one they preferred in their idols—smooth, hairless, lacking traditionally adult, masculine physical attributes, and, by implication, sexually unthreatening.

The bankability of these present-day movie stars also depends in part on their appeal to homosexual men, a large and wealthy constituency with disproportionate influence over all matters of style and taste in our culture.

The modern workplace has also been demasculinized. I spent

many years working in the offices of big corporations, among the vast clerical middle class of the Information Age. It has often struck me how much more suitable this work is for women than for men—how, in fact, men seem rather out of place among the "tubes and cubes" of the modern office. No masculine values are visible here. The mildness of manners, the endless tiny courtesies, the yielding and compromising, the cheery assertions of delivery-room stoicism ("Hangin' in there!") that are necessary to get this kind of work done, leave little outlet for masculine forcefulness.

Such outlets as did once exist have been systematically sealed off by the feminists and "sexual harassment" warriors. Twenty years ago my mixed-sex office in a big Wall Street bond brokerage celebrated the boss's birthday by bringing in a full-monty stripper to entertain us. Any firm doing that today would find itself looking at a big fat lawsuit, and probably a Department of Justice investigation.

The more boisterous manifestations of masculinity—physical courage, danger-seeking, the honor principle, belligerence, chivalry, endurance, small-group loyalty—that were once accessible to all men, in episodes of war or exploration if not in everyday life, have now been pushed out to the extremes of our society—to small minorities of, at one extreme, super-rich sports and entertainment stars, and at the other, underclass desperadoes.

There is no place now for a brilliant misfit like the Victorian explorer Sir Richard Burton, whose love of danger and of alien cultures led him to be the first, and quite probably the only, non-Muslim ever to penetrate the holiest sanctuary of Islam, the Kaaba in Mecca—he even had the audacity to make a surreptitious sketch of the place's interior while he was supposed to be praying. (Burton, by the way, was a holy terror as a boy. He would be a sure candidate for heavy Ritalin treatment nowadays.)

Even war, that most quintessential of masculine activities, is probably a thing of the past. For war you need a large supply of young men. With the great demographic collapse of modern times, that supply is drying up.

Soft, feminized, overcivilized, undermilitarized societies of the past were likely to be jolted back into vigor, or just overrun, by warriors from the wild places. Now there are no more wild places. While one should never be complacent about these things, and it's possible that a starship fleet of unwashed plunderers, cutlasses in their teeth and knives in their boots, is on its way from Alpha Centauri even as I write, the odds are good that the human race ain't gonna study war no more.

WHO NEEDS MEN?

It sometimes seems that sexual intercourse itself is on the way out. Think of the much-remarked and sudden (historically speaking) ubiquity of fellatio among young people. This is a genuine social phenomenon of our times. Its significance in this context is that fellatio is an act of condescension by a woman toward a man. The subtext, as we say nowadays, is "I am not willing to engage in full sexual congress with you. However, to maintain your affections, and pacify your beastly masculine nature, I will grant you this favor."

Rambunctious elementary-school boys are dosed with Ritalin to calm them. Fellatio is Ritalin for adolescents. What the mostly female staff of elementary schools is doing to eight-year-old boys, female high-schoolers are doing to their sixteen-year-old classmates, though the meaning of "orally administered" is of course somewhat different in the two cases. Along with the normalizing of homosexuality, we see here another sign that ordinary heterosexual intercourse is losing its market share. Sperm is no longer much in demand for its original purpose.

Males are, in fact, not biologically necessary. Plenty of species manage without them. One family of aquatic organisms, the bdelloid rotifers, seem not to have produced any males for about thirty million years, yet they are thriving. Whiptail lizards in the Arizona desert happily reproduce without sexual intercourse. The shuffling of genes that occurs in heterosexual pairing is useful to our somewhat more complicated species in keeping ahead of diseases and parasites, which base their attack strategies on the commonest genetic patterns of the previous generations. This shuffling can, however, be accomplished by fusing two eggs, instead of a sperm and an egg. There are some small points to be cleared up—the placenta produced in egg-egg unions is unsatisfactory—but these problems can no doubt be mastered. Or mistressed.

CAN MEN BE SAVED?

Back in 1962, Kirk Douglas made a movie titled *Lonely Are the Brave*. Twenty-six years later, in his autobiography *The Ragman's Son*, Douglas wrote that this was his favorite among all the movies he had made. That judgment looks pretty good to me: It's a fascinating movie.

Douglas plays the part of a cowboy who has outlived his time. He deliberately gets himself jailed to help a friend. Then, after escaping from jail, he heads for the hills on horseback pursued by various cops, rangers and soldiers, all riding in jeeps and helicopters. At last man and horse make an absurd, hopeless dash for freedom to a frontier that no longer exists. A truck driven by Carroll O'Connor hits them as they attempt to cross the Interstate. Horse dies, man dies. Moral of the story: There is no place for the free spirit of the old Range in today's documented, regulated, lawyered-up, securitized, overeducated modern state. Which of course is true.

In the long dark watches of the night, I sometimes think that we of the male sex are in the same situation as Kirk Douglas's cowboy, lingering on in a world that has less and less use for us. We may puff and preen and work out for a few more decades, but it will all be empty show. The world that is just over the horizon will be a woman's world. Then at last, when we and our Paleolithic skill set have fallen into complete desuetude, some Caroline O'Connor in a sixteen-wheel rig will come along and put an end to our sorry little performance. It was fun while it lasted—the patriarchy, the wars, the all-night poker games, the seductions—but now the game is up. Males are finished, and conservatism is finished with them.

Could this be right? Might there be a glimmer of hope? Well, just possibly. Some human-science researchers are mulling over a theory that goes roughly as follows.

- Before the rise of agriculture ten thousand or so years ago, when human beings lived in small hunter-gatherer groups, men and women treated each other in a fairly egalitarian sort of way, but innate male-female differences in traits like recklessness (more in men) and emotional responsiveness (more in women) were freely and fully expressed. Mating was based on straight-forward mutual affection, constrained only by incest taboos and tribal solidarity, but complicated, no doubt often fatally, by love triangles. Then . . .

- With agriculture came the higher-density, better-organized, hierarchical, and more constrained societies with which we are familiar. The sexes were less egalitarian in the way they treated each other. (Think of Chinese foot-binding.) On the other hand, paradoxically, innate male-female personality differences were squished down by all that social pressure: men constrained to be less reckless, women less emotional. Mating was way constrained: Think of the plots of *Romeo and Juliet* and *La Traviata*. The older, freer, wilder ways of mating lived on in myth and folk memory—think of the plot of *Tristan und Isolde*. Now . . .

- Modern postindustrial society is taking us back to the Pleistocene. Once again we are egalitarian in our treatment of each other; but our inner Mars and Venus are freer to express themselves without restraint than in those laced-up millennia of agricultural-industrial patriarchy. (Think of the plot of *Fatal Attraction*.)

John Tierney, science editor of the *New York Times*, covered this theory in September 2008. He quoted David Schmitt of Bradley University:

"Humanity's jaunt into monotheism, agriculturally based economies and the monopolization of power and resources by a few men was 'unnatural' in many ways," Dr. Schmitt says, alluding to evidence that hunter-gatherers were relatively egalitarian.

"In some ways modern progressive cultures are returning us psychologically to our hunter-gatherer roots," he argues. "That means high sociopolitical gender equality over all, but with men and women expressing predisposed interests in different domains. Removing the stresses of traditional agricultural societies could allow men's, and to a lesser extent women's, more 'natural' personality traits to emerge."

Note that phrase "to a lesser extent." Dr. Schmitt thinks it's men who are doing most of the changing.

The University of Iowa has been polling groups of students on their mating preferences since the 1930s. The preferences come under eighteen headings like "ambition," "similar political background," and "good looks." Men's preference for a woman who is "a good financial prospect" was second to last in 1939, and dead last in 1967, when you could still raise a family on one income. In 2008 it had risen to twelfth, and I think it's a fair bet it will rise further.

The big change in women's preferences concerned a man's niceness. "Women ranked 'pleasing disposition' as significantly less important in 2008 than they have ever before," the authors of the Iowa study tell us. "Pleasing disposition—presumably interpreted to mean being a nice guy—fell from a steady ranking of No. 4 throughout the second half of the 20th Century to a significantly lower rank of No. 7 in 2008."

So yes, there may be a glimmer of hope. Perhaps instead of killing, cooking, and eating us, women will keep us around, so long as we accept their supporting us, and cut down on the niceness. Drop those smiley faces, guys. Stop nodding eagerly in agreement like so many Labrador pups when the feminist harpies say that male-female differences are just imposed on us by "socialization." They're not—we never really believed it anyway, did we? Let your masculinity loose, guys, and *scowl*. It's our only chance.

6

EDUCATION: YALE OR JAIL

I believe that given the opportunity, most people could do most anything.

—*New York Times* REPORTER DEBORAH SOLOMON

TRIUMPH OF THE WILL

I took the epigraph for this chapter from an exchange in the *New York Times Magazine* of September 19, 2008. The participants were sociologist Charles Murray and the *Times* reporter Deborah Solomon. The latter was interviewing the former following publication of Murray's latest book, *Real Education*. The book argues, among many other things, that people have different innate abilities, and that a rational education system ought to acknowledge the fact. Solomon was scandalized by this idea. Here is the full exchange.

DS: Europeans have historically defined themselves through inherited traits and titles, but isn't America a country where we are supposed to define ourselves through acts of will?

CM: I wonder if there is a single, solitary, real-live public-school teacher who agrees with the proposition that it's all a matter of will. To me, the fact that ability varies—and varies in ways that are impossible to change—is a fact that we learn in first grade.

DS: I believe that given the opportunity, most people could do most anything.

CM: You're out of touch with reality in that regard.

Ms. Solomon may indeed be out of touch with reality, but she is very intimately *in* touch with the *Zeitgeist*. Foolishly optimistic liberal assumptions like hers—that "given the opportunity, most people could do most anything"—underlie all current thinking about education.

Surveying the field of modern educational practice, "in touch with reality" is not a phrase that leaps spontaneously to mind. There is no area of social policy where we see more clearly the destructive effects of the modern epidemic of happy talk, no area where the magical thinking of our intellectual cheerleaders is so clearly, painfully at odds with cold grim facts. Our educational practice is driven by our educational theory; and to enter the world of education theory is to leave the solid surface of the earth altogether, to float up to the Academy of Lagado in *Gulliver's Travels*, where learned men worked at extracting sunbeams from cucumbers. Let's float.

THE DREAM PALACE OF EDUCATION THEORISTS

As a single specimen of sunbeams-from-cucumbers education theorizing—I could equally well have chosen a thousand others—the excerpt on page 99 is from a long article that appeared in the *New York Times Magazine* of November 26, 2006. The piece is titled "What It Takes to Make a Student," and is by staff journalist Paul Tough.

The story is billed on the magazine's cover under the different heading: "Still Left Behind—What It Will Really Take to Close the Education Gap." Which gap would that be? "The achievement gap between black and white students, and the one between poor and middle-class students." Ah. So, two gaps then, actually. (I'll introduce a third one shortly. A huge chunk of education theory is about gaps.)

Let's cut to the chase here. What *will* it take to close those gaps? I turned to the end of Mr. Tough's article.

The evidence is now overwhelming that if you take an average low-income child and put him into an average American public school, he will almost certainly come out poorly educated. What the small but growing number of successful schools demonstrate [*sic*] is that the public-school system accomplishes that result because we have built it that way. We could also decide to create a different system, one that educates most (if not all) poor minority students to high levels of achievement. It is not yet entirely clear what that system might look like—it might include not only KIPP-like structures and practices but also high-quality early-childhood education, as well as incentives to bring the best teachers to the worst schools—but what is clear is that it is within reach.

"KIPP" is an acronym for the Knowledge Is Power Program, a network of intensive college-preparatory schools for inner-city kids started in 1994 by two idealistic young teachers, David Levin and Michael Feinberg, in Houston. There are now fifty-two of these schools nationwide. They get good results, but this is not very surprising. KIPP schools have long hours (typically 7:30 a.m. to 5:00 p.m.), a longer than average school year, and strict standards of behavior.

KIPP schools are covered in Abigail and Stephan Thernstrom's 2003 book *No Excuses: Closing the Racial Gap in Learning*, where more of the game is given away: "There is an application process that tends to—and is intended to—discourage families unlikely to cooperate with the school. Indeed, one of the five pillars upon which the KIPP schools rest is 'choice and commitment' . . . the fact that these are schools of choice is not incidental to their success." You can bet it's not.

All the recommendations offered by Mr. Tough—and by other education theorists, like the Thernstroms—have little trapdoors built into them like this. Look back at Mr. Tough's prescription: " . . . but also high-quality early-childhood education."

Oh, like Head Start? That landmark Great Society educational program, launched in 1965, is still going strong. The name of the program is still a magic charm among liberals. Their faces light up with virtuous certitude as they utter it—*Head Start!*—and the effect of the charm, they seem to imagine, is to silence their opponent. *You can't POSSIBLY be against Head Start!*

You should be. The Thernstroms reported that twenty million children had passed through it by 2003, at a cost to the federal taxpayer of $60 billion. They go on to report that while there is some slight, disputable evidence of marginal benefits for white children from Head Start, "it does not seem to have improved the educational achievement of African-American children in any substantial way." Whether it has done anything for Hispanic children is not known.

Similarly with "incentives to bring the best teachers to the worst schools." Setting aside the obstacles posed by the almighty teacher unions, even supposing you could establish a free market in public-school teachers, how could the worst schools—inner-city schools serving minority neighborhoods—ever outbid leafy, affluent suburbs for those "best teachers"? And how many "best teachers" are there, anyway?

As the Thernstroms point out, a lot of these prescriptions for school reform assume an unlimited supply of "saints and masochists"—teachers like those in the KIPP schools, who, Mr. Tough tells us, work fifteen to sixteen hours a day. I am sure there are some people who enter the teaching profession with the desire to crunch their way daily across the crack-vial-littered streets of crime-wrecked inner-city neighborhoods in order to put in fifteen-hour working days, but I doubt there are many.

That's ed theorists for you. They *love* to talk about how the top 1 percent of superbly excellent and inspired teachers can lift up the bottom 5 percent of students. That's interesting in its own way, but not very important as an issue in education. An example of an important issue would be: What can the average or mediocre teacher do for the average or mediocre student? Why is *that* question never asked? Because here in the Republic of Happy Talk, there is no such thing as an average—let alone mediocre!—student. "Given the opportunity, most people could do most anything."

Another important issue—Murray gives it a whole chapter in *Real Education*—is education of the gifted. Here you really get into sunbeams-from-cucumbers territory though, as no accredited education expert could ever admit, even under pain of torture, that any child is innately gifted at anything.

The way out of this conundrum is to argue that every child is innately gifted at everything—*given the opportunity, most people could do most anything!*—and that only the foolish cruelty of current education policy prevents struggling teachers from bringing out this universal giftedness. This is the actual working platform of the National Association of Gifted Children—I'll introduce one of their luminaries later.

What does the foolish cruelty of current education policy consist of? Why, it consists of not spending enough money! Let's take a look at what we currently spend.

THE MONEY PIT—LOWER LEVEL

Where I live, in New York's Suffolk County, we are pretty well protected from lawbreakers. In the opinion of some county residents, in fact, we are *too* well protected. Suffolk county cops are the envy of our region. New York City cops call them "the money boys." An officer with the NYPD earns a salary of around $60,000 after five years' service; our lads are at $98,000 by that point. They also get more than a hundred paid days off a year even outside their normal schedules, so a Suffolk cop works an average of 181 days a year. He's off-duty more days than he's on. He can retire on half pay after twenty years' service, cashing in unused days off (average payout $134,000). Benefits are extravagant. I tell you, people come from all over to take our police exam. There are lines around the block near county police HQ at exam time.

I'm therefore not very surprised to find, scrutinizing my current property tax statement, that a big chunk of my tax bill goes to the county police district: $765 this year. Library services ($443), garbage collection ($369), and highways ($264) are some way behind.

My total property tax bill is $6,545, though, so the police tab, over-the-top as it surely is, amounts to less than 12 percent of the total. Police, libraries, garbage, and highways all together add up to only 28 percent. Obviously there's a big-ticket item I haven't mentioned.

There sure is. When I open my property tax demand, the one item that leaps out at me from the page with fangs bared and claws reaching, hissing and rolling its yellow demon eyes, is SCHOOL DISTRICT. I don't know how things are in your neck of the woods, but here in the outer New York City suburbs, "property tax" is well-nigh a synonym for "education tax." This year's actual number for me is $3,979, which is 61 percent of my total tax bill.

In fact, that's the first thing you notice about education in the United States today: It's a money pit.

What do we get for all that money? The main thing we get is administration. My daughter's modest suburban high school held an orientation session for parents of freshmen. There all we parents were in the school auditorium facing a phalanx of school employees up on the stage, *not one of them a teacher*. Administrators, directors, advisers, psychologists, a dean, five guidance counselors (under, of course, a director of guidance), administrative assistants . . . All this for eleven hundred students. I cornered the director of mathematics, a very cordial fellow, to ask if he himself did any, you know, *teaching*. No, he regretted to say, he didn't. No time!

To me, child of another time and place, it is bizarre. I got a first-class education at a good boy's day school in England. We had about a thousand students. There was a headmaster, who did not teach. He was helped by a second master, who taught modern languages to juniors. The headmaster also had a secretary to do his typing and filing. There was a mysterious fellow called the bursar, occasionally glimpsed scurrying from his own tiny office to the headmaster's. A groundsman looked after the playing fields. "Dinner ladies" came in part-time to serve the cafeteria lunches, and there was a caretaker with a couple of cleaners, also part-time. The other forty-odd adults on the premises were all full-time teachers. The place seemed to work very well.

THE MONEY PIT—UPPER LEVEL

It's at our colleges that education spending really gets into its stride. I sometimes go to give talks at colleges and universities. My usual reaction on arriving at one of these places is "Okay, here's the construction site. Where's the college?" Our higher education system is awash in money, and colleges are building like crazy.

When I asked a knowledgeable friend what is going on, he explained thus: "Billy Bachelor graduates, does Wall Street grunt work for a few years, then starts a hedge fund. After a while he's Billy Billionaire. What's he gonna do with all that boodle? Have a building put up at his alma mater, that's what—*a building with his name on it.* That's what they all want, buildings with their names on them. Plus, his regressed-to-the-mean dimwit kids get legacy admissions."

Hard to object to that. Let people do what they like with their money. You'd think, though, that as flush with cash as they are, colleges would hardly need student fees. You'd think wrong. It is now routine for young people in their twenties to begin life loaded down with student-loan debt it will take them decades to pay off.

Things are so bad, they affect demography. A friend groans: "Our system sees to it that girls from middle-class families have to go to college and end up with a lifetime debt; which means few children. My youngest son's wife says she'd love to have a second child but she has to pay $990 every month until her daughter is in her second year of college. They can't afford a second child. It's like Roman times when you could sell yourself into bondage. Meanwhile we are taxed to support public colleges, which then take all that money and set up the loan system to get more."

The website CollegeBoard.com reports average annual tuition and fees at private four-year colleges as $25,143 for 2008–9. That's up 5.9 percent from the previous year, twice the consumer price index rate of inflation (which, in the opinion of many economists, understates true inflation by a lot). For public four-year colleges the figure is $6,585, up 6.4 percent on the year. That's just to feed the college; students still have to feed, house, and clothe themselves.

Yet some of these institutions are bloated with cash. Ivy League college endowments are stupendous. Even after the 2008 market crash, the eight Ivies ended the year with over $88 billion in endowments—that's about $1.5 million per undergraduate. If the Ivies with their 58,000 undergraduates were a country, they would rank way down at the bottom by population, along with micronations like Saint Kitts and Nevis (50,000) and Liechtenstein (35,365); but they'd be up at number 55 on the World Bank's list of 180 nations by gross domestic product, just behind Kuwait (population 2.9 million) and ahead of Slovakia (population 5.4 million). Yet still, tuition increases at twice the rate of inflation. What do they even *need* tuition fees for?

(Some colleges manage without them. New York City's Cooper Union; California's Deep Springs College; F. W. Olin College of Engineering in Needham, Massachusetts; the Curtis Institute of Music in Pennsylvania, and many other colleges are no-fee. For some reason, no-fee tuition hasn't caught on.)

At colleges the mania for administration is all raised to the fourth power. Pick an American college and wade into their website. There are the college employees smiling out at you from the thumbnail pictures in their little biographies on the site: the vice provost for academic affairs and international programs; the assistant vice president for labor relations and human resources; the director of residence life, with—of course!—her associate director and three assistant directors; the assistant vice president for affirmative action and multicultural programs . . . and so on, and on, down through the administrative food chain to lowly Financial Aid Advisers and Assistant Librarians.

I've seen it written somewhere that a typical big American university has more administrators running it than British India had. I wouldn't be surprised.

EVERYTHING'S UP THE SPOUT IN KANSAS CITY

Okay, you're probably thinking that when politicians and edbiz theorists talk about spending more money on education, they don't have leafy suburbs and ivy-clad universities in mind. It's those inner-city schools that are "failing our children." *That's* where we should be spending more money, right?

The optimists' faith that spending oodles of money will solve any problem is quite touching. In the case of education, though, the spend-more-money theory has actually been tested to destruction in several places. In *No Excuses*, the Thernstroms cover two of these tests in detail: in Kansas City, Missouri, and Cambridge, Massachusetts.

Kansas City is the more interesting case. The Thernstroms give it a page and a half, leaving out some of the juicier details. There is a much fuller report on the Cato Institute website, written by education reporter Paul Ciotti: Go to Cato.org and search on "ciotti."

In 1977, when the story begins, Kansas City's schools were in simply terrible shape. The city, like most others of its size (population 460,000), had experienced white flight from the 1950s on, and the school district even more so, with even whites residing in the city pulling their kids out of the public schools. By 1977 enrollment was 36,000, three-quarters of them racial minorities (which at that point meant mostly African Americans). The voters had not approved a tax increase for the district since 1969. In 1977 litigation commenced, members of the school board, district parents, and some token children suing the state and some federal agencies on the grounds that they had permitted racial segregation. Federal judge Russell Clark, a Jimmy Carter appointee, got the case.

After eight years of litigation, Clark gave the plaintiffs everything they wanted, and then some. He in fact ordered them to "dream"— to draw up a money-no-object plan for the Kansas City school system.

Dreaming is no problem for educationists. The plaintiffs— education activists and their lawyers—duly dreamt, with an initial price tag of $250 million for their dreams. This was twice the district's normal annual budget.

It proved to be only a start, however. Over the next twelve years the district spent more than *$2 billion*, most of it from the state of Missouri, the balance from increased local property taxes. Fifteen new schools were built and fifty-four others renovated. New amenities, Ciotti tells us, included

an Olympic-sized swimming pool with an underwater viewing room; a robotics lab; professional quality recording, television, and animation studios; theaters; a planetarium; an arboretum, a zoo, and a 25-acre wildlife sanctuary; a two-floor library, art gallery, and film studio; a mock court with a judge's chamber and jury deliberation room; and a model United Nations with simultaneous translation capability. [Students] could take courses in garment design, ceramics, and Suzuki violin . . . In the performing arts school, students studied ballet, drama, and theater production. They absorbed their physics from Russian-born teachers, and elementary grade students learned French from native speakers recruited from Quebec, Belgium, and Cameroon. . . . [T]here were weight rooms, racquetball courts, and a six-lane indoor running track better than those found in many colleges. The high school fencing team, coached by the former Soviet Olympic fencing coach, took field trips to Senegal and Mexico. . . . Younger children took midday naps listening to everything from chamber music to "Songs of the Humpback Whale." For working parents the district provided all-day kindergarten for youngsters and before- and after-school programs for older students.

The whole project was a comprehensive failure. After twelve years, test scores in reading and math had *declined*, dropout rates had *increased*, and the system was as segregated as ever, in spite of heroic efforts to lure white students back into the system.

Kansas City did all the things that educators had always said needed to be done to increase student achievement—it reduced class size, decreased teacher workload, increased teacher pay, and dramatically expanded spending per pupil—but none of it worked.

The great C-130-loads of money being air-dropped on the system also brought about waste and corruption on a heroic scale. Theft was rampant. So was overmanning: The project became a huge jobs and patronage program, with the inevitable mismanagement and scandals.

I have just (late 2008) been on GreatSchools.net, looking up Kansas City's Central High School. That's the one with the Olympic-size swimming pool; the school was rebuilt from scratch at a cost of $32 million under Judge Clark's supervision. Nine percent of students are testing "above proficient" on math, against a state average of 46 percent. For communication arts the corresponding numbers are 6 percent, 39 percent.

(The Cato Report has a postscript about the Sausalito, California, elementary school district, which serves not the prosperous white liberals of *that* Sausalito, but a mostly minority public housing project close by. Same limitless expenditures, same results. Kansas City is by no means the only case.)

With some honorable exceptions like the Thernstroms, who, as I have said, give the Kansas City experiment a page and a half in their book, this dismal story has mainly been flushed down the memory hole by education theorists. They would rather not mention it. A decade after the whole thing collapsed in grisly and obvious failure, politicians and edbiz bureaucrats are still routinely calling for more money to be spent on schools as a way to improve student achievement.

Barack Obama, for example. On the 2008 campaign trail, the day before the Martin Luther King birthday holiday, Obama told a swooning congregation at King's old church: "We must push our elected officials to supply the resources to fix our schools . . . We can't pass a law called No Child Left Behind and then leave the money behind."

Money is the answer! More money! That'll fix the schools! That'll close those pesky gaps!

Education theorists are great forgetters, and were even before Judge Clark came along. The first of the big modern government-sponsored papers on school reform, James Coleman's 1966 report titled "Equality of Educational Opportunity" (but almost always referred to as "the Coleman Report") surveyed 645,000 students in over three thousand schools nationwide. Coleman found almost no relationship between school quality—spending, newness of facilities, teacher credentials—and student achievement.

If you rank schools from worst to best by these measures of quality, then work your way up the ranking from low to high, logging student achievement as you go, once you get above a tiny proportion of really, *really* bad schools, nothing much changes. A truly excellent school with terrific facilities does somewhat better by its students than a mediocre school, but the difference is not great. What makes the difference is family background.

All this was discovered, at considerable effort and expense, in 1966. Apparently nobody told Judge Clark. Who knows?—perhaps some future government will commission some new study to find out how student achievement relates to school quality. Then, a decade later, perhaps some new federal judge will order some new spend-a-thon, beggaring the taxpayers of his state to no effect at all. Lather, rinse, repeat.

It is not quite true that there is nothing new under the sun, but there is nothing new in education theory, ever: just the same truths, revealed again and again, then pushed down the same memory hole by the same lying careerists, the same wishful-thinking fantasists, and the same parrot-brained politicians.

CHOOSE YOUR PARENTS WELL

The spending of more money isn't the only prescription on offer from education theorists. Parents, they tell us, should work harder at parenting. If there is a difference between left-liberals and smiley-face conservatives on education, it's that liberals lean harder on the spend-more-money solution, while conservatives are keener on be-better-parents. While a society with more good parents is surely a better place than a society with fewer, the parenting issue, too, is poisoned by optimism.

Paul Tough, in the *New York Times* article I discussed above, covers some of the research on parenting. However, all the research he cites is premised on the notion that parents can mold their children in different ways by treating them differently. Parents do *this* and the kids turn out like *this*; if the parents had done *that*, then the kids would have turned out like *that*.

He does not cite any of the research showing that aside from very extreme approaches—e.g., locking a child in a broom closet for the first four years of its life and feeding it cat food from cans—parenting style makes very little difference to life outcomes. (Though parental *decisions* about, for example, where to live, may make a great deal of difference indirectly, influencing what kind of peer group the child ends up among.)

Parents behave aggressively toward children: The children grow up aggressive. See!—the parents' aggression *caused* that outcome! Well, not necessarily. What about child-to-parent effects—innately difficult kids driving their parents to aggressive distraction? What about genes? The kids have a mix of their parents' genes, and most features of human personality—including aggressiveness—are partly heritable.

None of that for Mr. Tough. Genes? What are you, some kind of Klansman or Nazi? No, no, no, the kids are little blank slates for teachers, parents, and politicians to work their magic on. These undesirable outcomes—these mysterious test-score gaps, these dropping-outs and delinquencies—arise only because we are chanting the wrong spells!

A very good rule of thumb when reading child-development literature is that any study that has not taken careful account of heritable factors—by comparing identical twins raised together or separately, fraternal twins ditto ditto, nontwin siblings ditto ditto—is worthless.

The preceding sentence is (1) true, and (2) guaranteed to get you thrown out of a high window if spoken aloud at any gathering of education theorists.

Certainly Mr. Tough will have none of it. The child is a blank slate. Parents act on it, causing *this* and *this*. Then teachers act on it, causing *that* and *that*. Bingo!—you have a finished adult. Or, as Mr. Tough summarizes the interesting (but perfectly gene-free) work of sociologist Annette Lareau: "[G]ive a child X, and you get Y." So simple! One wonders if there has ever been an education theorist who has actually raised children, or retained any memory of his own childhood.

ONTOGENY RECAPITULATES IDEOLOGY

If you read much edbiz theorizing, you find yourself wondering how a single field of human inquiry can contain so much error and folly. One answer is that educationalists willfully—ideologically, in fact— ignore the understanding of human nature that the modern human sciences are gradually attaining, and cling doggedly to long-exploded theories about how human beings develop from infancy to adulthood. From false premises they proceed to false conclusions.

We come into the world with a good deal of our life course preordained in our genes. At age three or so we begin to interact with other children outside our home, with results that depend in part on us, and in part on where our home is situated. We pass through various educational processes—formalized extensions of that out-of-home environment, and also highly location dependent.

We end up as adults with personalities and prospects that are, according to the latest understandings, around half innate and preordained, around half formed by "nonshared environment" (not shared, that is, with siblings raised in the same home by the same parents—a somewhat controversial concept in its precise contents, but whose biggest single component is those out-of-home experiences), and 0–5 percent formed by "shared environment"—mainly parenting style.

(And we then, having reached adulthood, regress a little to our preordained shape, like one of those "shape memory alloys" that so fascinate materials scientists. These are metal alloys that "remember" their original geometry, and can be made to return to it, or something close to it, usually by heating, after any amount of deformation and pressure. It is a curious fact, well supported by a mass of evidence, that the heritable components of our personality and intelligence become more marked as we age. The IQs and personality characteristics of thirty-year-olds correlate better with those of their parents or siblings than do the IQs of fifteen-year-olds. The advice traditionally given to young men contemplating marriage—"Get a good look at her mother"—is very sound.)

You would never know any of this from reading edbiz propaganda pieces like Paul Tough's. Never mind that the spending-improves-education theory has been tested to destruction. Never mind that the demographics of the Western world are in free fall because of the ever-increasing demands in time and money placed on parents, and the cart-loads of debt young adults emerge from college with.

(Raising two children in suburban America, I dream fondly but futilely of my own 1950s English childhood, when by far the commonest words I heard from my parents were "Go out and play. Make sure you're back in time for supper." How on earth did civilization survive?)

Never mind that obstructionist, feather bedding teachers unions firmly control one of our nation's two big political parties. Never mind the mountains of evidence from the human sciences (next chapter) showing that everything education theorists and their liberal camp followers like Mr. Tough believe about human nature is false. Never mind, never mind. The edbiz show must go on—for the sake of the children, you know.

DOES EDUCATION MATTER?

Education is *important*—pretty much everyone agrees on that. Asked by the Rasmussen polling organization to rank which issues were "very important" to them, voters shortly before the 2008 party conventions put education at number four, tied with health care and the Iraq war, behind the economy, national security, and government ethics, but ahead of social security, taxes, and immigration. Fifty-nine percent of voters thought education a "very important" issue. For "somewhat," "not very," and "not at all" important, percentages were 27, 11, and 2 percent, respectively.

This is all the more striking when you consider that less than a third of voters have children in K–12 education, and one-fifth of *those* are being privately or parochially educated. These numbers tell us that there is a high level of public concern about education as a public policy matter, even among people not directly affected.

Whether education really *is* all that important, as a national matter, is a question that could use some discussion. I myself have lots of education—a degree and some postgraduate qualifications. I am also a home owner who often makes use of the services of plumbers, electricians, roofers, and other small contractors of various kinds, often having nothing more than a high school diploma apiece. They all, I notice, drive much nicer cars than mine.

It's certainly the case that citizens of a modern democracy ought to be literate, and capable of the sort of arithmetic involved in basic money-management skills, and aware of the outlines of their nation's history and the elements of civics. It's likewise indisputable that a modern economy needs a great many people who are understanding and skillful in a wide range of deep technical skills, from TV studio lighting to orthodontistry, from structural engineering to jurisprudence, from horticulture to aircraft maintenance, from crane operating to bond trading.

The first of those certainties, however, concerns skills that can be imparted to almost all children by age twelve. The second certainty mainly involves skills picked up by experience or job training, though some require a basis of long book learning—in history and law for jurists, in biology for orthodontists, and so on.

How much of that comes within the scope of what people mean by "education" when the Rasmussen pollster comes a-knocking, is debatable. If the authorities were to enforce compulsory education to age twelve then leave citizens free to purchase as much, or as little, further schooling or training as they wanted (with a loan or voucher system for equity), we might be no worse off than we are. There would be some loss of efficiency, since there is not much that twelve-year-olds can usefully do without close supervision; there would be some loss of socialization, with many youngsters missing the group-bonding aspect of high school activities (though others, of course, not missing them at all). Against those losses, think of the innumerable hours of boredom and frustration that America's young people would be spared, and the incalculable savings that would be made by dismantling the present apparatus of public secondary schooling.

I am of course dreaming. Hardly anyone wants such a regime. In telling pollsters they believe education to be important, parents are expressing a wish that their children join the middle classes, while both parents and nonparents alike are expressing wishes that their doctor, lawyer, airline pilot, and accountant be highly competent, and their nation economically competitive with other nations.

EDU-PATHOLOGY

My kids—girl, boy—have at this point passed most of the way through the public-school system of a middle-middle-class American suburb. Setting aside that Creature from the Black Lagoon that leaps out at me from my property-tax bill, it hasn't been a totally negative experience. What my kids got, I am sure they could have gotten for half the price in a saner educational system—one not controlled by a labor union armed with thermonuclear weapons and with one of the country's two major political parties securely in its pocket. Still, things weren't as bad as I expected.

The main problem with our public elementary schools is that they are feminized. The male elementary-school teacher is an endangered species, largely because of the child-molestation hysteria that seized the public imagination a decade or two ago, documented in Dorothy Rabinowitz's 2003 book *No Crueler Tyrannies*. A man who wants to teach small children is nowadays under suspicion of being a pervert.

This is a shame. In the first place, it deprives small boys of male instruction and guidance, of the kind I got from a cohort of demobilized World War II servicemen (mostly ex-RAF for some reason). In the second place, it gives those boys the impression that the norms of the world are female norms. One of my son's classmates was sent home by his outraged teacher for drawing a picture of a soldier firing a gun. This probably happens a hundred times a day at various elementary schools in the United States.

Once kids get up into the middle and high schools, the larger pathologies of the education system kick in. Boys are somewhat less expected to act like girls, though if they are *too* boyish they might be put back on Ritalin. Girls are now encouraged to act like boys, though, by taking up advanced science, math, and strenuous sports, which few of them have any liking or aptitude for; and boys and girls alike are indoctrinated in the dubious dogmas of Diversity and political correctness.

My own school district has been especially afflicted with all the rancor and waste of Diversity. Great numbers of Hispanics have come to Long Island in recent years, many of them illegally, and 12 percent of students in our school district overall now have limited English-language proficiency. The high school student body is 21 percent Hispanic. (The middle school is 24 percent; the elementary school, 31 percent. Can you spot a trend?)

Our high school principal was demoted last year by the school board. (You can't *fire* a high school principal, not for any offenses less grave than murder, arson, or piracy on the high seas.) The school board claimed that our principal was unduly favoring "disadvantaged and minority students," which is to say Sun People. The principal retaliated by playing the race card. She filed a federal lawsuit saying that she was being punished for trying to increase spending on special-education and English-language classes. Her demotion has now been canceled, and she has been fully reinstated, to ill feeling all around. The race card is a winner every time. The commonest observation about this principal on RateMyTeachers.com is that nobody at the school ever sees her outside her office.

The whole kerfuffle about the principal's demotion, lawsuit, and reinstatement was decorated with endless groveling protestations by the principal's school board opponents—"persecutors," I suppose she would say—that *no way* did they object to the Hispanic influx and *of course* they celebrated diversity, as all goodthinkful people should.

This PC butt-covering by the Ice People got a bit embarrassing, and eventually passed over into gibbering idiocy. The school board president did the full race cringe, as of course he had to. He was reported thus by the *New York Times:*

> If you live in Huntington and send your children to Huntington schools . . . you accept the way—so unusual for Long Island—they intermingle rich and poor, white, black and brown. If you don't like it . . . you move next door, to a place like Cold Spring Harbor.

So easy! Except for those numbers I showed in Chapter 2: In Cold Spring Harbor (Sun People 2 percent, Ice People 98 percent), the mean price for a detached house in 2007 was $1,089,622, while here in Huntington it is $777,772.

Celebrate Diversity! . . . if you can't afford to escape it. When did we become such a nation of hypocrites?

THE TEACHERS, AND HOW THEY GET THAT WAY

Our high school principal is a pretty typical product of the modern teacher-credentialing system. Notes Rita Kramer in *Ed School Follies,* her 1991 book on the training of teachers:

> Everything in the educationist mentality today is oriented to inner-city schools and their problematic students. There is an unquestioned assumption that it is the obligation of every teacher to take on those problems, to be first and foremost a social worker coping with the urban underclass.

Even in the leafy suburbs of Suffolk County, a high school principal can play at being a missionary to the underclass. Why not? Students from better-off homes are obviously "privileged" agents of "oppression," with innumerable historical crimes to answer for, at least as proxies for their race. Whatever happens to *them* is nothing but justice. They should suck it down without complaint. And if they *do* have the gall to complain, the Civil Rights Division of the U.S. Justice Department will step in to smite them.

I should say that within this warped, perverted system, and with due allowance for their function as dispensers of a socialistic extravaganza enforced on a public cowed by moral blackmail from the nation's richest, most arrogant labor union, individual teachers are usually pleasant enough. Some of them are very good indeed. There are many dedicated teachers in the United States, doing good and honest labor in the system.

Admirable teachers are only a part of the teacher corps, though. An article by a career high school teacher in the *London Spectator* some years ago set out the eight types of people to be found on a typical high school teaching roster. To abbreviate drastically, the eight types are:

1. *Evangelist*—wants to shape youth.
2. *Exhibitionist*—classroom as theater.
3. *Bureaucrat*—teaching as gateway to a career in administration.
4. *Scholar*—loves his subject but can't get a research post.
5. *Jock*—poor man's way of being a sports pro.
6. *Fascist*—loves power and discipline.
7. *Pedophile*—loves kids . . . the wrong way.
8. *Cynic*—short hours, long vacations, powerful union—hey.

The writer said that category 8 is "by far the largest" in England. I was once a schoolteacher in England myself. I think the man is right. Are things different here? I doubt it; although, given the colossal administrative superstructure of our schools, I'll bet category 3 is giving category 8 a run for its money in the United States.

Certainly there are gifted teachers—"evangelists" and "scholars"— who can work wonders. It nonetheless remains true, as Rita Kramer wrote in *Ed School Follies*, that, "although [inspiring teachers] exist here and there, they do what they do in spite of the present system of preparation and in spite of all the odds against them which that system presents."

Ms. Kramer's book is a depressing read altogether. Here she is at a national conference on "alternative teacher certification," a movement of the last twenty years to get more people from nonacademic backgrounds into the teaching profession. The conference is being addressed by an ed-school professor.

> He said he was going to read us some rules of good teaching. A good teacher, he read out in a deadpan voice, corrects mistakes right away; groups children in small homogenous groups; defines, explains, and gives examples; uses drills and practice; requires students to raise their hands before answering; praises students who do well . . .

When he's got his audience—the less clued-in members, at least—nodding along, the professor turns the tables on them. It turns out he was speaking ironically:

> "Teaching this way," he announced clearly and with emphasis, "is *unethical* and *immoral*." [Emphasis in original]

People tell me that things have improved somewhat in teacher training since the new emphasis on testing and "accountability" came in with the federal reforms of recent years, but I'm not so sure. It seems that anytime an institution of teacher education is in the news, the story concerns behavior, on the part of the teachers of teachers, out on the wilder shores of human strangeness.

There was, most recently, the peculiar little story about Madonna Constantine, a professor at Columbia Teachers College—one of the most prestigious teacher-training institutions in the country. In the midst of an investigation into charges of plagiarism against her, Professor Constantine, who is black, claimed to have found a noose hung on her office door in October 2007. This, in the most liberal department of the most liberal university in the most liberal district of America's most liberal city! A full police investigation came up with nothing, and Professor Constantine was fired a few months later based on the plagiarism charges. (Which involved, among other things, plagiarism *from one of her own students.*)

My favorite specimen of credentialed ed-school excellence, though, remains Dr. Kamau Kambon. Dr. Kambon has a quite remarkable number of degrees in education: a B.A. in education/history, a master's degree in physical education, both an M.A. and an M.Ed. degree in education/administration, and an Ed.D. in urban education/curriculum and instruction. He was Professor of Education at Saint Augustine's College in Raleigh, North Carolina, a historically black institution. Then he moved on to teach at North Carolina State University. This is one *very* thoroughly teacher-trained person. In September 2005, Professor Kambon enjoyed the proverbial fifteen minutes of fame when he declared, at a forum televised on C-SPAN: "The problem on the planet is white people," and: "We have to exterminate white people off the face of the planet to solve this problem."*

YALE OR JAIL

Towering over all these lesser pathologies is the college racket, a vast, money-swollen credentialing machine for middle-class worker bees. American parents are now all resigned to beggaring themselves in order to purchase college diplomas for their offspring, so that said offspring can get low-paying outsourceable office jobs, instead of having to descend to high-paying, unoutsourceable work like plumbing, carpentry, or electrical installation.

Any modern society needs some method for identifying talented adults and efficiently matching them with suitable employment. The rationality quotient of this process would be much increased if

---

* After this chapter was written, while in the last stages of preparing my book for the press in early 2009, I happened to meet Ms. Kramer, author of the aforementioned *Ed School Follies*, at a lunch in New York City. I complimented her on her book, and asked whether things had improved any in the eighteen years since she wrote it. She: "Improved? They're far *worse!*"

employers could just give aptitude tests to job applicants. Unfortunately most aptitude testing has been banned since 1971, when the U.S. Supreme Court ruled in the case of *Griggs v. Duke Power Co.* Duke had been using IQ tests to assign employees to positions, but this was found to have a disparate impact on minorities.

Lacking the ability to just test applicants in a straightforward way, employers need a proxy—something to tell them that this is a person of reasonable intelligence and diligence. The bachelor's degree from a four-year college has become that proxy for mid-level clerical work.

Griggs was a major landmark in the academic credentialing of middle-class America and the consequent tumorous growth of the college racket. In the United States of today, no personnel manager would ever dare rely on testing to select applicants for hiring or promotion. The threat of a discrimination lawsuit is too great. Much, much safer to go by the credentials. And after all, a person who has completed a four-year college course *has* shown some measure of intelligence and stick-to-it-iveness. A person who got into one of the Ivies must, in addition, have a high IQ. (The Ivies select by SAT scores; SAT correlates strongly with IQ.) To some degree, the college-credentialing system spares personnel managers the trouble and expense of administering IQ tests. It also wastes four years of the young job-applicant's life and puts him a quarter million dollars in the hole, but nobody thinks *that's* important.

At higher levels, professionals have their own credentialing systems. You may have graduated law school, but you'll still have to pass the bar exam, and so on. Then why make aspiring lawyers go to law school? Presumably for the same reason we insist on cube jockeys having bachelor's degrees from accredited four-year colleges—to keep the college racket going.

Why not let people study up at home from Teaching Company DVDs, or from broadcast lectures like Britain's Open University's? Then they could sit for a state-refereed common certification exam when they feel they're ready. Why not let lawyers learn by self-study, as Abraham Lincoln did, or on the job as articled clerks, like Calvin Coolidge? I don't know. College-going is just an irrational thing we do, the way upper-class German men used to acquire dueling scars, the way women in imperial China had their feet bound. The scarring process was occasionally fatal, and Chinese women were crippled for life, but hey, that's how we do things, because . . . that's how we do them.

The assumption is that if you don't have a college degree, you are not much good for anything other than selling crack. Human-sciences blogger Steve Sailer calls this the "Yale or jail" syndrome. Charles Murray's book *Real Education*, the book I referred to at the beginning of this chapter, makes a withering criticism of this whole Yale-or-jail mentality. The third chapter of Murray's book, titled "Too Many People Are Going to College," makes plain, across forty pages of data and argument, how supernaturally *crazy* the college obsession is.

> How smart do you have to be to cope with genuine college-level material? No more than 20 percent of students have that level of academic ability . . . For the student who wants to become a good hotel manager, software designer, accountant, hospital adminis-trator, farmer, high school teacher, social worker, journalist, op-tometrist, interior designer, or football coach, four years of class work is ridiculous. Actually becoming good in those occupations will take longer than four years, but most of the competence is ac-quired on the job . . . As long as it remains taboo to acknowledge that college is intellectually too demanding for most young peo-ple, we will continue to create crazily unrealistic expectations among the next generation.

Murray goes on to call for a system of national certification, for which students can study in any way they please—online, at home, even at a residential college if they like. He offers the CPA (certified public accountant) exam as a model.

> You can have studied accounting at an anonymous commun-ity college and be competing for a job with someone who stud-ied it at a prestigious university, but your CPA score is what it is.

This makes so much good sense, there is not the slightest chance of it ever coming to pass.

PROFOUND DEMOGRAPHIC DIVISION

As can be seen in some of the discussion above, the old American specter of race is lurking behind all educational theorizing. Mr. Tough does his best to fudge it up ("[T]he achievement gap between black and white students, *and the one between poor and middle-class students . . .*") but it's always there. [Emphasis added]

Conservative education policy debates are dominated by the idea of school choice, and most particularly by the concept of education vouchers. Peter Brimelow, in his 2003 book about teachers unions, *The Worm in the Apple*, makes a strong and detailed case for a voucher system of public schooling. As he says: "Washington is in the food stamp business, not the supermarket business."

He then confronts the rather touchy issue of the failure of voucher proposals when brought to the electorate. He suggests some secondary reasons. Then:

> The voucher movement's fundamental and unspoken problem, however, is race. Government schools in wealthy suburbs are already *de facto* private schools—and they are *de facto* segregated, by class if not completely by race . . . It may well be that a perfectly rational way of delivering government services is permanently crippled in America because of the country's profound demographic division.

The recent history of modern public-education reform in this country is very nearly a history of the determination on the part of white and East Asian parents that their children not attend schools with too many black and Hispanic students.

The 1966 Coleman Report argued for more racial mixing in public schools because, Coleman had found, black students achieved more in classes with a majority of nonblack students. This led to the busing programs of the early 1970s. *They* led to "white flight," non-black parents abandoning the schools to which black students were being laboriously bused.

So with the great Kansas City experiment of 1987–97. From the Cato Institute report:

> To entice white students to come to Kansas City, the district had set aside $900,000 for advertising, including TV ads, brochures, and videocassettes. If a suburban student needed a ride, Kansas City had a special $6.4 million transportation budget for busing. If the student didn't live on a bus route, the district would send a taxi . . . But despite a $900,000 television advertising budget . . . the district did not attract the 5,000 to 10,000 white suburban students the designers of the desegregation plan had envisioned. The largest number it ever enrolled was 1,500, and most white students returned to their old suburban schools or to local private schools after one year . . . [T]he cost of attracting those suburban students was half a million dollars per year per child.

Ice People (white and East Asian) parents simply will not send their children to schools with student bodies that are majority Sun People (black and Hispanic), not even ones like those in Kansas City, with Olympic-size swimming pools and planetariums. It's a fact of life in the United States, and a major determinant of our public-education system—and so, at one remove, of our residential-housing patterns. I mentioned this in passing in Chapter 2, but it is worth expanding on, as it shows the emptiness and dishonesty of our education theorizing.

The result is segregation—voluntary segregation, at least on Ice People's part.

OUR SEGREGATED SCHOOLS

The degree to which our public schools are segregated is very striking. My son plays on a Police Athletic League football team. I have gotten into the habit, before each game, of looking up demographics of the high school in the opposing team's town. One week in 2008 my son's team played a team from Commack; two weeks later they played Wyandanch. According to GreatSchools.net, the racial spread of Commack High School, in percentages of white-Asian-Hispanic-black, is 86-9-4-1, while Wyandanch Memorial High School's is 0-0-18-82.

It's like this all over. Up to a point, Ice People don't seem to mind schools that "look like America"—that would be around a quarter Sun People—but if the proportion gets up much above that, it reaches a tipping point, and the Ice People flee like lemmings.

Mainstream conservatives approach this whole issue, if you force them to (which isn't easy), with the whimpering terror they bring to all matters racial: "Oh please, mister, please don't call me racist! Beat me with this steel rod if you like, but for pity's sake, don't call me racist!"

Liberals are slightly more honest, being confident that no one ever *will* call them racist—though, of course, Ice People liberals are no more keen for their kids to attend majority–Sun People schools than are their conservative neighbors. There was a very neat illustration of this fact on the Upper West Side on Manhattan in November 2008.

The Upper West Side is a tony area, with condo apartments selling at around a million bucks each. The inhabitants are media, cultural, and academic types—high IQ, well-educated, prosperous, and liberal as all get-out, *New York Times* readers to a man and a woman. Well, New York City's Department of Education wanted to make some adjustments to school district boundaries in Manhattan. However, a lot of these people bought those million-dollar condos so that their kids could attend P.S. 199 on West Seventieth Street. It's a really good elementary school with great test results. If the proposed rezoning were to go through, their kids would have to attend P.S. 191 at West Sixty-first Street and Amsterdam Avenue. That's a lousy school with dismal test results.

Naturally these liberal, progressive, Obama-voting parents were furious. But what exactly was it about P.S. 191 that made it compare so poorly with P.S. 199 in these parents' eyes? Why did they think it's a bad school? Why didn't they want their kids to go there? What, actually, is the definition of the term "bad school"? What makes a bad school bad? Not to keep you in suspense, gentle reader, but I looked up the student stats for the two schools on the GreatSchools.net website at the time. For P.S. 199, the good school those parents shelled out a million bucks for: Ice People 80 percent, Sun People 19 percent. For the school our progressive, postracial, liberal citizens angrily did *not* want their kids to go to: Ice People 12 percent, Sun People 88 percent.

One liberal educationist, Jonathan Kozol, published a book on present-day school segregation in 2005, *The Shame of the Nation: The Restoration of Apartheid Schooling in America.*

Kozol's book is full of the kinds of facts I've been noticing. Of a school in South Central Los Angeles: "According to school documents, 99.7 percent of children in the school were black or Hispanic." The Business and Law Academy in New York's Bronx: "The 97 percent black and Hispanic school continues to be plagued with a colossal dropout rate." Chicago: "By the academic year 2000–2001, 87 percent of public school enrollment was black or Hispanic . . . Washington D.C., 94 percent . . . Detroit 95 percent . . ." Note that none of these inner-city schools is as segregated as Wyandanch Memorial, here in the bosky outer suburbs on Long Island.

Kozol is especially vexed that the schools named after African American heroes are invariably among the *most* segregated. He cites Thurgood Marshall Elementary School in a Seattle neighborhood where half the families are "Caucasian": GreatSchools.net shows the school's student body as 79 percent black and Hispanic. It seems that the local Armenians, Georgians, Ossetes, and Azerbaijanis prefer to enroll their children in private schools. Langston Hughes School (P.S. 233) in Brooklyn, New York, is 99 percent Sun People. New York has three schools named after baseball race-barrier-breaker Jackie Robinson: Sun People percentages are 98, 95, and 97. Fannie Lou Hamer, a heroine of the integration struggle (irony alert!) in the U.S. South, has two New York City schools named after her: Sun People percentages 98, 99.

Notes Kozol: "If you want to see a really segregated school in the United States today, start by looking for a school that's named for Martin Luther King or Rosa Parks." He gives many examples.

You will soon be able to add another name to this melancholy roll call. A school in a town (Hempstead, New York) near me has just changed its name from Ludlum Elementary to Barack Obama Elementary. The student body is, of course, 98 percent Sun People children. There will undoubtedly be Barack Obama schools all over the United States in years to come. Is it too much to hope that some of them, at least, will have student bodies that are less than 90 percent black and Hispanic? Yes, it probably is.

The edgier sort of comedian will soon have Barack Obama School jokes to go with his Martin Luther King Boulevard jokes. (*Q:* What do you do if your car breaks down on Martin Luther King Boulevard? *A:* Run!)

Is there anything that can be done about this? Kozol, an old-school leftist, offers social-engineering solutions: busing, more Section Eight housing in the suburbs, with "statewide laws that would *compel* municipalities to do this," [emphasis in original] much bigger and more authoritarian school districts, street protests, and so on. Lots of luck with those, guy. I note, by the way, that the great Kansas City experiment is not mentioned in Kozol's book. "The first thing a man will do for his ideal is lie." (Joseph Schumpeter, *History of Economic Analysis*). The second thing is, omit inconvenient facts.

What is the fundamental reason for all this segregation? Why *don't* the Ice People want their kids going to school with Sun People kids? As briefly as the question can be answered: because Sun People kids are, in the broad generality, unacademic and unruly.

THE ACHIEVEMENT GAP

The Ice People–Sun People academic achievement gap is a huge issue in educational theory, with regular conferences, programs, initiatives, interventions, restructurings, policy proposals, and so on, predicated on it. A Google search for the phrase "achievement gap" brought up nearly 750,000 hits. Opening up some of them, I found myself wading into a vast, turbid ocean of wishful thinking, special pleading, meaningless sociobabble, and the endless recycling of long-disproved theories. If you add "Kansas City" to the query, the number of hits drops very dramatically, to 13,000. Achievement gap theorizers don't talk about Kansas City.

The best book-length summary of the achievement-gap issue is the book I've already drawn data from, the Thernstroms' *No Excuses.* The authors famously called the achievement gap "the most important civil rights issue of our time." They are unusually honest, by the standards of educational theorizing, about the intractable persistence of the gap, and the failure of every attempt to tackle it: "The two largest federal programs serving a largely minority constituency— Title I [i.e., of the 1965 Elementary and Secondary Education Act] and Head Start—have accomplished very little."

The Thernstroms are briskly dismissive of the usual explanation for the gap: that it is a matter of class, not race. This is so much *not* the case that its not-being-the-case actually has a name: the Shaker Heights effect. This refers to an affluent Cleveland suburb where one-third of the families are black, and "the community is strongly committed to racial integration." Alas, in the 1999–2000 academic year, "more than half of all Shaker Heights whites passed [Ohio's statewide proficiency tests in basic subjects] with honors. For blacks, the figure was an astonishingly low 4 percent."

The Thernstroms' book offers a four-page Conclusion, but nothing much is concluded. Their proposals are feeble: "Choice [of where to live] should not be a class-based privilege." (Where has it ever *not* been? How will you stop people from moving, if they can afford to?) "Families must help their children to the best of their ability." (Oh.) "Vouchers are a matter of basic equity." (See Peter Brimelow's observation above.) "Big-city superintendents and principals operate in a bureaucratic and political straitjacket." (True, but Shaker Heights is not a big city.)

THE BEHAVIOR GAP

The unruliness of Sun People students has to be inferred, as school administrators are skilled at covering it up, for their own career reasons. If you trawl through news websites, in fact, there seem to be even more stories about the suspected covering up of violence in schools than there are stories about the violence itself. The best approach here is to read through both kinds of stories, looking up the named schools on GreatSchools.net to find the student demographics.

(You would be spared the trouble of all those lookups if news outlets reported demographic factors in criminal events. Of course, they very rarely do, believing these things best left unsaid. The assumption is, that if not told these things, the great slack-jawed, dimwitted, unwashed mass of Americans will make no assumptions of their own. Yet in fact every American can decode the subtext of reports like: "The robber was described as a tall man in his thirties." Reporters should get out more. I came home from work on the Long Island Railroad one day in December 1993. My train was right behind the one in which Colin Ferguson went berserk and shot twenty-five people. We were held up for a long time, and there were no cell phones. My poor wife was at home, watching news of the shooting on TV. For all she knew, I might have been among the dead. Kind neighbors came around to keep her company. Telling me about it afterward, she remarked: "They kept saying the same thing: 'It must be a black guy. If it was a white guy, they would have told us.'")

Thus, from a story in the *New York Times*, December 11, 2008, headlined "School Violence Data Under a Cloud in Houston."

On Oct. 3, 2000, a boy named Joseph Hamilton was "stomped and beaten" by another student in the cafeteria of Williams Middle School and was left injured on the floor, according to a school district memorandum, but the assault went unreported to Texas authorities. Last April, a 16-year-old boy was stabbed in the chest

by another student at Washington High School; that attack was
not reported, either.

Sun People percentages in the student bodies of the two named
Houston schools are 98 for Williams, 97 for Washington. So it goes.
(I have made no effort at selection here. Try the thing for yourself.)

THE MATH SEX GAP

I am sorry: I know how stressful it is to read about these race issues,
which we have all been bludgeoned not to notice on pain of being de-
nounced for doubleplus-ungood crimethink. For race-stress-free relief, here is a different educational gap: the math sex gap.

The starting point here is the January 2005 address by Harvard
president Larry Summers to the National Bureau of Economic Research Conference on Diversifying the Science and Engineering
Workforce. It included this little nugget of highly radioactive Political Incorrectness:

> It does appear that on many, many different human attributes—
> height, weight, propensity for criminality, overall IQ, mathemat-
> ical ability, scientific ability—there is relatively clear evidence
> that whatever the difference in means—which can be debated—
> there is a difference in the standard deviation and variability of a
> male and a female population. And that is true with respect to at-
> tributes that are and are not plausibly, culturally determined.

The outcomes certainly show a gap. Restricting the topic to
mathematics, where the gap is most pronounced, there were at that
time 143 Americans in the Mathematics and Applied Mathematical
Sciences sections of the National Academy of Sciences. Only 7 of
them were women. Even further out on the math-talent distribution,
the highest honor in mathematics is the Fields Medal, which has
been awarded to 49 mathematicians since its inception in 1936. *Not
one* Fields Medal recipient has been female.

That the cause of the gap might "not plausibly" be "culturally determined" is, however, crimethink. Nobody can be allowed to get away with making such evil, poisonous, *hurtful* remarks—certainly not the president of a prestigious university. For his offense, Summers was made the subject of a Two Minutes Hate by every feminist organization in the country, and eventually forced to resign his position.

There have since been heroic follow-up attempts to prove that the math-and-science sex gap is "culturally determined." Two major papers were published just in 2008. One was "Culture, Gender and Math," published in the May 30 issue of *Science*. The paper's four authors, all economists, argue that the math sex gap is the result of male prejudice against women. The second paper, "Gender Similarities Characterize Math Performance," authored by five feminists (all female—did I need to mention that?), was published two months later, also in *Science* (which is a bastion of political correctness). These authors were even more audacious, arguing that the math sex gap has actually been abolished, at any rate in the United States.

I have no space here to deconstruct these two papers. In any case, the deconstruction was done superbly well by the anonymous statistician who goes by the pseudonym La Griffe du Lion. I refer curious readers to La Griffe's website, lagriffedulion.f2s.com where he patiently exposes the many statistical errors in these papers.

La Griffe notes, for example, that No Child Left Behind assessments are designed to assess whether a student has reached some minimum level of proficiency. None of the questions requires complex problem solving skills—the area where sex differences are most apparent. They are poorly suited to the job of assessing the math sex gap.

The authors of the first of those two papers in *Science* addressed this issue by turning to the somewhat more difficult National Assessment of Educational Progress (NAEP) tests. There weren't any really complex problems there either, though. There were some *fairly* difficult questions . . . which showed a sex gap in favor of boys! "None of this," notes La Griffe drily, "appeared in the paper's conclusion or in post-publication publicity."

That publicity was, of course, ecstatic and widespread. That, in fact, is the main point here. Bogus studies turn up politically correct results and are joyfully trumpeted by all the media. The debunking of those bogus results has to be done by a guerrilla Internet intellectual using a pseudonym—probably an untenured academic who dares not let it be known that he is possessed by Bad Thoughts. This is the intellectual climate in the U.S. academy today.

A FEAST FOR PESSIMISTS

This whole topic of education is a glorious feast for pessimists of all kinds. Not only does no one have a clue regarding what to do about the achievement, behavior, and math sex gaps, but government programs to address them have just the kinds of results a pessimist expects when money and jobs are offered to people willing to say they will do something that nobody knows how to do. Those results will inevitably be: cheating, corruption, and cover-ups.

How, for example, does a schoolteacher, principal, or education bureaucrat close the Ice People–Sun People achievement gap in test scores? It is perfectly simple. There are in fact two ways to reduce the gap *all the way down to zero.* Way One: Make the tests so easy that everyone gets all questions right—gap zero! Way Two: Make the tests so difficult that nobody gets any questions right—gap zero!

Any actual test, of course, falls between these two extremes of difficulty and displays a nonzero gap. If you draw a graph showing size-of-gap (vertical) against degree-of-difficulty (horizontal), it's an inverted U, pinned to the zero points at each end. (That is, zero gap for tests of zero difficulty, zero gap for tests of total difficulty.)

There is some particular degree of test difficulty at which the gap is a maximum—the peak of the inverted U. If your actual test is more difficult than that, then making it yet *more* difficult will reduce the gap, sliding you down the curve toward the total-difficulty zero point. If your test is easier than that, making it yet *easier* will likewise reduce the gap, sliding you down the curve toward the zero-difficulty zero point. If your current test's difficulty is precisely at the maximum-gap point, *anything* you do will reduce the gap!

Do you think this little exercise in elementary calculus has escaped the attention of our nation's educators? Ha ha ha ha ha!

Calculus of course deals in small differences. The only way to *keep* reducing the gap all the way to zero is to make your tests metaphysically easy or metaphysically difficult.

That is of no consequence to your ambitious edbiz bureaucrat, though. In his two or three years on the job, he reduced the gap by a couple of ticks! He is now a prime candidate for promotion in the edbiz hierarchy, leaving someone else to face the problem of narrowing the gap further. Who knows, he might even ascend all the way to the position of U.S. secretary for education. No bureaucrat left behind!

DUMB AND DUMBER

The whole culture of professional educators is addled with chicanery, corruption, rent-seeking, time-serving, and lies. What I have given above is the merest glimpse. Reading through the literature of present-day edbiz, every time you think you've found an argument, assertion, or proposal than which nothing could possibly be dumber, something dumber soon shows up.

Did Donna Ford—professor of education and human development at Vanderbilt University, a Very Big Name Indeed in research on education of the gifted and talented—did she really say, in an interview videotaped and broadcast on the Internet, that black and Hispanic students don't do well on tests to identify gifted kids because "we've chosen the wrong tests"? Yes, she did. For forty years, apparently—including the past dozen or so when Professor Ford has been a big playah in the gifted-ed corner of edbiz—we've just been using wrong tests. So simple! Professor Ford is the proud recipient of a Distinguished Scholar Award (2008) from the National Association for Gifted Children.

Just when you've got your eyes back in focus after watching that video of Professor Ford, you read of a lawsuit in Tampa Bay, Florida, as a consequence of which, racial gaps in academic achievement may be declared *illegal*, with school officials confronted with the options of (1) cooking the books even more systematically than they already do, or (2) going to jail. Gee whillikers, I wonder which they'll choose?

You put *that* aside and pick up a report on a 2007 "Achievement Gap Summit" in Sacramento, California, attended by four thousand people. Addressing the massed educrats, California State Superintendent of Public Instruction Jack O'Connell announced the true cause of the achievement gap: black youngsters attend churches encouraging parishioners to clap, speak loudly, and be a bit raucous, behavior deemed inappropriate in schools. Therefore, said O'Connell, if teachers take sensitivity training to appreciate this behavioral style, test performances among black students will rise! It's as easy as that!

O'Connell is, I repeat, *California State Superintendent of Public Instruction*. He's responsible for *all the public schools in California*. It's around this point that Lou Costello used to grab the brim of his hat and scream: "HEE-AAAARRRRGGGHHH!"

Education is a vast sea of lies, waste, corruption, crackpot theorizing, and careerist logrolling. If, as H. G. Wells asserted, "human history becomes more and more a race between education and catastrophe," we have lost the race, and had better brace ourselves for the catastrophe.

Unless, of course, human beings are infinitely malleable—unless, as Deborah Solomon declared at the head of this chapter, "given the opportunity, most people could do most anything." Could this in fact be the case? Could human nature be what the smiley-faces tell us it is?

Charlie Allnut: A man takes a drop too much once in a while, it's only human nature.
Rose Sayer: Nature, Mr. Allnut, is what we are put in this world to rise above.

Plainly we can do *some* of that rising-above, though it might take a millennium or two. After all, we no longer (in most parts of the globe) enslave, eradicate, or eat each other. How much, though, can we reasonably hope to rise above our brute human natures? What *is* human nature, anyway?

7

HUMAN NATURE: ASK YOUR AUNT

It is impossible to live without a metaphysic. The choice that is given us is not between some kind of metaphysic and no metaphysic; it is always between a good metaphysic and a bad metaphysic.

—ALDOUS HUXLEY, *Ways and Means*

THE PROPER STUDY

Huxley was right: You can't think about society and politics unless you have some ideas about what it means to be human, and how we are situated relative to the rest of creation.

Our best shot at getting true answers in this zone, or in any other zone, is by methodical observation, classification, measurement, publication, criticism, and free discussion among investigators—in other words, by scientific inquiry.

"The proper study of mankind is man," said Alexander Pope; but the application of scientific method to that study has turned out to be much more difficult than an English gent of the 1730s could reasonably have anticipated. Objectivity is awfully hard when you're observing your own species.

We managed to make some progress in the twentieth century, though, and in the last half of that century real human-nature science began to pull ahead of pseudosciences like Marxism and Freudianism. We actually started to find out stuff.

Some of the progress was dramatic and headline making, like Watson and Crick's discovery of the structure of DNA in 1953. Most was gained by slow accumulation, like the years-long studies of identical twins raised apart, or the decades-long piling up of multigenerational data on human intelligence and personality.

A lot of what we've learned is still provisional and debatable. Some has crashed up against national or cultural prejudices. The broad picture of human-nature understanding in the United States today is a chaotic mix of long-standing, deeply rooted preoccupations, remnants of nineteenth- and twentieth-century pseudoscience fads, sentimental romanticizing, wishful thinking, guilt, fear, shame, and proper, nailed-down results from rigorous scientific inquiry. The state of modern educational theory, which I covered in the previous chapter, illustrates some of that. Here is a fuller picture.

That picture tells us mostly things an optimist would rather not hear: about human reason, about human differences, and about how human beings get to be what they are.

PICK ONE OF THREE

There are three theories of human nature enjoying widespread support at present. For convenience, I'll tag each one of them with a single adjective.

- *Religious.* Our species *Homo sapiens* is the special creation of God, either as a one-off miracle or by God-guided evolution. Human nature is a mix of attributes, some natural ones arising from plain biology, some supernatural ones inserted by God. We are the Chosen Species.

  The God-given attributes are unique to our species. They are the same in all human populations, forming the foundation of our essential equality. Their existence is independent of our biological nature, even to the degree that they can continue to exist after our deaths. Being nonbiological, they don't evolve, even if other features of the living world do, so that our evolution, if it ever took place, ended (except perhaps for some incidental biological features) when God decreed we have these supernatural attributes. These God-given attributes include the moral sense, which accesses transcendent truths—i.e., truths that do not dwell in the world of matter. God rules!

- *Cultural.* Our species arose, like all other species, from the ordinary processes of evolution. However, these processes ceased in the early history of the species, leaving us with a human nature uniform across all populations and unchanging over time, forming the foundation of our essential equality.

  This human nature has very little innate structure and is extremely plastic. By placing it in a suitable environment, or applying suitable pressures, the mind (and therefore the behavior, which issues from the mind) can be shaped in any way at all.

  "Human nature" does not really exist independent of the environment an individual happens to be in, especially that part of the environment made up of other human beings—"the culture." Moral standards are arbitrary, and are taken in by the individual from the culture. Culture rules!

- *Biological.* Our species arose, like all other species, from the ordinary processes of evolution, which have continued to the present day. Human nature is a collection of characteristics all susceptible to biological explanation.

  Some characteristics of a person's nature can be shaped to some degree by "cultural" (i.e., social or environmental) forces; some cannot. Human beings are a part of the living world, and nothing more. Our equality consists in being members of a single species; though our species, like any other with very wide distribution, exhibits regional differences.

  The characteristics of an individual human being are templated in his genome. They may be somewhat modified by womb events or life experiences; or they may need to be "instantiated" by postpartum environment. (An individual's genome may, for example, predispose him to be eloquent or tongue-tied when using language; but *which* language he uses will depend on his childhood environment.)

The repertoire of human behaviors, and of ideas, including moral ideas, about behavior, are innate, the result of evolutionary processes acting on our social lives across many generations. Biology rules!

For convenience in what follows, I'll label adherents of these three views with the more or less made-up words "Religionists," "Culturists," and "Biologians."

Each point of view has a history. Religionism emerges from core features of human thinking, as described by cognitive scientists like Pascal Boyer (*Religion Explained*, 2001), Scott Atran (*In Gods We Trust*, 2002), and Bruce Hood (*Supersense*, 2009).

Culturism has roots in the tabula rasa ("blank slate") theories of Aristotle and Locke. It was put into its modern form by German anthropologist Adolf Bastian (1826–1905). Bastian coined the phrase "the psychic unity of mankind." His student Franz Boas brought these ideas to the United States, becoming the most influential American anthropologist of the early twentieth century.

Biologism is just ordinary scientific method applied to humanity.

WHO THINKS WHAT

Broadly speaking, the religious view is most popular among ordinary citizens, the biological view is held by most actual researchers in the human sciences, and the cultural view is dominant—well-nigh exclusive, in fact—among our nonscientific elites and educators.

There's some qualification needed there. The "religious" tag should, strictly speaking, be "Abrahamic" (Judaism, Christianity, Islam), as non-Abrahamic religions have a different view of our spiritual nature. And there are exceptions to the previous paragraph. Some human-science researchers are religious, most famously geneticist Francis Collins, director of the Human Genome Project, who has written an eloquent book about his faith (*The Language of God*, 2006). Generally speaking, though, working biologists are irreligious.

In fact, biologists are the *most* irreligious among professional scientists. Reporting the results of their 1996 survey of National Academies of Science members, Larson and Witham tell us: "We found the highest percentage of belief among NAS mathematicians (14.3 percent in God, 15.0 percent in immortality). Biological scientists had the lowest rate of belief (5.5 percent in God, 7.1 percent in immortality), with physicists and astronomers slightly higher (7.5 percent in God, 7.5 percent in immortality)."

Similarly, some biologists are keen Culturists—most famously, the late Stephen Jay Gould, about whom I'll say more later. Culturism is in fact more than a mere opinion; it's the state ideology of most Western nations, and dominates academic life outside the human-sciences labs. Without a Culturist metaphysic to underpin them, multiculturalism and the Diversity Theorem (Chapter 2) are untenable. Having committed itself deeply and irreversibly to those things, Western society believes it must cling fiercely to Culturism. It does.

Harvard president Larry Summers found this out in the 2005 incident I mentioned in Chapter 6, when Summers suggested to an academic gathering that the paucity of women in high-end science and engineering positions might have non-Culturist causes. James Watson, co-discoverer of DNA's structure, learned the same sharp lesson two years later when a British newspaper quoted him as saying he was "inherently gloomy about the prospect of Africa" because "all our social policies are based on the fact that their intelligence is the same as ours—whereas all the testing says not really." That is indeed what the testing says; but to voice the fact out loud is a gross violation of Culturist protocols. Watson, like Summers, had to perform a full medieval-style recantation and penance.

In the social sciences, Culturism is compulsory, with vigilant policing to ensure total compliance. This is the case even in the older social sciences—economics, for example.

The results are sometimes comical. In December 2008, the Center for Economic Policy Research, a European academic think-tank, put out a report titled "Post-Columbian Population Movements and the Roots of World Inequality." By trawling through historical databases, the researchers put together a picture showing, for each part of the world, where the ancestors of that region's population were in A.D. 1500. For the current population of the United States, for example, about 4.4 percent of ancestors lived in France in A.D. 1500, 8.5 percent in Ireland, 1.1 percent in Senegal, and so on. Interesting, huh?

The researchers then crunched numbers to see if the current economic condition of the various regions had any relation to where those ancestors were five hundred years ago.

It sure did. Across the 125 countries they studied, they found a strong positive correlation between prosperity (year 2000 per capita GDP) and the share of the population's ancestors that lived in Europe back in 1500.

Pretty amazing. But why are the two things related at such a statistically high level? Why are people whose ancestors came from Europe in the last five hundred years better off than others? The authors speculate:

> The influence of population origins suggests that there is something that human families and communities transmit from generation to generation—perhaps a form of economic culture, a set of attitudes or beliefs, or informally transmitted capabilities—that is of at least similar importance to economic success as are more widely recognized factors like quantities of physical capital and even human capital in the narrower sense of formal schooling.

That's the kind of thing that makes your honest Biologian head for the liquor cabinet in despair. *There is something that human families and communities transmit from generation to generation.* There is, there is, indeed there is. What on earth can it be, though? Some mysterious substance—phlogiston, perhaps? A luminiferous æther? Dark matter? Ectoplasm? Such a mystery!

It's not that Biologians can't get a hearing. They have even appeared in the best-seller lists: most famously with Herrnstein and Murray's 1994 book *The Bell Curve*. Public displays of Biologism are, though, always sure to excite angry controversy. Compare the fevered responses to *The Bell Curve* with the placid reception given to

Culturist bestsellers like Jared Diamond's *Guns, Germs, and Steel* or Malcolm Gladwell's *Outliers*. A Biologian who wants to write a bestseller is well advised to just leave out the really fever-inducing stuff, however good it looks scientifically; or at the very least to put some Culturist lipstick on his Biologian pig.

Our country's high public discourse—politicians' speeches, corporate mission statements, newspaper editorials, and the like—is a bizarre mix of Religionism and Culturism, with Biologism completely taboo. Former president George W. Bush, for example, is a pious Christian, and therefore a Religionist. However, when he was not invoking God's blessings in his presidential speeches, he was enthusiastically pushing grandiose Culturist projects: the No Child Left Behind Act, democratization in the Middle East, relaxed credit standards for house purchases (apparently on the principle that becoming a home owner will transform a feckless proletarian into a sober bourgeois, and thence a Republican voter).

It goes without saying that not a word of Biologism ever passed this president's lips, or any other politician's. Should any of them ever be tempted to speak up for Biologism, they have the dreadful examples of Larry Summers and James Watson to deter them. Biophobia is as much a part of a politician's basic equipment as a sharp suit.

To get anywhere in American political life, you need to be a Religionist with some Culturist gloss, or vice versa. If the first, you are most likely a Republican; if vice versa, a Democrat. Biologians are unelectable. There is probably a sizable proportion of the population that wants them all rounded up and killed.

THE CASE FOR BIOLOGISM

As a pessimist marketing pessimism, I am naturally going to argue for the coldest, most realistic, and most depressing of the three metaphysics. That would be the Biologian view.

Religionism certainly has its consolations. Its consolations are, in fact, the main point of Religionism. I recall them well, and miss them. The world's great religions also have embedded within them many true observations about human nature. Those are only folkloric baggage carried along by religions for social utility, though. There are just as many of them in the proverbs of pagan peoples. You will have a better shot at a happy and useful life if you try to make the best of your innate abilities, however limited. That is a true observation; but I doubt that it first appeared among us when Jesus of Nazareth expressed it so memorably with the Parable of the Talents (Matthew 25:14–30).

Setting its consolations and folk wisdom aside, though, Religionism has a poor track record at telling us true facts about the natural world. Every tribe of headhunters, every settlement of subsistence farmers, every clan of herdsmen on the steppe, from the beginning of thought, has had a creation myth, an explanation for the succession of day and night and the rotation of the seasons, and something to say about the causes of natural disasters.

Alas, their theories were all wrong. The earth's surface is not the shell of a giant turtle; the sun is not pulled across the sky by a god in a chariot; earthquakes are not caused by the stirrings of subterranean dragons angered by human misrule.

What caused the turtles-chariots-dragons scenarios to be dropped was the rise, occurring mostly in Europe, mostly in the second half of the second millennium after Christ, of a new social phenomenon: science. Thoughtful people made careful observations of the natural world. They tried to classify and measure its various phenomena. Then they compared notes with others like themselves, in free discussion and exchange of ideas.

Societies and academies were organized as venues for these discussions, with qualifications for entry. To be admitted, you had to have a bundle of results from your observe-classify-measure activities, which must have been carried out by agreed methods that other inquirers could replicate. You should also, preferably, have some interesting ideas about *why* your data looked the way it did, ideas that your colleagues could test and apply, ideas that might lead to fruitful further investigations. This was science.

The success of science in explaining the natural world was

sensational. In the nineteenth and twentieth centuries it transformed human life, and the surface of the earth itself—for the better, much more often than not.

There was a unifying, civilizing effect, too. The explanations that came up were so convincing, they *detribalized* thought about the natural world. It ceased to be the case that every people had its own set of explanations. In traveling from China to Peru, you no longer went from the restless-dragon explanation for earthquakes to the wrath-of-the-goddess-Pachamama explanation. Everybody now had the *same* explanation: stresses on the earth's crust caused by slow movements of the semisolid magma beneath. This detribalization of truth, this unification of understanding, seems to me just as striking and wonderful as all the gadgets, cures, structures, and vehicles science has given us.

Now those same techniques of inquiry are being turned inward, to find out true facts about ourselves—our behavior, our abilities, our minds. Will these investigations be as fruitful, as unifying and civilizing? I don't know. They can't be stopped, though, any more than inquiries into nuclear fission could be. We shall just have to cope with the results as best we can.

Culturism? Just a fix—what computer scientists call a "kluge"— clung to by a society with a deep psychic need to justify the continuation of Diversity. The motivation for the clinging is mainly negative: fear of what might happen if we let go of the "psychic unity of mankind." Given the well-known horrors of the recent past, this fear is not unreasonable. Indeed, a superficial pessimist, expecting the worst of human nature, might approve Culturism on exactly those grounds.

The pessimism I am calling you to, however, goes deeper than that. There *is* an objective reality; we *can* uncover it by methodical inquiry; it *does* embrace human nature; and we *must* face it unblinkingly and courageously if it tells us that Culturism is false. It does.

THE 50 PERCENT RULE

Across the last third of the twentieth century, the human sciences were roiled by the nature-nurture war. Probably you're familiar, at least in outline, with some of the main incidents in that war. If not, there's a very good battle-by-battle account in the book *Defenders of Truth* (2000), by the Finnish sociologist of science Ullica Segerstråle.

In the terms I've been using, the nature-nurture war was a Biologian-Culturist controversy. All the participants were working scientists, or at least social scientists (Charles Murray) or political scientists (Tatu Vanhanen). There was no input from Religionists, who are generally indifferent to science, if not actually hostile, and so *hors de combat* here; though most Religionists, believing as they do in the transforming and improving power of faith, would put themselves on the nurture side.

The opening shots in the war—the Fort Sumter, so to speak—were fired in 1964, when biologist William Hamilton published two papers in the *Journal of Theoretical Biology*. Both papers were under the heading "The Genetical Evolution of Social Behaviour." Hamilton established a mathematical rule that brings social behavior firmly under the scope of evolutionary biology.

Hostilities then commenced under formidable generals on both sides. Most formidable of the Biologians (i.e., for nature) was Edward O. Wilson. His 1975 book *Sociobiology: The New Synthesis* announced a new discipline: "the systematic study of the biological basis of all social behavior." The book dealt mostly with social animals. Wilson had trained as an entomologist, specializing in ants. He followed up with *On Human Nature* (1978), which applied his ideas to human beings.

(Wilson featured in one of the more colorful incidents in the nature-nurture war. At an American Association for the Advancement of Science symposium in 1978, he had a pitcher of ice water dumped on his head by Culturists chanting, "Racist Wilson you can't hide, we charge you with genocide!")

For the Culturists (i.e., for nurture), the most brilliant strategist was paleontologist Stephen Jay Gould. A Chomsky leftist in his politics—though not, he always insisted, a Marxist—Gould was a skillful but unscrupulous propagandist. His 1981 book *The Mismeasure of Man* is to this day the best-known counterblast against Biologism in the cognitive sciences. This subtle and clever book managed to plant many false ideas that remain widely current today, e.g., that psychologist H. H. Goddard found early-twentieth-century Jewish immigrants to the United States to be of low average intelligence. (Goddard found no such thing.)

The dust of battle has pretty much settled now, in science departments if not in the popular press, and nature is the clear victor. Name any universal characteristic of human nature, including cognitive and personality characteristics. Of all the observed variation in that characteristic, very roughly half—from a quarter to three-quarters—is caused by biological differences.

You may say that is only a half victory for the Biologians, but it is a complete shattering of the Culturist absolutism that ruled in the human sciences forty years ago, and that is still the approved dogma in polite society, including polite political society, today.

Pull two adult human beings at random from the population and measure what we can measure about their minds and behavior. Their measurements differ. Why do they differ? A Freudian would say: "Because their parents treated them differently when they were infants." A Marxist would say: "Because of their different class backgrounds." A modern Culturist would say: "Because of the overall environment—familial, social, and material—in which they grew up."

The actual answer is: About half the difference between them has biological causes—either straightforwardly genetic or "womb events" that irreversibly affect the developing fetus. The other half is indeed "cultural," though not much of it has to do with parenting styles. The biggest contribution seems to come from childhood peer groups. (I have a British accent; my wife has a Chinese accent; our kids speak ordinary American English with no accent . . .)

That means we must lower expectations about how much we can change our individual selves, and other citizens, including even our own children. To the degree human beings can be changed, or change themselves, the methods of doing it are poorly understood. That's why social engineering is usually a bust: a good conservative lesson, but one rooted in pessimism about human potential.

LEFT CREATIONISTS, RIGHT CREATIONISTS

Stephen Jay Gould's leftism is worth a note here. Culturism is state dogma in the Western world, and to that degree is apolitical. All right-thinking people are supposed to subscribe to it, whatever party they vote for. It has particular appeal to the egalitarian Left, for obvious reasons, and the loudest propagandists for Culturism are on the Left. E. O. Wilson pointed this out in his book *On Human Nature:*

> The strongest opposition to the scientific study of human nature has come from a small number of Marxist biologists and anthropologists . . . They believe that nothing exists in the untrained human mind that cannot be readily channeled to the purposes of the revolutionary socialist state. When faced with the evidence of greater structure, their response has been to declare human nature off limits to further scientific investigation.

One way to scandalize a Culturist biologist of the left-wing Stephen Jay Gould type is to call him a "Left Creationist." Traditional Scopes-monkey-trial Right Creationists are those Religionists who insist that the living world, and all its great variety, could not have come about without miraculous intervention by God. The highbrow Culturists who dominate our intellectual scene regard these Right Creationists as ignorant straw-chewing hicks, so that to label someone a Creationist is a grave insult in highbrow Culturist circles.

Culturists, while scoffing at God, insist that the ordinary rules of biological evolution ceased to apply to *Homo sapiens* when our species emerged from Africa to populate the rest of the world, around fifty thousand or sixty thousand years ago.

Yet this is an appeal to the miraculous, too, just as much as is Right Creationism. That the laws of biology would suddenly *stop* like that is as inexplicable as that the sun should stop dead in the sky, as is told in the book of Joshua.

Basic biology tells us, for instance, that populations of a species that are long isolated from each other, each population starting off with a different "menu" of variations among its individuals, each breeding only, or almost only, within itself, and each subject to different environmental stresses driving natural selection this way or that, will *diverge*, each population developing peculiar characteristics. If the isolation goes on long enough—tens of thousands of generations in higher animals—the divergence will be so great that the populations can no longer interbreed . . . and that is the origin of species!

Even after mere tens of generations, group divergence can be detected. After the many *hundreds* of generations that Australian, East Asian, African, European, and indigenous American populations of *Homo sapiens* developed in isolation from each other, in different environments, there ought to be divergence aplenty, though nowhere near to speciation. And so there is. That is why a roomful of Australian aborigines looks nothing like a roomful of Hungarians, and neither looks anything like a roomful of Quechua-speaking South American indigenes.

That is a painful thought for Culturists. There is a way to escape from thinking it, though. The way is provided by science cartoonist Sidney Harris. One of Harris's cartoons shows two scientists at a chalkboard covered with equations. In the midst of the equations appear the words: "Then a miracle occurs." One boffin is pointing at these words, saying to the other: "I think you should be more explicit here in step two . . ."

For Religionist Right Creationists, the miracle is life itself, or human life (there are differences of opinion). For Culturist Left Creationists, the miracle is the abrupt suspension of biological laws fifty thousand years ago on humanity's behalf—more precisely, on behalf of twenty-first-century Western liberals who don't want to think uncomfortable and unpopular thoughts, or lose their shot at tenure, or be made the subject of a Larry Summers– or James Watson–style Two Minutes Hate humiliation. Even more precisely, since they can hardly deny obvious external differences, Left Creationists rule the brain off-limits. Evolution may have done its regrettable work on fingers and toes, even on body chemistry and digestive organs, but not on brains. Absolutely not!

At this point in our understanding, this Culturist Left Creationism involves willful self-deception. Willful self-deception is no problem for *Homo sap.*, though.

HOW WE THINK

For us Biologians there are no miracles and there is no need for self-deception, just the remorseless workings of nature's cold laws, without pause or interruption, indifferent to our dreams and hopes. None of the sugary, fortified-wine consolations of Religionism for us, nor the socially approved carrot-juice wholesomeness of Culturism. Ours is what Keats called "the true, the blushful Hippocrene," the sweet cool draft of indifferent Truth.

There is, however, a paradox here. Of the three points of view I have identified, the Biologian's is the *least* natural way for human beings to think. Cognition-wise, Biologians are freaks. "Belief in supernatural/religion" is number twelve on anthropologist Donald E. Brown's list of human universals, somewhere in there between "baby talk" and "body adornment."

There is nothing more human—nothing more irremovably, ineradicably a part of human nature—than a belief in miracles, souls, and supernatural agents. Those of us who eschew the consoling miracles of Religionism and Culturism are bucking our own human natures.

The ordinary modes of human thinking are magical, religious, social, and personal. We want our wishes to come true; we want the universe to care about us; we want the approval of those around us;

we want to get even with that SOB who insulted us at the last tribal council. For most people, wanting to know the cold truth about the world is way, way down the list.

Scientific objectivity is a freakish, unnatural, and unpopular mode of thought, restricted to small cliques whom the generality of citizens regard with dislike and mistrust. Just as religious thinking emerges naturally and effortlessly from the everyday workings of the human brain, so scientific thinking has to struggle against the grain of our mental natures. There is a modest literature on this topic: Lewis Wolpert's *The Unnatural Nature of Science* (2000) and Alan Cromer's *Uncommon Sense: The Heretical Nature of Science* (1995) are the books known to me, though I'm sure there are more. There is fiction, too: in Walter M. Miller Jr.'s 1960 sci-fi bestseller *A Canticle for Leibowitz*, the scientists are hunted down and killed . . . then later declared saints by the Catholic Church.

When the magical *(I wish this to be so: therefore it is so!)* and the religious *(We are all one! Brotherhood of man! The universe loves us!)* and the social *(This is what all good citizens believe! If you believe otherwise you are a BAD PERSON!)* and the personal *(That bastard didn't show me the respect I'm entitled to!)* all come together, the mighty psychosocial forces unleashed can be irresistible—ask Larry Summers or James Watson.

The greatest obstacle to calm, rational, evidence-based thinking about human nature, is human nature. Pessimism doesn't come easily. You have to *struggle* your way toward it.

INTO THE BRAIN

Why do we think the way we do? For good, evidence-based answers, we have to look to neuroscience, a big growth area in human-nature investigations. A lot of very smart young people are clamoring to get into mind studies. Some of the enthusiasm here is purely scientific— wanting to know how the brain does the amazing things it does. Some is medical—seeking cures for conditions like Alzheimer's and chronic depression. Some is metaphysical—trying to crack the age-old problem of consciousness.

I'll admit to a long-standing fascination with that last issue. What on earth *is* it, this thing that clicks on when my alarm clock goes off in the morning, and fades away after my second or third shot of single malt in late evening? Who *is* this little guy crouched inside my skull an inch or two behind my eyeballs, watching the passing scene, occasionally directing the action? (And who's directing *his* action?)

Consciousness is "a hallucination hallucinated by a hallucination," says Doug Hofstadter in his 2007 book *I Am a Strange Loop*. Not very helpful. Philosopher Daniel Dennett, interviewed in the *Science and Spirit* online magazine, is a little better: "Consciousness is not some extra glow or aura caused by the activities of the mature cortex. Consciousness *is* those various activities. One is conscious of those contents whose representations briefly monopolize certain cortical resources, in competition with many other representations" [emphasis in original]. Er, *who* is conscious?

It's still baffling to me. I've read a shelf of books on consciousness, listened attentively to Professor Daniel Robinson's "Consciousness and Its Implications" lectures from the Teaching Company, and even attended a one-week conference—"Toward a Science of Consciousness"—in Tucson, Arizona, April 8–12, 2008. (The eighth in a series under that same title. For an account of the first, in 1994, see John Horgan's pop-neuroscience classic *The Undiscovered Mind*, 1999. I blogged the 2008 conference—see my website www.johnder byshire.com/Opinions/HumanSciences, or the May 19, 2008, issue of *National Review*.) After all that, I am very little wiser.

I do have an outline picture of what we do and don't know, though, and a sense of which way the winds are blowing. They are blowing toward determinism, emotion, and error, and away from free will, reason, and judgment.

Take Benjamin Libet's results from the 1980s, for instance. Libet found that the subjective experience of willing an act is *preceded* by the brain activities required to initiate the act. The measured gap between unconscious initiation and conscious decision-making was less than a second in Libet's experiments, but later researchers have pushed it back to seven seconds.

Seven seconds! Your brain starts up the neural processes necessary for you to push a button. *Seven seconds later* you experience the wish to push that button. You then push the button. Where is free will? Where Schopenhauer left it, perhaps. Loosely translated: "We can do what we want, but we can't *want* what we want."

Libet's results haven't gone unchallenged, and there's now a vast amount of literature on volition. There is a good, though early, discussion in Chapter 6 of Daniel Dennett's 1991 book *Consciousness Explained*. Chapter 4 of philosopher Thomas Metzinger's 2009 book *The Ego Tunnel* has a more up-to-date survey of what the author calls "the fascinating and somewhat frightening new field of research into agency and the self." The results do, however, match what you see everywhere you look in the mind sciences. The ordinary notion of human volition—I perceive a choice; I choose; I act—is only what these neuroscience researchers cheerfully call "folk volition." It bears as little relation to the actual brain processes involved in volition as the crystal dome of ancient "folk astronomy" does to the actual night sky.

The idea that a lot of our mental activity is unconscious, is of course not new. It's implicit in Marxism, which holds that impersonal historical forces direct our fate. It's *explicit* in the theories of Freud, which claim that our conscious life is just a sort of outcropping of roiling subterranean urges shaped by our infant experiences then pushed underground by the socialization process.

Here's the data, though, written up in lab notes, timed to the tenth of a second. "You mean I'm just being dragged through life by a lump of meat?" I asked a researcher at Tucson, the one who'd presented Libet's findings. (Libet himself passed away in 2007.) "Probably," she replied, "but fortunately you'll never get yourself to believe it." Mind scientists tend to talk in paradoxes, perhaps to ease the pain of the pessimistic conclusions they keep coming to.

ON NOT KNOWING THYSELF

"Know thyself" goes the ancient maxim. That's the beginning of all deep understanding.

We don't, in fact, seem to know much about our own thoughts, though we're terrifically good at making up stories to kid ourselves that we know. University of Michigan psychologist Richard Nisbett (author of a good, though carefully Culturist, 2003 book titled *The Geography of Thought: How Asians and Westerners Think Differently . . . And Why*) has studied the reasons people give for their actions, and found that we hardly ever truly know why we act.

In one of Nisbett's early experiments (in collaboration with T. Wilson, 1977), the experimenters laid out many pairs of stockings, and asked female subjects to select which pair they liked the best. When the women were questioned as to the reasons for their selection, they volunteered all sorts of wonderful excuses about texture and sheerness. However, all the pairs of stockings were actually identical!

Here's Nisbett describing his work to the science-and-philosophy website Edge.org in January 2006:

> The most important thing that social psychologists have discovered over the last 50 years is that people are very unreliable informants about why they behaved as they did, made the judgment they did, or liked or disliked something. In short, we don't know nearly as much about what goes on in our heads as we think. In fact, for a shocking range of things, we don't know the answer to "Why did I?" any better than an observer . . .
>
> The idea that we have little access to the workings of our minds is a dangerous one. The theories of Copernicus and Darwin were dangerous because they threatened, respectively, religious conceptions of the centrality of humans in the cosmos and the divinity of humans.
>
> Social psychologists are threatening a core conviction of the Enlightenment—that humans are perfectible through the exer-

cise of reason. If reason cannot be counted on to reveal the causes of our beliefs, behavior and preferences, then the idea of human perfectibility is to that degree diminished.

I don't know that conservatives should shed any tears at losing the belief in human perfectibility; but if reason, like free will, is illusory, the foundations of our civilization are undermined. If reason is just a set of stories we make up to explain stuff that has happened in our brains as the result of molecules colliding, if it is nothing but the self-justificatory babbling of zombies, then where is liberty? Where is independence? Where is human dignity?

This determinism is gaining ground, as true ideas irresistibly will. This happens without our noticing much. We forget how alien such ideas would have seemed to our parents and grandparents.

Take homosexuality, for instance. Until a generation ago, homosexuality was widely assumed to be something you *did* because you chose to. That was the basis of public attitudes, and of our laws.

Now more and more of us are subscribing to the view that homosexuality is not something you *do*, it's something you *are*. A Pew survey in August 2006 found:

- The number of Americans who believe homosexuality to be innate rose from 30 percent in 2003 to 36 percent just three years later.
- The number believing homosexuality cannot be changed rose from 42 percent to 49 percent.
- These views have gained much more support among certain groups: college graduates (from 39 percent to 51 percent), liberals (46 to 57), mainline Protestants (37 to 52), and those who seldom or never attend church (36 to 52).
- Some other groups—white evangelicals and black Protestants of all kinds—changed very little in their views over the same three years (2003–6).
- A plurality of the public (49 percent) views sexual orientation as a characteristic that cannot be changed, a seven percentage-point increase since 2003.

In the November 2008 elections, the white-black split showed up clearly in California, where a ballot initiative banning gay marriage was rejected by a narrow majority of white and Asian voters, 51 to 49 percent, but favored clearly by Hispanics, 53 to 47, and overwhelmingly by blacks, 70 to 30.

(The actual science on homosexuality is unsettled. Male homosexuality, at least, seems to have some genetic component; but this is baffling, and nobody can make the evolutionary math work. Womb events are strongly suspected: the more older brothers a male has, the higher his probability of being a homosexual. This suggests that the prior carrying of male children has some effect on the mother's hormonal system which then affects later fetuses. There is also a disease theory, arguing that homosexual inclination is caused by an infectious agent . . . but it is all unsettled. I don't know the current science on female homosexuality.)

WHY YOU SHOULD CONSULT A MELANCHOLY PESSIMIST

Along with free will and reason, objectivity has been taking hits from the cognitive-science researchers. This started in the 1970s with psychologists Amos Tversky and Daniel Kahneman. Their field of study was human choice, judgment, and decision making. It begins with the notion, fundamental to cognitive science, of a *representation*.

The world we have to deal with is filled with extremely complicated objects behaving in extremely complicated ways. The quantity of mentation required to fully encompass every detail of, for example, the Japanese flowering cherry tree in my front yard, is far more, by a factor of *trillions*, than my brain can handle. Yet that is a comparatively simple case. What if I am thinking about, say, the Middle Ages, or the national economy (Kahneman won the 2002 Nobel Prize in Economics), or the earth's climate, or the fate of conservatism?

Being unable to cope with these floods of information, the brain builds a rough sketch of the thing being pondered—a *representation*. To get from the information-swamped sensory input to the pared-down representation sketch in the cerebral cortex, the brain has well-established little data-compression algorithms that it cranks through.

These compression algorithms are approximate rules of thumb—*heuristics* in the jargon. They often make mistakes; hence optical illusions. The patterns of these mistakes are called *biases*. This whole field is often called "Heuristics and Biases"; and that is also the name of a 2002 book, subtitle *The Psychology of Intuitive Judgment*, of which Kahneman was one of the editors.

Researchers like Tversky and Kahneman have identified dozens of different kinds of bias. Some of them have leaked out to become common knowledge: *confirmation bias*, for example—the tendency to give extra weight to facts that support our predesired conclusion. Others are more abstruse, like *self-attribution bias*—attributing good results to skill, bad results to luck.

Can we correct our biases? That depends on whom you ask. The overall picture that emerges from the cognitive science researches of the last half century is one of a brain that struggles to cope with reality, and rarely does very well at it.

Worse yet: Its not doing very well may be *adaptive*. That's a term of art in biology. A trait is adaptive if an organism that possesses this trait gets a reproductive edge thereby over an organism that doesn't.

Researchers like S. Taylor and J. Brown (*Illusion and Well-Being*, 1988) have found that a moderate degree of self-deception is normal in mentally healthy people, and is likely adaptive. Contrariwise:

"[I]t appears to be not the well-adjusted individual but the individual who experiences subjective distress who is more likely to process self-relevant information in a relatively unbiased and balanced fashion."

To put it slightly differently: Up to a point, the more depressed and maladjusted you are, the more likely it is that you are seeing things right, with minimal bias.

Or differently again: For a happy and well-adjusted life, practice self-deception. If it's the cold, unvarnished truth you want, seek out a melancholy pessimist. (Which, if you are reading this book, is what you have done.)

TRAGIC TRUTH, FEELGOOD FALSEHOOD

Every one of the results I've mentioned has been suspected by some thinker in some past age, long before the cog-sci lab rats came along with their scanners and electrodes and computers.

Come to think of it, the idea of sexual orientation as essence, not choice, has been around at least fifty years. This I know, because the first remark on the subject that ever registered on my brain was made by an aunt of mine at least that long ago. On it being mentioned that some acquaintance of the family was homosexual, my aunt remarked, "Poor things! They can't help it." Our jurisprudence may not have taken that point of view, but some good-natured ordinary folk like my aunt did. As I've said elsewhere, it would be surprising to find many surprises in the human sciences. We've known each other for too long. If you want to know about human nature, start by asking your aunt.

A century and a half before my aunt, here is the English writer and painter William Hazlitt, writing in 1821. The essay is titled "On Personal Character."

> No one ever changes his character from the time he is two years old; nay, I might say, from the time he is two hours old . . . the character, the internal, original bias, remains always the same, true to itself to the very last . . . A temper sullen or active, shy or bold, grave or lively, selfish or romantic, . . . is manifest very early; and imperceptibly but irresistibly moulds our inclinations, habits, and pursuits through life. The greater or less degree of animal spirits . . . the disposition to be affected by objects near, or at a distance, or not at all,— to be struck with novelty, or to brood over deep-rooted impressions,—to indulge in laughter or in tears, the leaven of passion or of prudence that tempers this frail clay, is born with us and never quits us. . . . The accession of knowledge, the pressure of circumstances . . . does little more than minister occasion to the first predisposing bias.

So much for the shelves of self-improvement manuals at your local bookstore. To the degree that it's possible to change yourself, Hazlitt implies, it's only walking north on the deck of a southbound ship. Hazlitt was an outlier in his time; but with the news coming in from the human sciences, we can all be Hazlittians now.

Can be. We can accept this grim determinism emerging from the human sciences, or we can decline it. If we accept it, there's not much left of the grand optimistic American dreams of equality, of autonomy, of government by free men following the dictates of reason.

My guess is, we'll decline it. Go on declining it, I mean, since outside the labs and research institutes, nobody much is accepting it. As Jack Nicholson famously said in some movie or other, we can't handle the truth.

After I'd written this chapter, and bandied the word "Culturism" about in some talks and published articles, I got sent a book with *Culturism* as its actual title. (Freelance writing doesn't pay worth a damn, but you get no end of free books.)

The author, John Kenneth Press (yes, that's the author, not the publisher—I checked) is definitely a Culturist in the sense I've used. "Racist books such as *The Bell Curve* are deplorable . . ." etc., etc. He takes the whole thing further, though, arguing that we should all unite under the banner of Western culture. If we don't, he implies, we shall slide into mayhem, racial pogroms, and cultural annihilation.

Perhaps he's right. Perhaps we don't have a choice but to cling to Culturism, even though it's false. But then, if we're stuck with Culturism, we're also stuck with Culturism's demon spawn, social engineering, with its north-of-90-percent failure rate. The thing does after all, as I mentioned above, have its roots in Marxism.

Discussing the thesis of my book with one of my friends—a conservative academic (political science)—I encountered total disagreement. He: "There's nothing about traditional conservatism that makes it truth friendly. In fact, it's the opposite. Historic conservatism is anti-science, prone to celebrate truth by authority, favors religion over rationalism and down deep sees unvarnished truth as corroding social cohesion—correctly, according to you. Keep the peasants happy with fairy tales and mumbo jumbo, if necessary."

If he's right, I'm arguing for a new conservatism. Of course I don't believe he *is* right, though I'll admit that thoughts like his sometimes disturb my rest. Human beings in the generality are prone to wishful thinking and comfortable consolations. "Human kind cannot bear very much reality," said T. S. Eliot; but my experience has been that conservatives can bear more than most. Wishful thinking about human nature and human potential is for leftists.

In any case, setting your face against truth is always a dicey business. Nature has a way of not being mocked. You can throw her out with the proverbial pitchfork, but she'll find her way back.

> *We now live in an age in which science is a court from which there is no appeal.*
> —from Tom Wolfe's *Sorry, but Your Soul Just Died*

Tragic truth or feelgood falsehood? I'll go with truth, however tragic.

RELIGION: WHAT SHALL WE DO TO BE SAVED?

Magna est veritas et praevalebit.
> —Thomas Brooks, *The Crown and Glory
> of Christianity* (1662)

The truth is great and shall prevail.
> —Correct translation of the above

The truth is great and shall prevail a bit.
> —Apocryphal schoolboy mistranslation of the above

CONSERVATIVES ♡ RELIGION

American conservatives love religion. This is even the case with irreligious conservatives, though their affection may be colored with cynicism. David Frum pointed this out in *Dead Right*.

> The conservative movement is secular to its toes. Even those conservatives, like [Irving] Kristol and Pat Buchanan, who believe that excessive secularism is a genuine problem, believe it for secular reasons. They expect that a more devout America would be a better-behaved America.

Conservative movers and shakers, Frum implies, are in the position of the magistrate in Gibbon's famous quip about the various modes of worship in ancient Rome, which "were all considered by the people, as equally true; by the philosopher, as equally false; and by the magistrate, as equally useful." To say this does not preclude individual cases of the magistrate himself being religious, as, for example, Pat Buchanan certainly is.

Religious and irreligious people alike may consider religion useful to social cohesion. I myself, when I was still a churchgoing Christian, wrote the following thing in a review of Michael Shermer's book *The Science of Good and Evil:*

> The problem with "science-based material analysis" is that it is a cold temple whose pale blue flame gives little warmth. However well Michael Shermer's provisional ethics may satisfy sanguine middle-class American intellectuals with a good grasp of the human sciences, no such system will attain widespread acceptance if it fails to nourish key components of the human personality.

I've since lost my own faith and joined the company of those sanguine intellectuals, but the words I wrote there still seem true to me. The human race won't be dumping the Supernatural anytime soon; and for most people, the Supernatural will nourish those key components better than any arguments from nature.

Human beings are religious. We don't all *have* to be, any more than we all have to be musical, or athletic, or humorous; but as long as there are human beings, there will be religion to offer warmth to those who can believe its stories and its metaphysics, while those who can't will be left with a paler, colder flame.

In the particular case of the United States, which an acquaintance of mine (moderately religious, Jewish) likes to call "this God-soaked country," nobody who seeks to influence our public life can ignore religion, whatever his personal doubts or inclinations. For forty years Gallup has been polling us on the question "If your party nominated a generally well qualified person for president who happened to be X, would you vote for that person?" X = "atheist" regularly occupies the bottom of the rankings, with only 45 percent of Americans willing to vote for an atheist in the December 2007 poll. The only avowed atheist currently seated in the U.S. Congress is San Francisco representative Pete Stark—a far-left liberal, of course.

Those conservatives David Frum wrote of, who expect that a more devout America would be a better-behaved America, may be on the wrong track, though. Irreligious regions of the United States, like the Pacific Northwest, have much better statistics on crime and other social dysfunction than religious regions like the Bible Belt. The least religious state of the Union is actually Oregon, 18 percent of whose inhabitants declare themselves as having no religious affiliation. For murder (2007, per 100,000), births out of wedlock (1995, percentage), and persons living with AIDS (2007, per 100,000), Oregon's stats are 1.9—28.9—76, respectively. The *most* religious state is Mississippi, with only 4 percent having no religious affiliation. Mississippi's stats are 7.1—45.3—109. Entire nations display the same trend, with very religious ones (Nigeria, Pakistan) exhibiting worse—often *much* worse—stats than irreligious ones (Japan, Norway).

That's not just back-of-envelope sociology, either. There are serious studies saying the same thing. Here's one from the *Journal of Religion and Society*, laboring under the title: "Cross-National Correlations of Quantifiable Societal Health with Popular Religiosity and Secularism in the Prosperous Democracies." The author, Gregory Paul, found: "In general, higher rates of belief in and worship of a creator correlate with higher rates of homicide, juvenile and early adult mortality, STD infection rates, teen pregnancy and abortion in the prosperous democracies." So much for religion making people better.

There's a tangle of demographic and cultural variables mixed in with those numbers, though. A conservative, religious or not, might still come up with some arguments for belief.

- The conservative preference for letting people lead their own lives and make their own arrangements for collective support, as opposed to having government bureaucrats organize their affairs, leads us to look favorably on churches, which are rather good at bringing people together without state assistance and organizing them in socially useful endeavors. (Not that churches will refuse such assistance if offered, which of course it never should be. George W. Bush's "faith-based initiatives" were a characteristically moon-booted attempt to violate this fundamental conservative—indeed *constitutional*—principle.)

- Our fondness for the past, and for traditional ways of doing things, embraces the religious outlook, which is a large part of America's past, and of the Western world's. (Though not as large a part as religious zealots sometimes claim. Of the people who made our nation, and our civilization, a hefty proportion were not perceptibly religious, including America's greatest writer, Mark Twain, and the West's, William Shakespeare. Our legal forms descend from pagan Rome, our philosophy from pagan Greece, our fondness for moots and parliaments—not to mention the names of our weekdays—from pagan Germany. All right, all right, I'll cut the quibbles.)

- The determination of conservatives to see humanity plain, and not in terms of some City of the Sun, New Soviet Man, "blank slate," wish-fulfillment fantasy, obliges us to respect the religious impulse as a core feature of human nature, and to be skeptical of any political scheme that ignores or denies it.

- Our devotion to the nation-state as a key organizing principle in large human affairs makes us cherish benign peculiarities of national character. Most of us count the "God-soaked" quality of the United States's national character as one such. We can cherish it from afar, as we may cherish other national peculiarities—college football, private firearms, the Delta blues, eating peanut butter with jelly—without being personally enthusiastic.

Conservatives, including irreligious conservatives, therefore have good reasons to smile on religion. Social and historical forces are afoot, though, that will wipe the smile off our faces.

I'll describe those forces in just a moment. First, let me detour through a couple of sections to take a closer look at the relationship between conservatism and religious belief in the United States.

FAITH AND CONSERVATISM

The association of religion with conservatism has always been a messy one. The old-world "throne and altar" conservatism of someone like Lord Salisbury or General Franco naturally embraced religion—or at least, in the spirit of Gibbon's magistrate, the social utility of religion.

American conservatism is a different matter. In this country, the connection between faith and conservatism is historically recent. It's occasionally been the cause of internecine warfare among conservative intellectuals, as with the early-1960s spat between the celebration of individualistic capitalism by fiercely atheistic Ayn Rand and her followers, and the emerging circle of conservative thinkers, most of them Christians, around the young *National Review*. (Bill Buckley offered a thinly fictionalized account of the fight in his 2003 novel *Getting It Right*.)

None of the three Abrahamic religions—Judaism, Christianity, Islam—is inherently "left" or "right." All three are capable of many quite different political interpretations—indeed, on the historical evidence, of any political interpretation whatsoever.

The Tenth Commandment ("Thou shalt not covet . . .") can be, and has been, read as a condemnation of the acquisitive spirit that animates capitalism. The Sermon on the Mount can be, and has been, read as a socialist—pacifist, redistributionist—tract. There is no more egalitarian sight in the world than the *tawaf*, the circumambulation of the holy Kaaba in Mecca at the end of a Muslim's ritual pilgrimage. All pilgrims, rich and poor alike, wear the *ihram*, which a standard guidebook describes as "two pieces of white, plain and unsewn cloth." I suppose that when the *tawaf* has been completed, the Saudi princes drive off to their palaces in chauffeur-driven limousines with solid gold trim, while the *fellaheen* shuffle away on foot to their crowded, insanitary pilgrim hostels. The egalitarian ethos is plainly there in the *tawaf*, though, and in Islam at large. It works its way through to the complaints about "corrupt, Western-backed rulers" made by Islamic fundamentalist militants.

In the United States, Christianity has often been a prop of liberalism, and even radicalism. It's not very long ago that Evangelicals were pounding the sidewalks and ringing doorbells on behalf of Jimmy Carter. I actually had my own doorbell so rung one evening in 1976. The Roman Catholic Church has produced radicals aplenty in recent decades, from the Berrigan brothers and "liberation theology" firebrands to Barack Obama's pal Father Pfleger. The Episcopal Church has been at the forefront of modern feminist and gay rights movements, infuriating many "values" conservatives. Establishment Methodism is practically synonymous with bleeding-heart liberalism: Hillary Clinton is a Methodist—a pretty typical one, I am told. Of all the United States' demographic subgroups, one of the strongest for redistributionist big-government socialism is African Americans . . . who are also one of our most religious subgroups. And so on.

Politically speaking, polls show that the *most* religious Americans tend to favor conservative-Republican candidates, while the *merely* religious are all over the place, with a general trend, if anwhere, considerably left of center.

The most intensely religious large group of Americans is Evangelical Christians. They form about 7 percent of the adult population. In the 2008 elections, according to the faith-trends-monitoring Barna Group, 88 percent of Evangelicals voted for John McCain, against only 11 percent for Barack Obama. That 88 percent is statistically the same as the 85 percent who voted for George W. Bush over John Kerry in 2004.

If you move down the scale of religious intensity you come to "born again" Christians. These are 43 percent of the adult population, a number that includes the 7 percent of Evangelicals. To put it another way, 36 percent of us are born again but not Evangelical. Of the overall 43 percent, there is a pretty even split in party registration: 18 percent Republican, 17 percent Democrat, 8 percent independent or other.

This means that among *non*-Evangelical born-agains, registered Democrats outnumber registered Republicans. The 2008 McCain-Obama voting split among all born-agains, including Evangelicals, was nonetheless 57–41. (The 2004 Bush-Kerry split was 60–36.) Subtracting out the Evangelicals gives about a 52–48 split in McCain's favor among non-Evangelical born-agains.

Out beyond the born-again Christians are the merely Christian voters, "notional Christians" in the pollsters' jargon. Barna doesn't break out the voting here, but they note that party registrations in this Christian-but-not-born-again group go 44–27 Democrat-Republican. Non-Christians—voters of other faiths, or no faith—split 62–36 Obama-McCain. Among atheists and agnostics the voting split was 76–23 Obama-McCain.

The bottom line on Barna's numbers is that the *most* religious Americans are strongly Republican, the *merely* religious tilt Democrat, and the *ir*religious are strongly Democrat.*

Religious Right? On the evidence of the pollsters, religious Americans lean rather hard to the Left.

MEET YOUR PAL THE METROCON

Thus the Right does not own religion in America—never has, never will. Nor will it ever, or should it ever, be the case that religion owns

---

* For a neat visual aid here, go to the "Comparisons" section of the Pew Forum on Religion and Public Life (religions.pewforum.org/comparisons), click on "Social & Political Views," then on "Party Affiliation." You are looking at a spreadsheet whose left-hand column breaks out respondents by religious confession. Each of the next six columns covers one political affiliation: "Republican," "Lean Republican," "Independent," etc. Each has a bar chart showing one bar per religious confession.

    The thing that jumps out at you is that the "Democratic" and "Lean Democratic" columns have far more color—that is, longer bars—than the others. Only Mormons (65–22) and Evangelicals (50–34) break Republican.

the Right. Some religious conservatives *think* it does, and even more *wish* it did. There are Evangelicals who think we irreligious conservatives will be Left Behind *en bloc* at the day of judgment to face the Tribulation along with liberals; and there are Roman Catholics who yearn for the American conservative movement to become a wholly owned subsidiary of the Vatican, as Damon Linker explained in his 2006 book *The Theocons.* The late Richard John Neuhaus, a leading theocon—he is the principal character in Linker's book—wrote a famous essay in 1991 arguing that it is not possible for an atheist to be a good citizen. (Neuhaus generously allowed that atheists should, nonetheless, be permitted to remain citizens.)

Sensible religious conservatives, though, know that irreligious ones need to be accommodated, just as sensible unbelieving conservatives understand that America's religious exceptionalism is, for the reasons I bullet-pointed earlier in this chapter, a key bulwark against a drift to the milk-and-water statist pseudoconservatism of, for example, modern Britain.

A digression within a digression here, before I return to my main theme. There's a big overlap between irreligious conservatives and a species I tried to pin down in an online column once, a column people still ask me about six years later.

This is the species "metrocon," short for "metropolitan conservative." My attempt to float this word back in 2003 was unsuccessful, mainly, I think, because people confused the word with "metrosexual," which was being launched at the same time, to much louder applause. I founded my argument in the contrast between the busy sophistication of the metropolis and the relaxed simplicity of the provinces, a contrast that goes way back in human history—at least as far back as Greek comedy, in which the city slicker and the country bumpkin were already stock figures of fun twenty-five hundred years ago.

Most of us are, in temperament and outlook, either metropolitan or provincial, either blue or red. I myself was raised in a small country town, but I have spent most of my adult life in big cities or their shadows, and have a mostly metropolitan cast of mind. (My sister, by contrast, who is a clever and well-read person of strong opinions, describes herself proudly as "a provincial lady.")

I dislike modern American liberalism very much, and believe it to be poisonous and destructive, as well as arrogant and false; yet I'm at ease in a roomful of New York liberals in a way that, to be truthful about it, I am not in a gathering of red-state Evangelicals. Setting aside our actual opinions about this, that, or the other, I'm aware that in the first gathering I'm among people with whom I have, at some level and in some key respects, a shared outlook; and in the second gathering, much less so.

I'll admit there's an element of condescension in the metrocon viewpoint. What the heroic worker was to an old-line Marxist, what the suffering Negro was to civil rights marchers, what the unfulfilled housewife is to Hillary Clinton, the Vietnamese peasant to Jane Fonda, the Palestinian rioter to Edward Said, so the red-state conservative with his Bible, his hunting rifle, and his antisodomy laws is to a metrocon. He is *authentic*, in a way we metrocons are not.

There's a faint odor of cynicism here—the cynicism David Frum identified in the quote I started from. Big political movements must be held together somehow, though. If there was ever one that didn't have a portion of cynicism in its glue, I never met it. Authenticity is in any case not to be sniffed at. My dictionary gives the antonym of "authentic" as "counterfeit."

You won't find many people willing to admit to being a metrocon, but the precincts I live and work in are thick with them. I conduct much of my social life among conservative journalists and editors. I know dozens of these folk. They are metrocon almost to a man. And of course woman, though the willing-to-admit quotient is even lower among gynometrocons.

Here, for example, is a question asked by the Gallup polling organization in May 2008: "Do you think homosexual relations between consenting adults should or should not be legal?" Forty percent of Gallup's respondents said "should not." Yet I'm pretty sure that *not one* of these journo-school metrocon acquaintances of mine would answer "should not" to that question. (Since 1977, when Gallup started asking that precise question, the "should nots" have never been less than 35 percent.)

I and my metrocon pals, including your favorite conservative TV pundit and the editor and staff of your favorite conservative periodical, therefore stand to the left of 40 percent of Americans on this key social-conservatism topic. Not just 40 percent of conservatives, 40 percent of *Americans.*

It's the same with many other issues. Did human beings develop from less advanced creatures, with or without God's guidance, or did God create Man in his present form? The public split 50–44 when Gallup polled that one, also in May 2008, whereas my guess for the metrocons would be more like 90–10 at worst. (Worst, I mean, for us scientifically literate metrocons. The with-without God's guidance split, by the way, was 36–14.) I once found myself in a roomful of mostly conservative New Yorkers who were expecting me to speak impromptu on some topic of my choosing. Having just recently fought a couple of bouts with the "intelligent design" people, I suggested that as my topic. Nobody was interested. One rock-ribbed conservative-Republican gentleman expressed the sense of the meeting with: "That intelligent design stuff is for the rubes."

There is, as I said, no use denying the condescension here. I don't think there is any cause for rancor or antagonism, though. Any movement that wants political influence must be a coalition of people with different interests and enthusiasms, town and country both. The metropolitan conservative and his provincial cousin both have their part to play in advancing common ideals. Sitting in New York or Washington, D.C., cooking up argumentative commentaries or organizing deep-brow conferences on "Whither Conservatism?" is as useful, in its own way, as running a Christian home-schooling group in Knoxville.

Those things are not as critical to the future of conservatism, though. Looking across the pond at the country of my birth, where there are no powerful conservative lobbies—no Second Amendment warriors, no Christian Conservatives, no Right to Life chapters—I see what happens when conservatism becomes a merely metropolitan cult. Conservative politics in Britain has become marginalized and impotent. Things aren't quite that bad here, and it hasn't been I and my metrocon pals who prevented it. It's been the legions of *authentic* conservatives out there in the provinces. Metrocons can't carry this thing by themselves. Carry it? We can't even pick it up.

And religion is the real ballast out there, keeping what remains of American conservatism upright and steady. Religion matters to conservatism in a way it does not to the Left. As I pointed out earlier, it is a friend to localism, voluntarism, mutual self-support, traditionalism, and patriotism. If it goes down the tubes, then so do they, sucking us wine-sipping, canapé-chomping metrocons in their wake. That won't matter to the religious Left, who are happy to see self-support delegated to government bureaucrats, who look askance at traditionalism, and who take patriotism to be an unacceptable affront to the Brotherhood of Man. It will matter to us, though. Which is unfortunate, because the omens for America's continuing religious exceptionalism are not good.

End of digression, end of digression. Return to main theme: America's religious exceptionalism is doomed, and American conservatism with it.

THE END OF EXCEPTIONALISM

There's no up-front reason to suppose that religious exceptionalism will be a permanent feature of our country. Things come and go. The Frontier, along with most of the Frontier Spirit, came and went; the three-martini lunch came and went, to the regret of some people still among us; so did the exceptional levels of chastity and sexual innocence in both sexes noted by de Tocqueville and other nineteenth-century visitors. (Traveling in the United States in 1896, a few months after the Oscar Wilde trial, Bertrand Russell was pestered with questions by young men who had not been able to fathom what it was that Wilde had *done*.)

If we lose our religious exceptionalism, American conservatism will have had a key prop knocked out from under it. Can this really happen? Can a nation as "God-soaked" as ours really turn religiously indifferent? It certainly can. I have myself watched it happen in my own lifetime to two Christian nations, one Catholic and one Protestant, both as "God-soaked" as you please.

There never was—well, not in the modern world—a country more steeped in Christianity than the Ireland of my youth. The 1951 census showed only 64 atheists in the Republic of Ireland. They could all have met together in one of those famous Dublin pubs. This intense devotion to the Church continued into the 1980s.

Nowadays the strikingly low religious numbers coming out of Ireland are for vocations: 9 priests ordained in 2007 (when 160 died or quit), and just 2 nuns taking final vows (228 died or quit). You could cram *them* into a single confessional. The average age of Irish priests is currently sixty-one. Regular attendance at mass has dropped from 85 percent in 1985 to below 60 now, according to the Dublin Archdiocese; and that latter figure is propped up by an influx of Polish workers.

It's not just Catholicism that has taken a hit. The other paragon of intense religiosity in my youth was Methodist Wales. When we sang hymns at morning assembly in my English-Midlands schools, the voices of the Welsh schoolmasters—schoolmasters being the principal export of Wales—could be heard above all the rest. Every one of them had sung in a chapel choir; every one could tell you his voice register to a fine precision; none of them needed to look at the hymn book for the words (which he could have sung equally well in Welsh, also without a prompt book).

Now the chapels of Wales are empty and derelict, where they have not been bought up or demolished. In 2001 they were closing at the rate of one per week. Wales, like Ireland, is becoming just another hedonistic, religiously indifferent European welfare democracy.

It can happen anywhere. It can happen here. Will it, though? Yes, it will. The forces eating away at our religious exceptionalism are working away in plain sight. Some of them were set in motion by an event in *very* plain sight, an event that was hard to ignore.

THE SHOCK OF JIHADISM

Every so often the kaleidoscope of social and political attitudes gets a good hard smack, causing all the little fragments of colored tinsel inside to rearrange themselves in new patterns. The great smack event of the last few years was the one we call "9/11"—the multifold attacks of September 11, 2001, on our country by Islamist fanatics.

What did that attack do to the prospects for conservatism in the United States? It helped doom them, of course. I shall say something about the policy implications of 9/11 in the next chapter. Here I just want to make some arguments about the effect on our national psyche of what was indisputably an act of religious passion.

Prior to 9/11, hardly any Americans thought about Islam from one year's end to the next. The white-hating and anti-Semitic Nation of Islam gangster-cult had long been a fringe phenomenon among African Americans. It was occasionally in the news, as when the boxer Cassius Clay joined them, becoming Muhammad Ali, in 1964, or when Louis Farrakhan made an inflammatory speech, as he did from time to time, and still does. There have always been cults aplenty in the United States, though, and this one was no wackier than most. (Though it *was* a bit more homicidal than most.) In any case, anyone who looked into the matter would quickly learn that the Nation of Islam is regarded by mainstream Muslims as an ignorant and heretical aberration.

After 9/11 we were obliged to do a lot of thinking about Islam. Obviously those atrocious suicide attacks carried with them some kind of message about religious belief. What was that message?

Two answers came up in short order from two quite different groups: atheists and Islamophobes. The atheists told us that the 9/11 attacks proved the wickedness and folly of all religion; the Islamophobes, that the attacks proved the wickedness and folly of *one particular* religion, the religion of the attackers.

Both groups had been around for a while, of course, catering to small audiences. Now, after the attacks, they stepped to the front of the public stage and addressed us through bullhorns. Both found receptive audiences. Neither is through lecturing us yet. When they are, we shall be a less religious nation.

ATHEISM'S NEW CHURCH MILITANT

There have always been atheists in the United States. Much entertainment was provided in my own London college days by Madalyn Murray O'Hair, plaintiff in the lawsuit that eventually (1963) caused the U.S. Supreme Court to rule that prayer in public schools is unconstitutional. Ms. O'Hair's 1965 *Playboy* interview was circulated with much glee among the kinds of English people—it's around 50 percent, rising to 90 in the intelligentsia, of which I at that time fancied myself a postulant—who think the United States is full of Holy Rollers who spend their Sunday mornings fondling snakes while speaking in tongues.

In the interview, Ms. O'Hair pondered the idea of publishing a book to be titled *Letters from Christians*, made up from the hate mail she'd received. She offered some samples: "Somebody is going to put a bullet through your fat ass, you scum, you masculine Lesbian bitch!" . . . "You will be killed before too long. Or maybe your pretty little baby boy. The queer-looking bastard. You are a bitch and your son is a bastard" . . . "Slut! Slut! Slut! Bitch slut from the Devil!"

And there have of course been many other notable American atheists. The Wikipedia index for "Category: American Atheists" has 315 entries, from novelist Ernest Hemingway to movie star Katharine Hepburn, from sci-fi author Isaac Asimov to martial arts legend Bruce Lee, from physicist Richard Feynman to baseball superstar Ted Williams. If you stretch the definition a little to include "functional atheists"—people who, though religion plays no part at all in their lives, might prefer to tag themselves with something a little less emphatic, like "Deist," "agnostic," or "Mysterian"—you could pull in far more, including some of the Founding Fathers, most twentieth-century writers and intellectuals, and, well, me.

Below the ranks of the famous, there have always been the types that religious people like to scoff at as "village atheists," though I don't know why a village atheist should be any more contemptible than a municipal or metropolitan atheist.

Atheists never made such noise as they did in the years immediately following 9/11, though. Sam Harris was first out of the gate with his 2004 book *The End of Faith*. Daniel Dennett and Richard Dawkins followed in 2006 with, respectively, *Breaking the Spell* and *The God Delusion*. The following year Christopher Hitchens brought out *God Is Not Great*. The phrase "celebrity atheist" entered the language somewhere along the way.

Some of these authors had advertised their atheism before. Hitchens had published a book taking down Mother Teresa in 1995, and a scathing article on the Dalai Lama in 1998. Dawkins had described himself as "an intellectually fulfilled atheist" in a 1986 book about biology. None of this got much attention until after 9/11, though. On that dreadful day we were given an illustration of a truth about religion: that profound religious belief can drive people to do utterly crazy things, including very wicked things. So that proved what? That religion was horrid and dangerous? Or just that *some* religions were horrid and dangerous, while others were benign? Naturally there was a market for both points of view, and the celebrity atheists stepped up to offer their wares on behalf of the first.

The celebrity atheists prompted a Newtonian reaction from intellectual believers. An overreaction, in fact: There seem to be far more of these books countering atheism than there were in the original atheist tranche. As a point person for conservative unbelief (and a founding member of the SecularRight.com blog), I get 'em all, usually with very pleasant covering notes from the authors urging me to read with attention. Just for 2008, I have logged in David Aikman's *The Delusion of Disbelief*, Vox Day's *The Irrational Atheist*, Michael Novak's *No One Sees God*, and Edward Feser's *The Last Superstition*. Perhaps the WWE could organize some tag-wrestling matches, in the spirit of Monty Python's German versus Greek philosophers soccer game.

The thing you heard a lot was that none of those polemical atheist books really changed anyone's mind. This I doubt. If you talk to people about their religious beliefs, the strongest impression you get is one of vagueness. Most people have no taste for abstract thinking and can't be bothered to ponder such matters, so that if you probe them or poll them, you get muddled and contradictory assertions, mixed up with half-remembered things they learned from parents, teachers, or clergymen. D. Jason Slone covered this ground in detail in his 2004 book *Theological Incorrectness: Why Religious People Believe What They Shouldn't*.

The aforementioned Barna Group, for instance, reports that two-thirds of atheists and agnostics believe in an afterlife! My own father was an unbeliever, a "village atheist"; but when filling out a form, he would put "C of E" (that is, Church of England) in the Religion box.

Most English people did the same, and for all I know still do, whether churchgoers or not. Their self-identification as Christians has very little to do with Christ or the Bible. They were no more Christian than British astronomer Martin Rees (nowadays Lord Rees), who told Richard Dawkins that he goes to church "as an unbelieving Anglican . . . out of loyalty to the tribe." (Compare English *über*-patriot George Orwell's remark that "I like the Church of England better than Our Lord.") Roman Catholic friends tell me that many Americans who identify with their Church are likewise only "tribal Catholics," who hardly ever, perhaps never, think about God, Christ, or the Holy Spirit.

The 9/11 attacks clarified some of that vagueness. People who had never before really pondered, now did. Some of them, to aid their pondering, picked up one of the celebrity atheist books, and found themselves responding affirmatively to it.

It happened: I know cases. Before 9/11 the U.S. population consisted of a few percent who were knowledgeable about their faith and unshakable in it; a few percent who were unapologetic and immovable unbelievers, and several dozen percent whose beliefs were mostly a matter of habit and upbringing, rarely reflected on or thought deeply about, largely muddled and incoherent. The events of 9/11 sent some shafts of light through the vagueness, pushing some of the unreflecting into the unbeliever camp. Possibly a few at the other side had their faith strengthened by 9/11, but it's hard to see why.

And then, for those unwilling to believe that all religion stinks, there was an alternative lesson from 9/11: No, it is not the case that all religion stinks, but it *is* the case that Islam stinks. This position is also corrosive of faith in general, if less obviously.

ISLAMOPHOBIA—THE NEW CRUSADERS

The Islamophobes come in a wide variety of types. Some are lapsed Muslims, fallen from the faith, always (it seems) into agnosticism or atheism. The best-known of these is Ayaan Hirsi Ali, the Somali-born Dutch author of the 2007 bestseller *Infidel.* Ibn Warraq, a Pakistan-born British writer, is another case: His 1995 memoir *Why I Am Not a Muslim* got a new lease of life after 9/11.

Jewish writers have been prominent too, understandably enough given the high levels of anti-Semitism in the Muslim world. The Egyptian-born British-Jewish writer Bat Ye'or gave us the word "Eurabia," and popularized the notion of *dhimmitude*—that is, the second-class status of non-Muslims in a Muslim society. British Zionist Melanie Phillips caused a stir with her 2006 book *Londonistan.* American scholar Daniel Pipes contributed *Militant Islam Reaches America* (2002), but angrily denies he is an Islamophobe, arguing that he has taken pains to separate out Muslim fanatics from moderate, mainstream Muslims.

(To which my comment would be: Human history would have been a dull and featureless affair if moderate, mainstream people had been its driving force. Bolsheviks were a tiny minority of Russia's population in 1917. Most Russians were no doubt moderate and mainstream . . .)

There are Islamophobic websites, too. I actually used to contribute to one: the rather good *New English Review*, run by an energetic Christian lady in Tennessee. They have the good sense to leaven their pages with some non-Islamophobic literary, historical, and social commentary, but the main mission is to get everyone knowing how horrible Islam is and what a monster Muhammad was. I was voted off the site after eighteen months for not being Islamophobic enough.

That's all right. In matters editorial, I am a believer in totalitarian despotism. Most writers are lazy, difficult, selfish, thoughtless, and unreliable. This is especially the case with freelance writers, the people lesser outlets like *NER* must rely on. For trying to get anything out of us feckless, alcoholic, bohemian scribblers, the "herding cats" metaphor is barely adequate. Herding gnats, perhaps. Editors everywhere have my sympathy. (And the Tennessee lady still sends me Christmas cards.)

In any case, the decision was a fair one, as I am *not* particularly Islamophobic. All religions look wacky to an unbeliever, even to one who does not, like the celebrity atheists, consider religion a menace. Islam, in its present frustrated state, is doing more harm than most, but that's historically contingent.

It may indeed seem wacky for a suicide bomber to expect he will find seventy-two virgins waiting for him in the afterlife; but what is it that Christians expect? Here is one of them, an exceptionally brilliant, literate, well-educated, and theologically erudite one, the English-Catholic historian Paul Johnson in his 1996 religious apologia *The Quest for God*:

> Those who find themselves in Hell—if anyone does—will include painters and composers and writers and philosophers as well as dictators and tyrants. A man, like Beethoven, who saw himself, through the sublimity of his work, as an intermediary between God and man, was walking close to the precipice. So was Tolstoy, whose idea of his own moral righteousness and importance led him, at times, to see himself . . . as "God's elder brother." Picasso, in his old age, fancied himself as an art-god, a painter endowed not just with skill and intelligence . . . but as a special being.

Beethoven! Tolstoy! Picasso! Sounds like Mark Twain was right: "Heaven for climate, Hell for company."

To an unbeliever, different faiths merely display different degrees of preposterousness: seventy-two virgins here, Beethoven roasting on the spit next to Lenin there. (More charcoal!)

A believer is naturally reluctant to think like that. When the absurdity of other people's beliefs is a common topic of conversation, though, it must surely be hard to keep at bay the dread thought: *Isn't that what* my *faith might look like to an outsider?*

One way to shut down that thought is to adopt the posture that the other guy's religion is a monstrous perversion. If my revelation is *true! true!* then your different revelation must be *false! false!* Not for believers the calm, parsimonious luxury enjoyed by us heathens of thinking that all religions are equally false.

It follows that the strongest Islamophobia issues from the firmest adherents of other religions. In the United States that means Christians. I am sure that devout Hindus have their own beefs (wrong word . . . never mind . . .) with Islam. Do they?

> A screaming mob of thousands of Hindu militants stormed a 16th-century mosque here [in Ayodhya, northern India] today and demolished it with sledgehammers and their bare hands, plunging India into a political and religious crisis. [*New York Times*, December 7, 1992]

Yes, I guess they do. I can't imagine Buddhists are very happy with what Afghanistan's Muslim fanatics did to the great ancient Buddha statues of Bamyan in 2001, either. (The Taliban dynamited the fifteen-hundred-year-old statues as "idols," forbidden in strict Islamic law.) In the United States, though, strong religion is Christian, and one would expect to find the strongest Islamophobia among devout Christians.

So it proves. The star performer here is Robert Spencer, author of a shelf of books with titles like *Islam Unveiled: Disturbing Questions About the World's Fastest Growing Faith* (2002), *The Truth About Muhammad: Founder of the World's Most Intolerant Religion* (2006), and *Religion of Peace?—Why Christianity Is and Islam Isn't* (2007).

Spencer is a Melkite Christian with family roots in the Middle

East. Melkites are a very old sect in communion with Rome (and so can correctly be described as Roman Catholic), but much of whose ancient literature is in Syriac, a language related to Arabic. Spencer, though firm in his own Christian faith, has been fascinated by the Koran (though he annoyingly spells it "Qur'an," as if any Western reader has a clue what to do with that "Q" and that apostrophe) since his college days around 1980, and is very thoroughly familiar with it, as well as with the secondary scriptures of Islam. He is also a gifted and engaging writer, some of whose books have been bestsellers.

I'll admit I find Spencer quite persuasive on at least some of his topics. Here he is in a September 2007 interview with the Liberal Institute making an important point:

> *LI:* You defend Western civilization vigorously and hero-
> ically—but you call it "Judeo-Christian." Isn't it more accu-
> rate to call our Western World "Greco-Roman" or
> "Enlightenment liberal"?

> *Spencer:* I don't see this as an Either/Or proposition, but as a
> Both/And one. I focused on the Judeo-Christian aspect be-
> cause that is both the element of Western civilization most
> frequently attacked by the jihadists (cf. Adam Gadahn of Al-
> Qaeda in his extended critique of Christian doctrine last year),
> as well as by atheists in the U.S. (Dawkins, Harris, Hitchens)
> who see Christianity and Christians as part of the problem
> along with the Islamic jihadists, not as part of our civilization
> that is worth defending.
>
> But I myself have no problem working with atheists and
> with anyone who is interested in defending the West from the
> jihad.

That is a *very* good point, one I haven't seen any of the celebrity atheists answer. Unbelievers may think—all right, we *do* think—Christianity is only slightly less nutty than Islam; but Christianity is *ours.* We've got along with it for several centuries; and the relation-ship between Western unbelievers and Western Christians, if not always polite, is stable and comfortable. Can we fit Islam in like that? Spencer is sure we can't, though he is coy about making the obvious conclusion.

(Which I will make for him here. Western countries should severely restrict settlement of Muslims. There are fifty-seven member nations in the Organization of the Islamic Conference. Any Muslim who is dissatisfied with the country he finds himself living in, is spoiled for choice. There are fifty-six other nations hospitable to Muslims that he can emigrate to, including many with excellent climates—Yemen, Uzbekistan, Guinea-Bissau. Western nations are under no obligation to accommodate him, and we should not.)

For all the intelligence being exercised here, though, from both celebrity atheists and Islamophobes, the effect is the same. The more exposure we get to other people's religions, the harder it is to push away the thought voiced by David Hume: that while it is not possible that all the world's religions are true, it *is* possible that they are all false.

To keep a faith strong, it's best if believers don't think about it too much, especially in comparison with other faiths. One way or another, Americans have been getting a seminar in Comparative Religion since 9/11, and that cannot help but weaken the faith of many, as the religious wars of the devout seventeenth century ushered in the Enlightenment of the skeptical, disillusioned eighteenth.

9/11 AS AN ACCELERANT

The post-9/11 exposure of religious faith, both ours and theirs, was not the beginning of religious decline in the United States. The 9/11 attacks were only an accelerant. They happened when belief was already retreating.

The 2001 American Religious Identification Survey found: "The greatest increase in absolute as well as in percentage terms has been among those adults who do not subscribe to any religious identification; their number has more than doubled from 14.3 million in 1990 to 29.4 million in 2001; their proportion has grown from just eight percent of the total in 1990 to over fourteen percent in 2001."

There was never any good reason to suppose that American religiosity would resist the forces that have eroded faith elsewhere in the Western world. With mass communications and cheap long-distance travel, we are all just more worldly than our parents and grandparents.

You can see the worldiness effect at work in individuals. I recently read David Aikman's 2007 biography of Billy Graham. I'd had a vague notion that Graham had drifted somewhat from his original fundamentalism, and an even vaguer memory of some theological conflict between him and Bob Jones University back in the 1970s. I hadn't realized just how far Graham had drifted, though. The Gospels?

> He has leaned towards a vision of the Gospels which, if it excluded the Hitlers and Pol Pots of the world, seems to be entirely accessible to just about everyone else.
>
> *Billy Graham: His Life and Influence*

(That quote and all the following are from Aikman's book, with Graham himself in quotation marks.)
Hell?

> "Hell means separation from God. We are separated from his light, from his fellowship. That is going to hell."

Sounds a lot more comfortable than Paul Johnson's vision. Muslims, Hindus, Buddhists?

> "I used to think that pagans in far-off countries were lost—were going to hell—if they did not have the gospel of Jesus Christ preached to them. I no longer believe that. I believe there are other ways of recognizing the existence of God—through nature for instance—and plenty of other opportunities, therefore, of saying yes to God."

Abortion?

"There is a Christian position, I think. But I'm not prepared to say what it is."

Fundamentalist? Ol' Billy sounds like he's auditioning for a job as archbishop of Canterbury.

How does this happen? Where has the thunder and hellfire gone? I suppose Graham has just been out in the world too much. That Old-Time Religion can stay intact only if you remain among people with more or less the same kind of faith. A couple of decades of hobnobbing at interfaith gatherings with the Dalai Lama, the Grand Mufti of Jerusalem, rabbis and swamis and Catholic archbishops, and things just don't look so cut and dried anymore.

If a man as devout and *American* as Billy Graham can, under the pressure of worldly modernity and acquaintance with other faiths, drift that far from good old Bible Belt hellfire dogmatism toward vague, fluffy spirituality, the rest of America can too, and will.

As Billy Graham goes, so goes the United States.

THE RISING TIDE OF UNBELIEF

Everything in our world works against our religion, most especially against unquestioning faith in miraculous events. The strict evidentiary standards that were once the property only of lawyers, engineers, doctors, and working scientists, are now the property of everybody—basic grounding for the "symbol-manipulating" work most of us do in postindustrial society. Watch one of the lawyer, doctor, or dead-whore TV shows; pick up one of the proliferating pop-science books or magazines; listen to citizens discussing their medical complaints and diagnoses . . .

William Clifford's dictum that it is an intellectual sin to believe in something for which there is not sufficient evidence has seeped into the general consciousness. We're all Missourians now.

The National Opinion Research Center put out an interesting

little graph in February 2008. The graph showed the relative strength of three religious affiliations from 1972 to 2006. The three were Protestant, Catholic, and None. The line for "None" was pretty flat until the early 1990s, when it began to climb. It flattened for a while in the early 2000s as the shock of 9/11 was absorbed, then continued its upward climb.

What happened in the early 1990s to cause religion to take such a hit? My best guess would be: the Internet. With sudden fingertip access to all the opinions in the world, on a fashionable medium that is likely installed in your workplace, as well as your home, one's own ideas are bound to come in for some self-scrutiny. What happened to Billy Graham happens to any regular Internet user.

And then, to return to the cases of Ireland and Wales, there is welfarism. Some portion of what sustained the Catholic parishes of Ireland and the Methodist chapel-communities of Wales was the support their churches supplied in times of trouble or distress. The Catholic faith of the Irish sustained them through famine and oppression. And watch the mine-disaster scene in John Ford's 1941 movie *How Green Was My Valley*, the men trudging back from their rescue work singing the lovely old Welsh hymn "Cwm Rhondda."

The modern welfare state knocks away that communal prop for organized religion. It did so in Wales and Ireland—everywhere in Europe, in fact. It will do so in the United States, as we sink ever deeper into welfare socialism and the managerial state under the socialist triumphalism of the Obama presidency and its compliant Congresses.

We are Europeans too, we of the dwindling majority; and those swelling numbers of us who are not European are mostly Sun People, with a political center of gravity far to the left even of Europe. In the long years of economic decline we now face, we shall become as welfarized as any Scandinavian nation, looking to the federal government for that security and stability we once spurned as a people of proud restlessness; or, if we sought it, found it in communal life and worship.

Note please that what is weakening here is not the human instinct to spirituality. That is, as I said above, a core feature of human nature, and not likely to go away, however much the celebrity atheists wish it to. Billy Graham, for example, has not lost it.

What is weakening is organized, churched religion, based on stories about things that are supposed to have happened in human history—the kind of religion that conservatives ought to smile on.

Just about the least churched country you could name is Iceland, where only 2 percent of people attend religious services weekly. Yet "four out of five Icelanders say that they pray, and the same proportion believe in life after death." (That's according to Paul Bloom's article "Is God an Accident?" in the December 2005 *Atlantic Monthly*.)

We're all becoming Missourians, yes; and soon we shall all be Icelanders, nursing vague dreams of transcendence while the state takes over the social role of our churches and conservatism dies a slow death. Well, let's try to look on the bright side: If that study I quoted at the beginning of this chapter is right, perhaps we shall at least be better behaved. In fact . . .

Hang on a minute, who's this coming up my driveway? Some strange-looking fellow in a nineteenth-century outfit, muttering to himself in what sounds like German. Wow—check out that *mustache!**

---

* "I don't get it," grumbled one of the people who looked over the manuscript of this book. That leaves the poor author torn between pleasure in the contemplation of his own wit, and chagrin at the necessity to explain a joke. I'll give a clue. The position I ended up with there is close to that arrived at by a nineteenth-century German philosopher who I supposed was best known for the humongous mustache he sported. I'm not the only person who supposed that, either. Professors Robert Solomon and Kathleen Higgins begin their course of Teaching Company lectures on this philosopher with some remarks about his mustache. The philosopher's name is an anagram of CRITICIZED FRESH HEN.

9

WAR: INVADING THE WORLD

Nuke 'em, bribe 'em, or leave 'em alone.
— Gary Brecher, "The War Nerd"

CONSERVATIVE UTOPIANISM

A key document in the annals of smiley-face conservative utopianism is George W. Bush's second inaugural address, delivered in front of the U.S. Capitol on January 20, 2005. I remember being startled by it at the time.

> The survival of liberty in our land increasingly depends on the success of liberty in other lands. The best hope for peace in our world is the expansion of freedom in all the world.

So the liberty Americans enjoy, and which I personally take as the foundation of my own conservatism, depends on what happens in Albania, Bangladesh, and Cameroon? Over which we have *how much* control? How did liberty survive in our land for two and a quarter centuries while most of the rest of the world was sunk in despotism?

> It is the policy of the United States to seek and support the growth of democratic movements and institutions in every nation and culture, with the ultimate goal of ending tyranny in our world.

That's a heck of a goal. Isn't there an issue of means and ends there somewhere?

Eventually, the call of freedom comes to every mind and every soul.

No it doesn't. Numberless people have lived and died—and live today, and will die tomorrow—more concerned with advancing the interests of their tribe, nation, or faith, or just with surviving and supporting their families, than with pursuing individual liberty.

We do not accept the existence of permanent tyranny because we do not accept the possibility of permanent slavery.

A *non sequitur.* There is plenty of daylight between what a modern American might call "tyranny"—nonconsensual forms of government—and the proper meaning of the word "slavery": the lawful ownership as property of one human being by another.

It has, for example, been the common opinion of mankind down the ages that a lesser degree of liberty under native rulers is preferable to a greater degree under foreign occupation. The Greek poet in Byron's *Don Juan,* living under Turkish rule around A.D. 1790, looks back wistfully to a predecessor who lived in the golden age of 500 B.C.,

> *He served—but served Polycrates—*
> *A tyrant; but our masters then*
> *Were still, at least, our countrymen . . .*

Modern political scientists, like Barrington Moore in *Social Origins of Dictatorship and Democracy* (1966), have shown how undemocratic rulers can enlist a population's support by skillful manipulation of class interests, appeals to nationalism, and well-managed economic progress. That's how mid-twentieth-century Germany and Japan ended up fascist. Present-day China teaches the lesson all over again. That "call of freedom" easily takes second, third, or fourth place to the call for national independence, religious duty, victory in war, or just economic security.

IF WE LOVE THE WORLD, THEY'LL LOVE US BACK!

In fairness to Bush, he was speaking in an oratorical tradition that has always favored gassy declarations about the brotherhood of man and universal aspirations to liberty. Even Ronald Reagan, in his own second inaugural, said that "freedom is one of the deepest and noblest aspirations of the human spirit . . . America must remain freedom's staunchest friend." Reagan, however, was at least facing what he had rightly called "an evil empire," armed with thousands of thermonuclear ballistic missiles. Bush faced nothing but a rabble of crazy religious terrorists with box cutters.

For anything equivalent to the wilder assertions in Bush's second inaugural, you have to go back not just to times of real war (or cold war) with real nations, but to liberal and "progressive" presidents fighting those wars. Woodrow Wilson told Congress in January 1918: "The people of the United States . . . are ready to devote their lives, their honor, and everything that they possess" to vindicate "the principle of justice to all peoples and nationalities." John F. Kennedy declared in his own inaugural: "We shall pay any price, bear any burden, meet any hardship, support any friend, oppose any foe, in order to assure the survival and the success of liberty."

Bush (or his speechwriters: Michael Gerson, Matthew Scully, and John McConnell) seemed to be dimly aware of the problem. After every proclamation of intent to "end tyranny," or to liberate Muslim women from "humiliation and servitude," there was a little escape clause. That ultimate goal of ending tyranny "is the concentrated work of generations." Phew!—so we don't have to get on it, like, right *now*. That call of freedom? "Liberty will come to those who love it." Oh, it's a sort of God-helps-those-who-help-themselves deal, so we may not have to do the heavy lifting after all. Liberating those gals from their burkas? "When the soul of a nation finally speaks, the institutions that arise may reflect customs and traditions very different from our own." Best not cut up those burkas for halter tops just yet, ladies.

That second inaugural showed that the president regarded foreign policy as another aspect of the principle he had offered us here at home: "compassionate conservatism," which my *National Review* colleague John O'Sullivan correctly tagged as "less a political philosophy than a romantic cult of sensibility."

I think even *that* is making too much of it. While "compassionate conservatism" began its life as a kind of orthodox-Catholic response to leftist liberation theology, as practiced by the Bush administration it was really just an outgrowth of Boomer hedonism. If it feels good, do it! And: If it sounds good, say it! Rational calculation of the national interest was barely present. The driving force here was feelings, wo wo wo, feelings.

If it feels good, and you do it, you will surely be *doing* good. People in other countries will see this, and love us for it. "Americans want to be loved, the English want to be obeyed," observed English Americanophile Quentin Crisp. We have built a great nation under grand ideals, and kept our Constitution intact for a remarkably long time. Why would foreigners *not* admire us, and wish to follow our example?

Alas, they don't. The Global Attitudes Project of the Pew Research Center showed "favorable opinions of the U.S." dropping from 83 percent to 56 percent in Britain across the years 2000–2006. For France the corresponding percentages went from 62 to 39; for Germany, from 78 to 37; for Turkey, from 52 to 12; for Japan, from 77 to 63. Those are seismic numbers. The first decade of the twenty-first century ushered in a new era of anti-Americanism.

The world loved us once, though. I was there: I remember it.

AMERICA'S GOLDEN AGE, 1945–65

I got to know Americans when I was a small child, growing up in a sleepy English country town in the 1950s. There was a big USAF base a few miles away, and we often saw Americans around the town.

If I had to encapsulate those early impressions in a single word, the word would be "extravagant."

They were so *big* (corn-fed farm boys from the South mostly, I suppose) and so *rich*. Their cars were *enormous*, festooned with chrome decoration and painted absurd colors—pink, peach, powder blue, *yellow*. They had endless supplies of candy, which they would hand out to you for the asking.

(We natives were still living under wartime austerity. Candy was actually rationed until February 1953, when I was seven years old. You had to tear off a coupon from your ration book and present it at the store. That great postrationing candy splurge was the origin of all my subsequent dental problems.)

The Yanks seemed to own excessive amounts of time as well as space. They spoke very s—l—o—w—l—y and walked with a peculiar easy rolling gait that told you they were never in a hurry. It wasn't really a swagger, whatever the forty-third president said. There was no real arrogance to it, just an attitude-free rolling of the hips. (Malcolm Muggeridge noticed that gait too, watching the GIs parade through Paris in 1944.)

Extravagant. Americans were rich. The salary of a USAF technician in 1950 put him in the English upper-middle class. In their home country they lived in enormous houses filled with gadgets. They all had telephones! Refrigerators! Washing machines! *TV sets!* Their cities boasted skyscrapers hundreds of feet high! And *automats!* I read about automats—I suppose it was the original Horn & Hardart automat—in a magazine my father took, and was entranced by the idea. There was no picture of the thing, so my imagination supplied one: a sort of robot waiter. What a country! What a people!

And then came the music. Through the wall. Our house was semidetached, sharing a living-room wall with the family to our west, who had a late-teenage son. His pleasure was to play gramophone records at high volume, and the songs came through the wall. (My father used to grumble that the wall was so thin, if our neighbors plugged in an electrical appliance, it pushed the plug out of our receptacle. This was not actually true.) This next-door teen favored what we would nowadays call country-and-western music, though to

the benighted British adults we lived among, all American vocal per-
formers were just "crooners." Thus I made the acquaintance of
Frankie Laine, Tex Ritter, Gene Autry, and the greatest of them all,
Hank Williams.

Then pop music began, *real* pop music. In his invaluable 1968 history of pop, irresistibly titled *Awopbopaloobop Alopbamboom*, British
writer Nik Cohn dates the beginning of real pop from Bill Haley's
"Rock Around the Clock," recorded in 1954. Elvis Presley soon followed; then the deluge: Little Richard, Buddy Holly, Jerry Lee
Lewis, Gene Vincent, . . . We Brits had our competing pop stars, but
nobody—except of course their promoters—took them seriously.
Nik Cohn: "British pop in the fifties was pure farce. Nobody could
sing and nobody could write and, in any case, nobody gave a
damn . . ." America was the real thing, the real place.

The hero of David Gerrold's 1973 sci-fi novel *The Man Who
Folded Himself* inherits a time-travel device from a mysterious uncle
and explores the past and the future. At last, tired of exploring, he
settles in 1956 Los Angeles.

> The fifties are as early as I dare go without sacrificing the cul-
> tural comforts I desire. They are truly a magic moment in
> time, a teeterboard suspended between the wistful past and the
> soaring future . . . The fifties are a great time to live. They are
> close enough to the nation's adventurous past to still bear the
> same strident idealism, yet they also bear the shape of the de-
> veloping future and the promise of the technological wonders
> to come.

To be sure, Americans of the 1950s were extravagant only by the
flat-broke standards of 1950s England. An American of today, or
even an Englishman, transported back by David Gerrold's time-
travel device to the America of 1953, would find life intolerably bare
and frugal, even in the middle class. No central air? No dental floss?
Party line phone? Only three TV channels? *Linoleum?*

We have our own discontents, though, and human beings quickly adjust to a narrower scope. I wouldn't gainsay the judgment of David Gerrold's time traveler.

I saw it all only from a distance, through a glass darkly, with the eyes of a child, but I know that with all their blemishes and short-comings, these two postwar decades, the ones from Hank Williams to Bob Dylan, were as close as the United States has come, perhaps as close as nations are permitted to come, to a golden age.

When I put that sentiment into a column once, a thoughtful reader sent me the following. It's from James Baldwin's 1956 novel *Giovanni's Room*, which is about homosexual life in post–World War II Paris.

> Nobody stays in the garden of Eden . . . they have scarcely seen their garden before they see the flaming sword. Then, perhaps, life only offers the choice of remembering the garden or forgetting it. Either, or: it takes strength to remember, it takes another kind of strength to forget, it takes a hero to do both. People who remember court madness through pain, the pain of the perpetually recurring death of their innocence; people who forget court another kind of madness, the madness of the denial of pain and the hatred of innocence; and the world is mostly divided between madmen who remember and madmen who forget.

My reader added the following comment: "In the context of your remark, the 1950s would be 'Eden,' conservatives would be those going mad with the pain of perpetually remembering that Eden, and liberals would be those going mad by trying to forget it."

ANTI-AMERICANISM, THEN AND NOW

Not everybody loved the United States in the fifties. To the commu-nist nations, or at least to their ruling classes, America was the enemy. In Latin America, this was the age of "Yanqui Go Home!" as

Vice President Richard Nixon discovered in 1958 when a mob attacked his motorcade while he was visiting Caracas, Venezuela, as part of a subcontinental goodwill tour. Latin Americans disliked us because we were the regional hegemon. The Germans were unhappy about having been defeated. The French were unhappy about having been liberated by a nation ignorant of real philosophy, literature, and cheese.

Even in England there was anti-American grumbling. Those upper-middle-class USAF grease monkeys would come into our little town in their astonishing huge cars, head for their favorite pub, and monopolize the very limited local supply of loose women. There were occasional fights, and instead of employing fists and bottles for the purpose like honest English lads, the Yanks brought out knives. They fought among themselves, too, sometimes—most commonly, blacks against whites. The blacks and whites hated each other, everybody said.

Movies were another issue, though English children and English adults parted company here. We kids couldn't get enough of Abbott and Costello and Flash Gordon, and there was a general opinion that the B-feature westerns were usually better fun to watch than the main features our parents took us to see—sappy things with songs, dance routines, and squirm-inducing romance.

Adults had a different point of view. They seemed to like American movies well enough, especially the musicals. This was, though, a time when great numbers of war movies were being made, and our elders grumbled about the Yanks—in particular, for some reason, John Wayne—thinking that "they won the damn war all by themselves."

Was there an element of great-power envy at work in these adult reactions? You bet there was. Sellar and Yeatman's 1930 classic humor book *1066 and All That*, which I mentioned in Chapter 1, was still widely enjoyed. It was a spoof account of English history: "James I slobbered at the mouth and had favourites; he was thus a Bad King . . ." etc., etc. The book's last chapter follows a send-up of Woodrow Wilson's Fourteen Points at the end of World War 1, and reads in its entirety as follows:

Chapter 62

A BAD THING

America was thus clearly top nation, and History came to a .

(That final punctuation mark is called a "full stop" in British English, not a "period.") Britain was in even worse shape in 1950 than she had been in 1930, so that the United States was even more incontrovertibly the new "top nation." British adults, some of the time, minded that.

As American life has scaled new heights of extravagance these past fifty years, so the rest of the world has become more anti-American. Not that this is just envy of American wealth, though that's one element. There's the pacifism, intellectual snobbery, and business-hostile "cultural Marxism" of the college-educated class that every advanced nation is now afflicted with. (Including the United States herself. "This is the most evil nation that ever existed," an American college lecturer—white, midwestern—remarked to me once.)

Nations with a strong sense of their own identity, particularly non-European nations with historical grievances, resent American cultural and military dominance. In nations with corrupt and unpopular governments who are allied with the United States, the common people blame us for their political misfortunes.

That brings us of course to the 2001 attacks and the wars that followed. Osama bin Laden's big beef against America was that we propped up Middle East dictatorships that had abandoned their Islamic heritage for dollars and fleshly pleasures. On September 11, 2001, anti-Americanism became a mighty historical force.

BEFORE THE DELUGE

Just by way of illustrating that anti-Americanism was alive and very well prior to 9/11, here is a story about that very day. It is the story of my one appearance on a lecture stage with Dr. Henry Kissinger; or rather, the story of how that appearance failed to happen.

The U.S. State Department runs a Foreign Visitors Program, under whose auspices people from various parts of the world, people distinguished in the arts or professions, are brought to the United States to meet with American counterparts from their own lines of work. I suppose the idea is that mutual understanding will be created thereby, the veil of ignorance lifted, the fetters of ancient prejudice struck off, the dogs of war silenced, and so on. Whether this result is actually attained in many cases, I cannot say. In the particular case I am going to tell you about, it never had a chance to happen.

As a journalist who has often written about Chinese affairs, I am sometimes asked to participate in these functions. The usual course of events is that the State Department will call me to tell me that such and such a person is being brought over from China under the Foreign Visitors Program, and they think it would be a good idea for me to meet with him or her. They tell me who the person is. If the name is not familiar to me (which, I am sorry to say, is more often the case than not), they give me the visitor's résumé. If I then express interest, a date is set up, almost invariably a lunch date. I hasten to add that this is unpaid work. I do it for the opportunity to meet interesting people, and in the hope that I might get a column out of it.

Well, one day in the summer of 2001 I took a call from my contact—I had done this often enough that we were on first-name terms—at the Foreign Visitors Program. They had a major event coming up, he told me. A large group of Chinese media people, TV producers and the like, were coming over in a single batch. "The cream of thirty- to forty-year-olds at major Chinese media outlets," he gushed. A series of discussion groups and lectures was being arranged. Would I care to address these people? I said I'd like to see names and titles. He e-mailed me a list. Scanning it, I was impressed. These were indeed heavy hitters in Chinese media circles. News director, Shanghai Broadcasting Network . . . Deputy editor-in-chief, China *Newsweek* magazine . . . Editor, international affairs, *Global Times* . . . News anchor, CCTV . . . I called the guy back. Yes, I'd definitely be interested.

In the fullness of time, arrangements were made, a program published. There would be an event at the State Department's New York

City office (which, students of biblical numerology might care to note, is at 666 Fifth Avenue). I would speak for an hour, 10:30 to 11:30 a.m., on the subject "Perceptions of China in America's Right-Wing Press." I would then be the guest of the Department for lunch. There would be an honorarium of $250! And the speaker right before me, 9:30 to 10:30, would be Dr. Henry Kissinger. The date: Tuesday, September 18.

On the Friday following the September 11 attacks, I got a call from my man at State. The whole thing was off, he said. Why? I naturally wanted to know. "I can't tell you, *really* can't tell you. Anyway, it's off. We've told Kissinger." Where were the media hotshots? "Gone back, gone back to China, the whole lot. It's all off."

In the weeks that followed, I was able to piece together what had happened. This, I should say, was from informal sources, whose versions of events did not always agree in precise detail. All the accounts told the same basic story, though.

The Chinese media types came over on September 8. They were in a room together with some State Department minders, receiving some kind of cultural acclimatization, when the World Trade Center was hit. There was a TV set in the room, and everyone got to see the second plane hit. When this happened, some of the Chinese party stood up and cheered. My informants differ on how many, from a lower bound of "only three or four" up to "at least half a dozen." (The list of participants I had been given contained fifteen names.) This made the State Department minders very angry. A shouting match broke out. A report went up the chain of command. Whether it went all the way to the secretary of state—Colin Powell at that point—I am not clear. It certainly went as far as Richard Armitage, Powell's second-in-command. The Chinese media people flew back to China shortly afterward—whether voluntarily or not, my informants did not agree.

INVADE THE WORLD

The notion that the 9/11 attacks elicited broad sympathy in the rest of the world therefore needs some qualifying. The later unpopularity of the United States in the world was built on a solid foundation of preexisting anti-Americanism. If those Chinese media types were representative, between 20 and 40 percent of the world thought the attacks served us right. In some places the proportions were much higher: People danced in the streets of Arab cities.

What soured things even further was of course the Iraq war. I belong, together with many much smarter and better-informed people—the late William F. Buckley Jr., for example, and Dr. Kissinger—to that sad contingent of conservatives who supported the war at first, but soon came to regret having done so.

A couple of years ago my son passed through that very annoying stage of development in which a child discovers that language is not so much like a solid landscape of rocks and trees, but much more like a well-equipped theater stage, fitted out with screens, doors to nowhere, trick lighting, turntables, trapdoors, and wires to lift you up into the flies. He had, in short, discovered ambiguity. Asked whether he had finished his homework, he would furrow his brow and say, "Define 'finished'."

I retreat to that developmental phase myself when people ask me whether I feel embarrassed at having supported the Iraq war. "Define 'war,' " is the thing I want to say. I don't say it, of course, exactly because it sounds like an irritating eleven-year-old, but it's really the essence of the matter. Did I support the 2003 invasion of Iraq? Yes I did. Did I support the subsequent effort to get civil society going in Iraq? No I didn't.

I saw the attack on Iraq as an exercise in gunboat diplomacy. Iraq was a nuisance to us; and our intelligence agencies told us it was a future threat. We'd send an expeditionary force, break their stuff, kill a few of their leaders, put some friendlier gangster—"*our* son of a bitch," in Lyndon Johnson's memorable words—in power, then get the heck out. Had not George W. Bush said: "I don't think our troops ought to be used for what's called nation building. I think our troops ought to be used to fight and win war. I think our troops ought to be used to help overthrow a dictator . . . when it's in our best interests."? (Yes he had, in the October 11, 2000, presidential-candidates debate with Al Gore.)

Then, as 2003 passed on to 2004, that was no longer operative.

We were busily nation-building: drawing up a constitution, installing leaders, scheduling elections, suppressing insurrections, wading blithely into the snake pit of Arab political culture, the ancient, lethal culture of "money-favoring" and "power-challenging" described so graphically in David Pryce-Jones's 1989 book *The Closed Circle*.

Not only was the U.S. government ignoring reality in Iraq, it was *boasting* of doing so. In October 2004 an unidentified aide to President George W. Bush told *New York Times* reporter Ron Suskind that

> guys like [Suskind] were "in what we call the reality-based community," which he defined as people who "believe that solutions emerge from your judicious study of discernible reality." . . . "That's not the way the world really works any-more," he continued. "We're an empire now, and when we act, we create our own reality. And while you're studying that reality—judiciously, as you will—we'll act again, creating other new realities, which you can study too, and that's how things will sort out. We're history's actors . . . and you, all of you, will be left to just study what we do."

I'll confess, again, that I was slow off the mark, wrapped up in the 2004 U.S. election campaign. It wasn't until September that year that I published a column calling for prompt, unapologetic withdrawal from Iraq. I wish it had been sooner. I wrote then: "The lazy-minded evangelico-romanticism of George W. Bush, the bureaucratic will to power of Donald Rumsfeld, the avuncular condescension of Dick Cheney, and the reflexive military deference of Colin Powell combined to get us into a situation we never wanted to be in, a situation no self-respecting nation ought to be in, a situation we don't know how to get out of."

I was by that point wondering why I had supported this gross blunder in the first place. I had explained myself a few months before, in an April 2004 column on the VDARE website:

> My attitude to the war is really just punitive, and Iraq was a target of opportunity. I am not a Wilsonian nation-builder. I

don't want to "bring democracy to Iraq." I don't, in fact, give a fig about the Iraqis. I am happy to leave barbarians alone to practice their unspeakable folkways, so long as they do not bother civilized peoples. When they do bother us, though, I want them smacked down with great ferocity. Saddam Hussein had been scoffing for years at the very concept of international order, in the belief that we would never pass from words to deeds. I wanted to see that belief confounded, and I am pleased that it has been. If the civilized world is never willing to back up its agreements, resolutions, and communiqués with force, then those fine documents are all worthless and civilization is impotent against its enemies. I am very glad to know that we have not yet reached that sorry pass.

There were particular and personal motives at work, too. Midway between the 9/11 terrorist attacks and the beginning of the war in March 2003, I became a naturalized U.S. citizen. (My wife, who is more efficient with paperwork than I am, was naturalized the Friday before 9/11.) I had the new citizen's exaggerated enthusiasm for my adopted country, with the correspondingly heightened outrage at what had been done to her.

So all right, I supported the damn fool Iraq war. I acknowledge some tiny particle of guilt for my error in lending my voice to this folly. I was therefore glad when, in 2007, the Bush administration finally heeded the wise words of Gary Brecher, who blogs as The War Nerd (and whose real name is not "Gary Brecher"). Gary's prescription for dealing with Third World rat-holes like Iraq is the one I put at the head of this chapter: "Nuke 'em, bribe 'em, or leave 'em alone."

We were never willing to nuke Iraq, and would not have been justified in doing so. The era of leaving them alone ended in 2003. That left bribery, and I am glad to see it has worked so well. At the time of writing, Iraq is quiet; quiet enough for us to negotiate withdrawal terms with the Iran-friendly stooges we installed as a "government" of Iraq. When we leave, civil war will no doubt commence, with the Kurds trying to secede, the Sunnis reverting to power-challenging mode, and the Iranians and Saudis pulling whatever strings they can get their respective hands on. That's their business. It always was.

SMILE AND THE WORLD SMILES WITH YOU

It's a mess out there, all right. Liberal internationalists like George W. Bush actually have a point, or half of a point. Societies with consensual forms of government *are* more stable and less dangerous than tyrannies. (Though there are no strong reasons to believe that *every* nation is capable of consensual government.) The older, Kissingerian, *our*-son-of-a-bitch "realist" school of international relations *did* throw up some nasty problems. (Though it solved many others.) The jihadists got much of their energy and support from widespread Muslim fury at the corruption of the Islamic homelands by undemocratic rulers like the Saudis, who were—and still are, as I write—*our* sons of bitches.

And the cheery Wilsonianism of what their conservative enemies call "neocons" was not totally misplaced in its time. Hadn't the world seen a wave of democratization from the 1970s on? If Poland, Argentina, and Uganda could become democracies, why couldn't Iraq and Afghanistan? Neoconservatism was too optimistic, but it wasn't barking mad.

You can also make a case that the misguided optimism of George W. Bush and his neocons concerning their power to transform the world in America's image was grounded in an *under*estimation of the wonderfulness of democracy, a species of pessimism in itself. Political scientist Charles R. Kesler argued this in the Summer 2007 *Claremont Review of Books*:

> Paradoxically, their biggest mistake is not thinking too highly of democracy, but not thinking highly enough of it. By underestimating it and what it requires of its citizens, they conclude that democracy is more easily exportable and transferable than it really is. And they neglect all the other forms of government

between the best and the worst—forms that might be more congenial to many countries capable of something better than tyranny but incapable, at least now, of the best sorts of republicanism.

These expeditions and debates will seem pretty academic five or ten years from now. By that time, the United States will be so obviously broke, there will be no question of our sallying out on trillion-dollar adventures to democratize other people. The trillion dollars won't be there. In point of fact, they weren't even there when we marched into Iraq in 2003. America's been broke for quite a while. We just haven't been noticing.

The other great bone of contention among conservatives will likely still be in play, though. The wild optimism of George W. Bush's administration abroad, the Yes-we-can! conviction that the United States can and should spend her wealth converting inconsequential Third World sand-pits into Western-style nation-states, had its domestic counterpart in immigration policy.

Smiley-face logic not only suggests that everyone everywhere is really just a freedom-loving American—that, to slightly adapt what the Colonel says in *Full Metal Jacket*: "Inside every Middle East Muslim there is an American trying to get out"—but also that America's future is exactly like her past, with tens of millions of tired, poor, huddled masses yearning to breathe free here, in the United States.

Whether or not there is an American trying to get *out* of every Middle East Muslim, it is certain that every Middle East nation, and every other nation everywhere else too, has a million or so trying to get *in* to the United States. Let 'em come! say the smilers. Ten million, twenty million, fifty million—let them in! What could possibly go wrong?

10

IMMIGRATION: INVITING THE WORLD

First, our cities will not be flooded with a million immigrants annually. Under the proposed bill, the present level of immigration remains substantially the same . . . Second, the ethnic mix of this country will not be upset . . . Contrary to the charges in some quarters, [the bill] will not inundate America with immigrants from any one country or area . . .

—SENATOR EDWARD KENNEDY, SPEAKING AS
FLOOR MANAGER OF THE 1965 IMMIGRATION ACT

Forcing Mexico to deter its citizens from emigrating . . . will make social peace in the barrios and pueblos of Mexico untenable.

—JORGE CASTAÑEDA, SHORTLY BEFORE BECOMING
MEXICO'S FOREIGN MINISTER IN 2000,
QUOTED IN HUNTINGTON'S *Who Are We?*

GOODNESS HAS NOTHING TO DO WITH IT

Immigration's no problem, say the happy faces, because we will absorb and assimilate them. We did it before, didn't we?

Well, yes, we did, when we were an empty nation with plenty of room, and no welfare state, and innumerable low-level manual jobs, and when the great immigrant flows were of European Christians and Jews not very different in their outlook, allegiances, and ancestry from our settled population, and with the commitment of a great ocean between their old homes and their new ones. That was then, this is now.

Immigration is a difficult topic to discuss, though. The reason it is so difficult is that it has, more I think than any other aspect of U.S. policy, been moralized, in fact *hyper*-moralized. I have covered some of this ground in Chapter 2. The complicity of cheerily optimistic conservatives in that hypermoralizing is perhaps their greatest sin against good sense and proper conservative skepticism.

According to this hypermoralized point of view, current policy is an expression of America's Intrinsic Goodness and High Principle. Any policy more generous would be an even more emphatic expression of our I.G. and H.P. Persons who object to generous immigration policy are bad persons with malign intentions—"nativists," *eiuw!*

That liberals, who have treacle for brains, should strike these self-righteous poses is no more than one would expect of them. That conservatives should join with them in denouncing immigration restrictionists as wicked people with sinister intentions, is scandalous. Conservatism is the cold-eyed, skeptical, data-driven approach to national policy. Romantic moralizing belongs on the political Left.

And immigration is just a *policy*, like farm supports, military recruitment, national parks maintenance, and income tax rates. Goodness, as the lady said, has nothing to do with it. Immigration is, in fact, one aspect of population policy.

OUR POPULATION POLICY

The United States, like every other nation, has a population policy. You can't *not* have a population policy. To *not* have any laws at all concerning immigration and settlement, for example, to train yourself and your fellow citizens never to think about such matters at all, *would itself be a population policy*—in the case of a rich and stable nation like ours, it would be a policy of very fast and unlimited population growth. That Americans are embarrassed to be heard talking about our national population policy doesn't mean we don't have one. As with metaphysics (Chapter 7), you have a population policy whether or not you know you do, and whether or not you feel comfortable talking about it.

Those USAF personnel who so impressed my infant self in the middle of the last century came from an America with a very different population policy. The country was at that point thirty-odd years into a great immigration lull started off by restrictionist legislation in the early 1920s: the Emergency Quota Act of 1921 and the Immigration Act of 1924. That latter act limited legal immigration from all sources to 150,000 annually. Thanks to that lull, the Great Wave of 1890–1920 had time to assimilate fully into American life.

By way of contrast, the Department of Homeland Security reports 1,052,415 immigrants given permanent residence in fiscal year 2007. In 1960 less than 6 percent of the U.S. population was foreign born, with the leading birth countries being Italy, Germany, Canada, and Britain. Today the foreign-born are nudging 13 percent, and the leading birth countries are Mexico (*way* out ahead), China, the Philippines, and India.

Much of the nervousness about speaking of immigration issues arises from discrimination being a key feature of any immigration policy. Just as a nation can't *not* have a population policy, so immigration laws—if there are any—can't *not* discriminate. Any immigration policy short of completely open borders must select immigrants *somehow*, thereby discriminating against the unselected!

Current U.S. policy mostly allows each intake of immigrants to select the following intake. Of that 1,052,415 for fiscal 2007 mentioned above, two-thirds—689,820—were sponsored by family members already settled here. This discriminates rather severely against foreigners, however worthy or talented, who don't currently have family members settled in the United States. Our government's very lackadaisical approach to immigration law enforcement in recent decades has also discriminated massively against foreigners who are scrupulously respectful of other people's laws.

Is this the discrimination that American citizens want? It's hard to know. Discussion of this topic has become so hypermoralized that citizens fear to speak critically of current policy—or, in the case of gross and widespread failure to enforce the people's laws, antipolicy.

Kumbaya conservatives breezily assure us that all is well; that the current great wave of immigrants are "good-hearted people" (George W. Bush) who will assimilate just as the 1890–1920 Great Wave did.

That this is not happening jumps out at you from the figures, if you bother to look at them. This is most notably so with Hispanics, as political scientist Samuel Huntington documented at length in *Who Are We?* U.S.-born Hispanics of the third and higher generations, for example, drop out of high school at twice the rate of white Americans. The illegitimacy rate for children born to Hispanic mothers passed 50 percent in 2007, heading upward—double the white rate; of Hispanic men aged 25–29, 3.9 percent are in prison or jail, versus 1.7 percent of non-Hispanic whites (and 11.9 percent of blacks); etc., etc.

ABSIMILATION

The English word *assimilation* derives from the Latin prefix *ad-*, which indicates a moving toward something, and the same language's verb *simulare*, "to cause a person or thing to resemble another." You can make a precisely opposite word using the prefix *ab-*, which marks a moving away from something. Many immigrants of course assimilate to American society. I think I have. I *hope* I have; I've tried to. Many others, however, especially in the second and following generations, *ab*similate.

One sad story of absimilation is told in the 2008 book *Generations of Exclusion: Mexican Americans, Assimilation, and Race*—remarkably, as the authors, Vilma Ortiz and Edward E. Telles, are left-wing Hispanic sociologists (at UCLA). Sample quote: "Despite sixty years of political and legal battles to improve the education of Mexican Americans, they continue to have the lowest average education levels and the highest high school dropout rates among major ethnic and racial groups in the United States." Ortiz and Telles blame the schools. Gosh, when are we ever going to get those schools right? More money! More money! (Chapter 6.)

Absimilation seems to be rather common, though you don't read much about it. I noticed it years ago in England. The first generation of black Caribbean immigrants to my native land strove to be as English as possible. They worked hard at low-paying jobs—the black bus conductor was a stock figure in English life by the mid-1960s—bought old houses and spruced them up, dressed in immaculate "Sunday best" to go to church, and kept on the right side of the law. Doing unskilled summer-vacation construction jobs at the time, I was often in work gangs with black laborers. They were popular and good workers, fun to be around. Those island accents apart, they were as English as they could be. I still get fond nostalgic feelings when I hear a voice with that Caribbean lilt.

It was dismaying, in the 1970s and 1980s, to see a large piece of the second-generation cohort break off and slip into crime, idleness, and social dysfunction. Those spruced-up houses became ganja dens; daughters of the elegant church ladies became welfare queens. A stock joke among Londoners in the 1980s was: "*Q:* How do you reduce street crime in London? *A:* Close down the Northern Line." That is the subway line that goes to Brixton, a district of concentrated black settlement.

It's the same with Muslim immigrants. Of the four men held responsible for the London terror bombings of July 2005, three were English born. (The fourth immigrated at age five from Jamaica.) In December 2008, writing in PajamasMedia.com, terrorism expert Patrick Poole noted that many U.S. citizens of Somali origin were leaving the country to train as terrorists in Somalia.

The funeral for Shirwa Ahmed last week in Burnsville, Minnesota, punctuated a growing national security threat metastasizing inside the U.S.—one Homeland Security and law enforcement authorities have quickly taken note of. Ahmed, who killed himself in a suicide bombing attack in Somalia in October, is just one of up to 40 men from the Twin Cities area who have disappeared and are feared to have returned to their homeland for training with the al-Shabaab terrorist group to wage jihad.

Assimilation, absimilation: If you let great numbers of foreigners settle in your country, you will surely get both.

REFUGEES AND PSEUDOREFUGEES

The only area of immigration policy where goodness *does* have something to do with it, is the resettlement of refugees. The United States is extraordinarily generous toward refugees. In 2006, the last year for which I can find numbers published by the UN High Commissioner for Refugees, we took 41,300 refugees for settlement. The next four receiving countries were Australia (13,400), Canada (10,700), Sweden (2,400), and Norway (1,000).

(For a curiously similar list, see the beginning of the next chapter.)

If you scale by the receiving country's population, we don't look so exceptional. There were about 7,300 Americans per refugee accepted in 2006. Australia is the clear leader on this basis, with only 1,522 citizens per refugee. Still, we are very generous by the standards of the advanced world. "For the past three decades the United States has resettled more refugees from around the world than all other developed nations combined," reports the Center for Immigration Studies (CIS).

We might be wise to take a break from contemplating our own goodness to peer a little more closely at the refugees we are taking in. The whole system is addled with fraud. Also from the CIS:

> Spend enough time talking to people in the refugee resettlement business and you will hear the story, by all accounts true, about a surprise encounter the Kenyan ambassador to the United States had one day in Washington, D.C. While making their way through a D.C. airport, the ambassador and his nephew spotted a group of students from the nephew's elite school in Nairobi. It turned out the privileged youths had managed to pass themselves off as "Somali refugees" and were on their way to new homes and a new life in Minnesota.

Even when the person resettled is a genuine refugee, the following "chain migration" is full of chicanery.

Once settled in the United States, a refugee is entitled to apply for permission to bring a spouse, minor children, parents, and siblings. This is "chain migration." In mid-2008 the State Department actually had to suspend this aspect of its refugee program for Kenya, Ethiopia, Uganda, Guinea, and Ghana, after DNA testing revealed widespread fraud. Unrelated Africans were posing as family members to gain entry. At the time of writing, the whole family reunification program for African refugees is in a state of limbo.

Charity is a noble virtue, which has my keen approval. It needs to be tempered with some pessimistic realism about human nature, though. The problem with being openhanded toward strangers, when you are rich and the strangers mostly poor, is that in the matter of openhandedness, supply can never match demand.

The supply of openhandedness in fact *generates* demand. A 2006 report by David Martin, former general counsel of the Immigration and Naturalization Service, makes it clear that once some displaced group is designated for resettlement to the United States, the size of the group at once begins to increase rapidly. People with comfortable and peaceful lives will actually uproot themselves and move to a refugee camp, if they believe that will increase their chances of resettlement to the United States.

Everybody wants to come to the United States. A quarter century ago, when refugees were streaming out of the newly communized nations of Southeast Asia, I knew an Irishman who actually worked for the UNHCR. (The Irish are, or were, heavily overrepresented in UN institutions.) He told me of his frustration that people in squalid camps in Thailand would not accept offers of resettlement in Ireland. They preferred the mere possibility of an offer from the United States to the certainty of one from the Emerald Isle (admittedly not yet at that time the "Celtic Tiger").

The well-intentioned family unification policy compounds the problem. Every Third World immigrant is regarded by his family, extended family, or clan back home—refugees or not—as a foot in the Golden Door. Then, when enough refugees from some nation or group are present here, they can organize as an ethnic lobbying group for yet more to be admitted. Our refugee program—to the degree that it *is* ours: key decisions are made by the UNHCR—is an immigrant-generating mechanism.

And charity proverbially begins at home. Our refugee-settlement policy also shows up one of the most infuriating aspects of happy-clappy, multi-culti immigration cheerleading: the insults it throws in the faces of American citizens. This is, in fact, one area of immigration policy where citizens have actually put up a fight, and had policy changed.

Somali Bantu immigrants, and those masquerading as such, were scattered to towns and cities around the United States in the early 2000s, in accordance with long-standing (since 1980) federal policy. The fact of the refugees being Muslim, uneducated, and mostly non-English-speaking caused several of the towns selected for resettlement to feel they were being imposed upon.

One refugee group was sent to Buffalo, New York, an economically struggling place, where the resettlement agencies' attempts to place the Bantus in jobs aroused great resentment among unemployed locals (of whom, by the way, 38 percent are African American and another 8 percent Hispanic).

The small town of Holyoke, Massachusetts, was so fiercely opposed to the program that resettlement agencies changed their minds about sending Bantus there.

Cayce, South Carolina, also put up a fight. "We don't feel we should be the dumping ground," said a city official. They won their fight, too: no Bantus were settled there.

It's all very well to frown at the lack of charity here, but the concerns of these townspeople are reasonable. A BBC report on Somali-Bantu resettlement noted of the refugees: "Though many are keen to work, they can not do so until they learn some English and to read and write."

I bet the townsfolk of Buffalo, Holyoke, and Cayce were glad to hear that many of these Somalis were keen to work, but . . . how many is "many"? And who are the ones *not* keen to work? Perhaps the ones mentioned in a Church World Service report on the topic: "Struggling the most are single mothers with several children—most of them the former second wives of men who had to break with Somali Bantu culture and divorce them in order to qualify for U.S. resettlement."

(Note that refugees, unlike other types of immigrants, are immediately eligible for all forms of welfare on the same basis as U.S. citizens. In addition, they are fawned over by the charities and religious groups who help drive the whole business.)

Furthermore, given the well-publicized problems and frictions caused by Muslim communities in non-Muslim nations, even in the native-born second and subsequent generations, it's reasonable to ask whether perhaps it wouldn't be better for all concerned if Muslim refugees were settled in Muslim nations. Several Muslim nations are quite prosperous—far more prosperous than India was in 1959 when, out of religious fellow-feeling, she took in thousands of penniless Tibetan refugees and gave them a town of their own. (I have heard Tibetans express their gratitude very eloquently, speaking with reverence of "Mother India.") Doesn't the Koran contain injunctions to charity and religious solidarity among Muslims?

Our cheery conservative optimist will wave all this away. What's the problem? Why should not 12,000 (the actual number) of illiterate Somali-Bantu Muslim villagers settle down happily to useful and productive lives here in the United States? Didn't the Irish? Didn't the Italians? Didn't the Germans and the Poles? Problem? There is no problem! All together, now: "Kumbaya, Lord, kumbaya . . ."

THE IMMIGRATION FACTOR—A TRUTH SANDWICH

Robert Putnam's Uppsala paper, which I covered in Chapter 2, has much to say about immigration as a prime source of modern diversity, which of course it is. What does Putnam tell us about immigration policy?

That Uppsala paper is, as I showed, a kind of truth sandwich, made with happy-talk bread. The happy talk—presumably the component that Professor Putnam labored over in such psychic anguish for six years—is flimsy stuff, looking even flimsier in proximity to the real social-science meat in the middle. Putnam is a rigorous researcher, and did his work well. The filling of the sandwich is good nutritious stuff. The bread, however . . . Well, here's an excerpt from the top slice of bread:

> Immigrants have accounted for three to four times as many of America's Nobel Laureates, National Academy of Science members, Academy Award film directors and winners of Kennedy Center awards in the performing arts as native-born Americans.

Just checking the handy Wikipedia list of Nobel Prize winners by citizenship and nation of origin (and ignoring the Peace Prize, which is merely political), I see that of the seventeen American winners listed for the years 2005–7, four are indeed immigrants. They came from Russia, Italy, England, and Germany. Of the thirteen U.S.-born awardees, three are from immigrant-Jewish families, one from an immigrant-Portuguese family, the others of older Anglo- or German-American stock.

The seventeen names are: Hurwicz, Maskin, Myerson, Capecchi, Smithies, Kornberg, Mather, Phelps, Smoot, Fire, Mello, Aumann, Grubbs, Schrock, Schelling, Hall, and Glauber. You have to read down through fifty-three names before you get to the first American of other than European origins: Egypt-born Ahmed Zewail (Chemistry, 1999), followed by China-born Daniel Tsui (Physics, 1998).

Without exploring Putnam's other categories, the Nobel Prize list does indeed make some kind of case for immigration . . . from Europe, with strong preference to be given to Jewish immigrants. There *may* be a case for immigration from Somalia, Iraq, and the Dominican Republic, but the Nobel Prize list doesn't make it. In fact, it rather argues against it.

Similarly with a Duke University study, "America's New Immigrant Entrepreneurs" (2007), which counted up the patent applications filed by immigrant noncitizens in the years 1998–2006, breaking them out by the applicant's country of citizenship. The top twenty contributing countries filed over sixty thousand applications altogether.

That sure is an impressive number, and immigration enthusiasts will chortle over it as evidence for the revitalizing power of immigration. Perhaps it is; but what *are* those top twenty countries? Since you ask, they are, in order: China (including Taiwan), India, Canada, United Kingdom, Germany, France, Russia, Korea, Japan, Australia, Italy, Israel, Netherlands, Swizerland, Spain, Sweden, Turkey, Ireland, Greece, Iran.

I dunno, there's something about that list that's hard to square with the realities of recent mass immigration. Can't quite put my finger on it . . .

Or take this, from the lower layer of Professor Putnam's sandwich:

> A century ago America also experienced a large, sustained wave of immigration that massively increased our ethnic diversity in traditional terms, with the arrival of millions of immigrants of different "races"—a term that then referred to the Italian and Polish Catholics, Russian Jews and others who were swarming into a previously White Anglo Saxon Protestant (WASP)–dominated society. Though I have not found any comparable survey evidence for that period, my strong suspicion is that that period also witnessed a good deal of hunkering, even within the immigrant communities. Yet fifty years later, the grandchildren of the WASPs and of the immigrants were comfortable in one another's presence.

That's all quite true, but what does it prove? Does it prove the Diversity Theorem?

It's often claimed that it does. The "Great Wave" of immigration from 1880 to 1924 did indeed assimilate, as did the earlier German and Irish waves. Since they assimilated, so—we're assured—will any current or future mass immigrations.

Possibly they will. We don't know. At any rate, those of us whose brains have not been addled by the Diversity happy talk don't know.

The happy talkers *do* know—new Great Waves will assimilate just fine, like the old ones! "We wish it to be so—therefore it will be so! We *know* it will!"

Are there reasons to think otherwise? Well, yes. As immigration scholar Mark Krikorian says in his recent book *The New Case Against Immigration:* "Americanization is much more difficult under modern conditions than in the past." The United States of 2009 is unlike the United States of 1909 is some important ways.

- It is a welfare state. One little-remarked feature of the earlier Great Wave of immigration is that many of the immigrants eventually went home—as many as a third of the 1890–1924 immigrants did so. Immigrants who fail here nowadays have no incentive to go home. The welfare state will care for them.
- We have a diminishing number of low-skill jobs in manufacturing and agriculture. The number would likely be diminishing even faster—yielding to automation—without a plentiful supply of cheap, low-skill immigrants.
- Large segments of elite culture—in the universities, for example—are hostile to the naïve "Americanism" of our great-grandfathers, and to the assimilationist ethic that went with it.

And, as with the Nobel Prize remark in the top layer of Professor Putnam's sandwich, it has to be noted that the nineteenth- and twentieth-century Great Wave was pretty solidly European—94 percent for 1880–1920. Allowing for a scattering of Muslims from the Balkans, the overwhelming majority of those immigrants would have been of Christian or Jewish heritage.

So both sides of the immigration equation have changed drastically since the Great Wave. Today's America is not the America of 1900; and today's immigrants don't much resemble the immigrants of 1900.

What the Great Wave proves is that in the social and economic conditions that prevailed a hundred years ago, big numbers of Christian and Jewish Europeans assimilated well into WASP America, with hearty assists from:

- the national solidarity enforced by participation in two world wars;
- the experience of common suffering through the Great Depression;

and, of course:

- the near-total freeze on immigration from 1924 to 1965.

Again, more than that *may* be true; but that is all that can fairly be deduced from the Great Wave experience. You can deduce more only if you light up your opium pipe and drift off into wish-fulfillment dreams, or bring in some other data. The Great Wave experience certainly does not prove the Diversity Theorem.

RHAPSODIZE, MORALIZE, DEMONIZE

A dismaying proportion of people who call themselves conservative are no-problem-here smiley-faces on the immigration topic. Not all of them lead sheltered elite lives with a regular requirement for low-wage household help. Some are quite ordinary middle-class types, locked into the sentimental, moralistic position for psychological or social reasons.

If you let an immigration enthusiast just rattle on about the topic, the rattling generally proceeds along the lines: rhapsodize, moralize, demonize. First comes the rhapsodizing about the speaker's Ellis Island or Famine Ship ancestors. Then the moralizing: We are a *good* nation—let the whole world know how good we are! Let them come! Lift the lamp beside the Golden Door! Then the demonizing of any kind of immigration restrictionist as evil, filled with cruel intentions, plotting to . . . to what? Bring back the slave trade? I really don't know what these moralizers have in mind. I've hung out with immigration restrictionists a lot. They are very nice people, mild and thoughtful. I haven't spotted any horns or cloven hooves at all.

The urge to demonize sometimes has odd results. An editorial in the *New York Times* (January 31, 2009) called immigration restrictionist Marcus Epstein, who is a friend of mine, a "white supremacist." Marcus has a Korean mother and a Jewish father. Funny sort of person to be a white supremacist.

The whole topic, though, is soaked with moralizing and sentimentality. Immigration advocates have their eyes fixed firmly on the past—Ellis Island, Famine Ships. Yet population policy is really all about the *future*—not about indignities suffered by our grand-*parents*, but about the kind of nation our grand-*children* will live in. Conservatives should be the realists here, the number crunchers and green-eyeshade talliers of debits and credits, of assimilations and ab-similations, making the most pessimistic assumptions when the projections are unclear.

Instead, too many conservatives have been cheerleaders for a vast experiment in social engineering. Rather than carefully project the results of the experiment, they simply declare those results to be inevitably good, on no grounds at all but their own vapid optimism and wishful thinking. Aren't conservatives supposed to be *hostile* to social engineering schemes? Why do so many conservatives swoon with approval at this one, while snarling at immigration skeptics as heartless xenophobes? The question is rhetorical. I have no idea what makes people so stupid and dishonest.

"A nation is a fragile thing." (Huntington.) Yes it is, except in the imaginations of blithe optimists, who believe that if a million immigrants are good for your country, then ten million will be ten times as good. Is that how they salt their stew, these people who call themselves conservatives? Fools!

FOREIGNERS: INSPECTING THE WORLD

I have lived 78 years without hearing of bloody places like Cambodia.

— WINSTON CHURCHILL, APRIL 28, 1953

Politics in the Third World starts with a soap box, proceeds to a ballot box, and ends with a cartridge box.

— PROVERBIAL AMONG JOURNALISTS

JUST LOOK AT IT!

My 1911 *Encyclopedia Britannica* lists 152 countries in the world. Question: How many of those countries made it from 1911 to today, nearly a century later, with their systems of government and law intact (allowing for minor constitutional adjustments like expansion of the franchise), without having suffered revolution, civil war, major dismemberment, or foreign occupation?

I'll stand open to correction here, but I make it six: Australia, Canada, New Zealand, Sweden, Switzerland, and the United States. Not even Britain qualifies, because of the secession, accompanied with revolutionary violence and a brief but nasty civil war, of the Republic of Ireland, nearly 30 percent of the area of the 1911 United Kingdom. (There are a scattering of marginal cases you might lawyer into the list, South Africa for example, but I'm going to apply a strict standard.)

Plainly a person alive in 1911 who wished to see his nation get clear through to 2009 without suffering any of the above-mentioned traumas needed to be a citizen *either* of one of the big British-settler nations, *or* of a smallish, out-of-the-way European country speaking mainly some language of the Germanic family and having a name beginning "Sw—."

I mention this only to point out that while it is certainly true, as Adam Smith said, that "there is a deal of ruin in a nation," it is also true that the modern age has brought with it a deal of exercises in nation-ruination, albeit often of only a temporary kind.

To put it another way: To get a nation up and running under a stable, modern constitution and legal system, and to keep the whole thing on the tracks for a few decades, is no mean feat. If you are not a nation of the British-settler or Sw— type, in fact, it needs something close to a miracle.

Brit-settler and Sw— nations aside, the political history of the twentieth century was a bit of a train wreck. To a conservative, this is not very surprising. To a conservative informed by the view of human nature I sketched a couple of chapters ago, what is surprising is that there are any societies at all that can keep themselves intact and stable across an entire century.

And to a conservative it is obvious that, if you have the great good fortune to live in such a society, you should leave well enough alone, and not go attempting revolutionary overhauls of (for example) your population by (for example) uncontrolled mass immigration from absolutely everywhere. In saying that, I am of course expressing an older style of conservatism, the one we had before the happy clappers took over.

Let's take a look at the world to see if there is anything much to hope for beyond America's shores, and whether this nation can keep its footing in the big global movements of the near future. The spirit of the inquiry here is taken from that old Yiddish joke about a fellow who goes to a tailor to be measured for a suit.

Customer: "How long will it take to make the suit?"
Tailor: "A month."

Customer: "A *month?* Come on! It only took the Good Lord six days to make the whole world."
Tailor: "Yes, and just look at it!"

EUROPE—A BUSTED FLUSH?

There is a view of Europe that is common in American conservative circles. It goes something like this:

Europe is dying. Extravagant welfare states and long decades of peace guarded by the U.S. military have destroyed the continent's moral fiber. Birth rates have plummeted so that Europe is graying. Mass immigration from Muslim countries has planted a fifth column in Europe's cities—a hostile subpopulation that is outbreeding the natives. Soft, easy living has stripped Europe of religious faith. As a dwindling, graying population slips deeper into hedonism and sloth, the place will implode and the jihadis will take over.

The best—I mean best written, the *literarily* best—expression of this view known to me is Mark Steyn's 2006 book *America Alone.* Europe's a goner, says Mark, and soon only the United States will remain as a rearguard remnant of Western civilization. America will stand alone because the malign trends seen in Europe are not seen here, or at least not in such pronounced forms.

Mark has to fudge some numbers to make it all work. For example, on page 48 of *America Alone* he describes the United States as a "[partial] exception to the softening of the West: a nation that still breeds . . ."

Take a close look at that "partial." Our overall 2007 total fertility rate, children per woman, is 2.1—just about replacement level. If you break out the rate by race, however, as the National Center for Health Statistics has done, you get 2.959 for Hispanics, 2.115 for non-Hispanic blacks, 1.864 for non-Hispanic whites. The figures for Sweden, Norway, Finland, and Iceland are 1.67, 1.78, 1.73, and

1.91. Iceland has a lush welfare state, and is (see Chapter 8, page 182) the least religious of all European nations, yet Icelanders—among whom are very few Third World immigrants—are actually broodier than white Americans. Hmm.

(On the facing page of his book, page 49, Mark scoffs at a British writer's claim that all Western democracies subscribe to ideas that are liberal or leftist, raising his own home state of New Hampshire as a counterexample. Hmm again: In the presidential election of November 2008, New Hampshire went for liberal-leftist Obama over John McCain by 384,826 votes to 316,534. Hmm, hmm.)

One counter to the Steynian Europe-is-doomed scenario has been offered by columnist and author Ralph Peters. In a November 26, 2006, *New York Post* column titled "The 'Eurabia' Myth," Peters prophesied that John/Jean/Josef/José/Giuseppe Q. European will eventually get in touch with his inner fascist.

> Don't let Europe's current round of playing pacifist dress-up fool you: This is the continent that perfected genocide and ethnic cleansing, the happy-go-lucky slice of humanity that brought us such recent hits as the Holocaust and Srebrenica. The historical patterns are clear: When Europeans feel sufficiently threatened—even when the threat's concocted nonsense—they don't just react, they over-react with stunning ferocity.

Like Mark Steyn, though, Peters clings to American exceptionalism.

> I have no difficulty imagining a scenario in which U.S. Navy ships are at anchor and U.S. Marines have gone ashore at Brest, Bremerhaven or Bari to guarantee the safe evacuation of Europe's Muslims.

None of that beastly "genocide and ethnic cleansing" in *our* "historical patterns"!

Comparing and contrasting the Steyn and Peters prognostications, the *Wall Street Journal*'s James Taranto remarked: "Think about this: Peters is predicting a rebirth of European fascism, possibly including genocide—and he's the *optimist* of this pair" (emphasis in original).

From where I sit they are both optimists so far as American exceptionalism is concerned. Steyn rests his argument ultimately on birth rates. Responding to Peters on PowerLineBlog.com, he wrote: "When you've demographically checked out of the future, why fight for it?" The fertility data is nothing like that conclusive, though, as I have shown above. Has Finland (1.73) really "demographically checked out of the future," but white America (1.864) not? The answer here, I can sadly predict, will be that I am a wicked, wicked person to have quoted the racial breakdowns, and that black and Hispanic Americans are just as resistant to advancing welfarism and mass immigration as are white Americans. Uh-huh.

Not only is America's white population actually less broody than some of those irreligious, hedonistic European nations, it is not clear that the Islamo-demographic threat to Europe is real.

Demographers Charles F. Westoff and Tomas Frejka, in a paper tiled "Religiousness and Fertility Among European Muslims," published in the *Population and Development Review* at the end of 2007, throw plenty of cold water. After presenting a wealth of supporting data, they conclude the following:

> The study confirms the perception that Muslim women have more children than non-Muslims in Western Europe, but shows that the gap is not as large as many believe. And, similar to other immigrants in other countries, Muslim fertility rates tend to fall over time, narrowing the gap with the non-Muslims who make up the vast majority of the European population now, and for the foreseeable future.

Muslims are not even demographically vigorous in their own countries. All over the Muslim world, total fertility rates are plummeting. Kuwait (2.81), Egypt (2.72), Morocco (2.57), Jordan (2.47), and the United Arab Emirates (2.43) all have rates lower than the one for Hispanic residents of the United States (2.959). In Algeria (1.82),

Tunisia (1.73), and Iran (1.71), the rates are at positively European levels.

The United States doesn't look so exceptional to me. A Muslim-demographic takeover of Europe? Doesn't look likely. (And if welfare-state security saps away at religious faith, why wouldn't Europe's Muslims follow Christians into vague, nonobservant spirituality?) Absimilated Muslim terrorists? They've got 'em, sure, but so have we: those Minnesota Somalis in the previous chapter, for example, slipping out of the country to train as terrorists. And in the news as I write is the conviction in federal court of five Muslims for conspiring to murder U.S. troops at Fort Dix, New Jersey. Three of the conspirators are illegal immigrants, one is a legal resident alien, one is a naturalized U.S. citizen.

The outstanding feature of the West over these past few decades has been our demographic bust. As the numbers show, it has occurred in the United States just as much as in Europe. Here, as there, politicians responded by admitting millions of Third World workers to keep the national economies humming. This has stressed society everywhere in the West.

European nations find their identity in deep common ancestry—"ethnonationalism" (Chapter 2). We Americans find ours in shared commitment to abstract principles, the principles of our Founding Fathers and our Constitution. Which kind of identity is better suited to weather the stresses of population aging and mass Third World immigration? I think I know the answer; but in any case, we shall find out.

Did we ever really have a choice, though? Is there any way to cope with demographic decline *other* than by permitting mass immigration? Is anybody trying? Yes they are.

THE OTHER ICE PEOPLE

The other Ice People are the East Asians—the Chinese, Japanese, and Koreans. *Their* demographics make Europe look like a rabbit farm. The Chinese "Special Administrative Region of Macau" actually has the lowest total fertility rate of any territory listed in the CIA World Factbook: 0.91 children per woman. Hong Kong and Singapore are little better at 1.02 and 1.09, respectively. (And yes, I know, Singapore's on the equator, which makes "Ice People" look like a pretty daft demonym. Their Paleolithic ancestors were up there chasing mammoths around the Arctic tundra, though—trust me.) There's more room to breathe, and breed, in Taiwan, but even there the TFR is a feeble 1.13. South Korea is 1.2, Japan 1.22, mainland China 1.77, which is a tad below Norway.

None of these nations shows the slightest inclination to turn to mass immigration as a counter to their demographic decline. Most immigrants to Japan, Taiwan, and South Korea are other East Asians, and the numbers are in thousands or tens of thousands, not millions and tens of millions. Ethnonationalism is very strong, and the Diversity cult has made little headway even in Japan, the most developed, sophisticated, and pacifistic East Asian nation. If there is any demographic exceptionalism to be noted in the world, it is East Asia's: low birth rates, stiff resistance to mass immigration.

(A couple of years ago I wrote a column titled "When Foreigners Were Funny," looking back wistfully to the days before the Diversity cult fixed its clammy grip on our society, the days when it was still okay to laugh at foreigners. I happened to mention the article in an e-mail to an American friend living in Japan. Do the Japanese find foreigners funny? I asked him. He: "Oh yes! Comedians on TV are forever dressing up in white face or black face, and everyone falls around laughing.")

From time to time some Japanese politician will call for a relaxation of the immigration laws, in order to boost the workforce. He is listened to politely, but nothing ever happens.

It is a plausible general principle that, when the human race in its overall development comes to some kind of bridge, the first nation to cross the bridge successfully has a great advantage over other nations. Britain was the first nation to industrialize, and dominated world affairs for a century afterward. If demographic decline is inevitable—which of course it is: the earth must have *some* maximum carrying capacity—the first nation to get through the transition intact, and conquer the associated problems, will be at a huge advantage. On current showing, that will be Japan.

China will be a generation or so behind, but the demographic cliff edge is already in sight. Not long ago, giving some talks after returning from a trip to China (my wife's home country), I was asked about the possibility of a future Japan-China conflict. I replied that unless it happens very soon, any such conflict will have to be fought out on the shuffleboard court. While there is still some demographic vitality in the deep countryside, in China's cities the official one-child policy is not even needed. Careerist young urban Chinese women simply have no interest in childbearing. A Chinese friend joked to me that the one-child policy slogan will soon be rephrased as: "Have one child— *please!*"

I once tried to float the idea of an Arctic Alliance, the Ice People of Europe and north Asia uniting to preserve their numbers and civilizations against the Sun People of further south. The idea had no takers. Going over the numbers again—especially those plummeting birth rates for the Muslim world—I think perhaps I was alarmist. I am still sure, though, that anyone who looks to American exceptionalism as a bulwark against the great demographic changes of our era, is practicing Wrong but Wromantic wishful thinking. The problem is a common one, whether the Ice People unite to confront it or not.

Meanwhile, how are things going in the Sun People homelands?

LATIN AMERICA, ATAHUALPA'S REVENGE

An interesting question for the next few years is whether Bolivia will survive as a nation. In common with most Latin-American countries, Bolivia's population is partly of European ancestry, partly of indigenous "Indian" ancestry, and partly mixed—"mestizo." The percentages are about 15-55-30, European-indigenous-mestizo.

The separating-out of people that I noted in Chapter 2, the ethnic disaggregation that seems to be an inevitable feature of modern life, is going on in Bolivia, aggravated by economic issues. The eastern third of the country is more white and mestizo than the western highlands, which are heavily Indian. That eastern third is also more prosperous, with some good farmland and reserves of oil and natural gas.

This makes for obvious tensions, especially since the nation got its first fully indigenous president in 2006. Evo Morales is a pure-blood Aymara Indian. In common with practically all Sun People, he is a socialist, and has been pushing through a program of nationalization, anti-Americanism, constitutional change, and "decolonization"—for example, by the promotion of indigenous languages over Spanish. Morales, in fact, came to power in 2006 talking about "uniting Latin America's 135 Indian nations to expel the white invasion, which began with the landing of Columbus in 1492."

This has not sat well with the prosperous easterners, and they have been agitating for more autonomy. The country is now in a state of more or less continuous unrest, with strikes and protests.

The Bolivian story is just one chapter in the recent rise of indigenous peoples everywhere in Latin America where they are numerous. (Which isn't everywhere. Argentina and Uruguay are less than 5 percent indigenous-plus-mestizo; Brazil has far more black citizens than Indians.) Hugo Chávez, president of Venezuela since 1998, got the ball rolling, and Morales is following in his footsteps—has actually proposed an "Axis of Good" with Venezuela to oppose "neoliberalism and U.S. imperialism."

What this rising tide of Sun People socialism will do to Latin America is anyone's guess. Given the track record of radical socialism, and the opportunities for Bolivia-style racial conflicts over resources, my own guess would be that Latin America will end up poorer and more chaotic.

For the United States there is nothing good here. Our own Hispanic immigrants are largely Mexican, with a mix more indigenous and mestizo than Mexico's own, since white Mexicans do disproportionately well in their own country. (Mexico's population is roughly 10-30-60, white-indigenous-mestizo.) A movement of aggressive race consciousness among Latin American indigenes is the last thing the United States needs to import.

Listening to immigration-friendly Americans, it's hard to avoid the impression that they see Hispanic immigrants as cheerfully subservient, doing those "jobs Americans won't do" with willing industriousness. To be even more blunt about it, it's hard to avoid the impression that a great many prosperous white Americans view cheerful, willing Hispanic gardeners, fruit pickers, and child minders as an agreeable replacement for surly, attitude-loaded African Americans.

Which, if I am right, raises the interesting question: What if the Hispanics get attitude? Way down south in the other half of our continent, they have. Perhaps Evo Morales is to your cheery, obliging indigenous-Peruvian child-minder as Robert Mugabe is to Aunt Jemima. This, of course, is a thought that no smiley-face conservative can think.

AFRICA, BREEDING FOR HUNGER

You'd think that the smile on even the smiliest of faces would freeze at the sight of Africa, with its apparently endless problems of poverty, disease, dictatorship, massacre, and war. That would be to underestimate the power of idiot optimism.

The George W. Bush administration, for example, was very busy in Africa, at the president's own insistence. When I say "busy," I mean of course busy handing out cash, in accordance with the First Law of optimistic statecraft, i.e., "Any problem can be solved if you spend enough money." In a seven-day, five-country trip around black Africa at the end of February 2008, President Bush scattered aid money like confetti. Benin got $307 million, Tanzania $698 million, Rwanda a "bilateral investment treaty" and $100 million for troop training, Ghana $547 million, Liberia more military aid, and also a million textbooks and ten thousand desks and chairs for its schools.

This was all on top of "regular" aid sluicing steadily out through the U.S. Agency for International Development. In yet another category are single-issue programs like the President's Emergency Plan for AIDS Relief (PEPFAR), a 2003 brainchild of Bush's that had cost

U.S. taxpayers close to $20 billion at the five-year mark. Africa's hard up, goes the thinking; therefore Africa needs aid.

Most parts of Africa are indeed in a sorry state. Individual citizens in more prosperous countries should respond according to the promptings of their individual consciences, and many have. For the past thirty years, in fact, private acts of assistance to Africa have been all the rage, from Bob Geldof stalking the rock concerts of the world urging patrons to "Give us yer fockin' money" to the movie-star fad for adopting winsome African babies.

It's hard to find fault with any of that. Private citizens should be left to do as they please with their own time and money. The money George W. Bush was spraying around in February 2008 was, however, government money, ripped from taxpayers' pockets by force of law. Was it well spent?

Not likely. The near-universal opinion among economists is that government aid does more harm than good to recipient countries. There is now a paper trail on this topic stretching back decades to the researches of British economist Peter Bauer in the 1960s and 1970s. Bauer was the originator of the apothegm that foreign aid is "a transfer of money from poor people in rich countries to rich people in poor countries." Among those influenced by his arguments was Ronald Reagan. Bruce Bartlett, who worked in the Reagan White House, tells us in his 2006 book *Impostor:*

> One of Reagan's first actions was to commission a Treasury Department study of the multilateral development banks, which found them to be almost a complete waste of money. When Reagan spoke before the first joint meeting during his administration of the World Bank and the International Monetary Fund, he made it clear that what developing countries needed wasn't foreign aid, but economic freedom.

(Another person influenced by Bauer was Margaret Thatcher. She raised him to the British peerage in 1983 as Lord Bauer.)

The smileys of course have an answer to all that. The kind of aid Bauer scoffed at, they will tell you, was the *wrong kind* of aid.

Nowadays the aid biz is much more sophisticated! Those nine-digit bundles of cash I quoted Bush as handing out to Benin, Tanzania, and Ghana, for example, were all grants under a program called Millennium Challenge Accounts. The idea is that to qualify for the aid, a nation has to meet benchmarks and pledges covering quality of governance, education spending, regulation, corruption, and so on.

Unfortunately the Stalin principle kicks in here. It's not who votes for whom that matters, said the old tyrant, it's who gets to *count* the votes. In the case of these "benchmarked" aid programs (as with that other pet project of George W. Bush's, No Child Left Behind), it's who gets to gather the statistics—which in most cases is the very people who will qualify for cash if the statistics look good.

Dress it up as you please, there is a fundamental problem with all aid, pinpointed by William Easterly in his 2006 book *The White Man's Burden.* Easterly, who spent sixteen years doing economic research for the aid-dispensing World Bank, says there is an "aid curse," like the much-commented-on "natural resource curse." Being an aid recipient is, says Easterly, like having oil under your territory: it frees governments from the need to tax their people. With no need to tax, there is no need to consult, or seek consensus. Thus aid actually decreases democracy and makes government worse.

It's not even clear that the much-praised PEPFAR program to combat AIDS in Africa has done net good. PEPFAR has made expensive retroviral drugs available where they were not before, but the program comes with moral strings attached. Of the funds disbursed, one-third must to go to programs promoting sexual abstinence, and none may be spent on activities that suggest approval of prostitution.

But abstinence education hasn't been shown to have any effect on sexual behavior. (An extensive 2007 study by Dr. Kristen Underhill of Oxford University offers the latest confirmation of this.) One-third of the PEPFAR funds are therefore spent to no purpose—other than, of course, to shore up the president's standing with U.S. morality lobbies.

The prostitution bar leaves out a large pool of susceptible Africans, since prostitution is a much more commonplace affair in Africa than it is in Western countries. This aspect of PEPFAR also became something of a joke when Randall Tobias, who as Bush's global AIDS coordinator had been responsible for disbursing PEPFAR funds, was obliged to resign in April 2007 after his name turned up on the Rolodex of a Washington call-girl service.

There have also been criticisms from within Africa that PEPFAR distorts and corrupts health care in the continent. Well-funded AIDS programs draw nurses and doctors away from more mundane work. Comments a Tanzanian observer: "It is not uncommon to find swanky air conditioned buildings with several expensive 4-wheel drives parked outside in local hospitals with dilapidated maternity beds, no water, and no medicines. As billions are spent on funding these single-minded . . . projects emblazoned with U.S. flags, primary health care systems are decimated and children die needlessly from diarrhea."

The real heart of pessimistic darkness about Africa was reached by veteran Irish journalist Kevin Myers, writing in the Dublin *Independent*, July 10, 2008, in response to an appeal for aid to Ethiopia, which was undergoing another famine. Myers noted that Ethiopia's population had grown from 33.5 million to 78 million across the quarter century since Bob Geldof had begun his charity campaigns—campaigns Myers had responded to with donations. So, he asked:

Why on earth should I do anything to encourage further catastrophic demographic growth in that country? . . . How much morality is there in saving an Ethiopian child from starvation today, for it to survive to a life of brutal circumcision, poverty, hunger, violence and sexual abuse, resulting in another half-dozen such wide-eyed children, with comparably jolly little lives ahead of them? Of course, it might make you feel better, which is a prime reason for so much charity. But that is not good enough.

For self-serving generosity has been one of the curses of Africa. It has sustained political systems which would otherwise have collapsed . . . It is inspiring Bill Gates' programme to rid the continent of malaria . . . If his programme is successful, tens of millions of children who would otherwise have died in infancy will survive to adulthood, he boasts. Oh good: then what? I know. Let them all come here. Yes, that's an idea.

I hope it is no very cynical asperity on my part to suspect that in the smug minds of love-the-world conservative optimists like George W. Bush—not to *mention* the even smugger fantasies of Africa sentimentalists like Barack Obama—this actually *is* an idea, and a jolly good one. Why shouldn't thirty million Ethiopian goatherds settle in the West? Who but a stone-hearted racist would object?

THE MIDDLE EAST—ETERNAL RECURRENCE

Oh, the Middle East. Do I really need to sell you on pessimism about *them?* Is there anyone who doesn't contemplate the whole region with utter despair? Anyone who doesn't think that the Middle East is the leading candidate for the title Region Most Likely to See a Megadeath Nuclear War? It's all too horrible to think about.

The main thing that comes to my mind when I am forced to think about the Middle East is our mustachioed friend Nietzsche's idea of eternal recurrence—the same darn thing happening over and over again, forever. I go way back with the Middle East—always the same arguments, the same voices, the same grievances, the same horrors.

I see the younger me, in my mind's eye, riding the New York subway in fall of 1973, on my way to a one-day dishwashing gig in Brooklyn, Rockaway, or the Bronx, following the progress of the Yom Kippur War in the dense, dull, smudgy print of the *New York Times*.

Further back yet, here I am sitting in the student cafeteria at Liverpool University with some friends, listening to news of the 1967 war, which the college was relaying to us on the PA system. One of those present was a Jewish girl who had spent time on a kibbutz. She kept shushing us to hear what had happened; then, when nothing new was being said, giving us long and passionate expositions of Israel's case. I was rather keen on that girl. Sad: now I can't even remember her name.

Further back yet, to volunteers in the streets of 1950s England, rattling cans and asking for donations on behalf of the Arab refugees.

And still further back. A few years ago my sister bought me, as a birthday present, the actual issue of the London *Sunday Times* for the day of my birth, June 3, 1945. I have the paper in front of me right now, discolored and rather fragile—a little slice of the world as it stood in the closing weeks of World War II. And there the wretched place is, under a headline: DE GAULLE ON LEVANT CRISIS.

> Gen. de Gaulle, addressing a Press conference in Paris yesterday afternoon on the crisis in the Levant, said that events there had an international and not merely a local importance . . . France, he said, was ready for negotiations on the question as a whole, not only concerning Syria and the Lebanon but the whole Eastern Arab world, for America and Russia were also interested in this . . .

You don't say. "Levant" is an old term for the Middle East. (After it was the Levant, it was the Near East. In my childhood geography lessons, the Middle East referred to places like India, contrasted with the Far East—China, Japan, etc. I wonder if there was something deliberate in the change of name—pushing the whole accurséd place a bit further away from Near to Middle.)

The context to that *Sunday Times* news story is the reluctance of de Gaulle to altogether let go of the French mandates in Syria and Lebanon, mandates awarded to France in 1918 following the defeat and disintegration of the Ottoman Empire. He blamed all the problems on Britain, of course. Hey, about having saved your bacon in two world wars, pal: YOU'RE WELCOME.

Not only the lead front-page headline is concerned with "the Levant," but the lead editorial on the Op-Ed page, too: THE TROUBLE IN THE LEVANT. Over on the inside Foreign News page, the main story, datelined Washington, D.C., is headed: AMERICAN DISMAY OVER SYRIA. (Says the story: "The headline 'French Bomb Damascus' produced the same feeling of dismay here as did that announcing the arrest of the 16 Polish leaders by Russia a few weeks ago.")

Syria . . . Lebanon . . . crisis . . . bomb Damascus . . . Egypt, "Irak," and Palestine . . . America and Russia also interested . . . Oh boy. A date plucked at random from sixty-odd years ago, and the names, even some of the issues, are all so drearily familiar.

My health is pretty good, thank heaven, and if my kids don't drive me to suicide, and Al Qaeda doesn't pop the big one in New York City (my house is right under the fallout plume), I have an actuarially excellent chance of living for another twenty years. I confidently expect that when at last I shuck off this mortal coil, kick the bucket, get my ticket punched, hand in my lunch pail, and go off to join the Choir Invisible, the newspaper headlines will still be saying AMERICAN DISMAY OVER SYRIA, and editorialists will still be pondering THE TROUBLE IN THE LEVANT, though unless it is true that absolutely everything comes back around sooner or later, they'll likely refer to the place as something other than the Levant.

A hundred years ago people of a geopolitical inclination used to amuse themselves by saying that the Balkans produced more history than they could consume locally. The Levant was at that point vegetating quietly in the embrace of the Ottoman Empire. When, after World War I, the region at last emerged from its chrysalis, it proved capable of generating a quantity of history that makes the Balkans look like North Dakota.

Does anyone else feel, as I do, an almighty weariness with the Levant and its intractable problems, its immemorial rancors, its savage rivalries, its unappeasable grievances? Back when Henry Kissinger was secretary of state he used to tell his aides that if he ever showed signs of taking an interest in the Cyprus problem, they should immediately put him in a straitjacket. If only we could be that indifferent to the Levant!

I know, I know, we can't. Oil; nukes; Islam; terrorists; Russia and China—the Great Game of our time. We can't ignore the damn filthy loathsome place. Our statesmen have to come up with policies; we journalistic thumb-suckers have to come up with opinions; all we citizens have to come up with taxes to pay for the warships and armies, the bribes and subsidies, the front men and stool pigeons, the soldiers, spies, and diplomats. No, we can't ignore the Levant. But Lord, how I wish we could!

Postscript. A couple of years ago, I took my family on a vacation to Montana, to give them a look at the West. One feature of the trip was a ghost town—the town of Garnet, just off I-90 out of Missoula. Garnet was a gold mining town in the late nineteenth century. It had a little revival in the 1930s when the price of gold soared. The post office finally closed for good in 1942, though some inhabitants lingered on for a few years more.

The place is kept in pretty good shape by some kind of preservation group. You can go inside some of the old buildings, and peer into their rooms from behind bars across the doorways.

Mooching around in the Garnet hotel I spotted, on a table in one of the bedrooms, an old newspaper. Leaning over the bar across the doorway, I could make out the front page above the fold. This was:

THE MONTANA STANDARD
Butte-Anaconda, Montana
Wednesday Morning, June 2, 1948   Price 5¢

And what do you think was the main headline above the fold?

JEWS AND ARABS ACCEPT U.N. ARMISTICE PLEA

Their replies leave unanswered such questions as when the shooting in Palestine will stop. . . .

No-o-o-o- . . .

It will never stop, unless the whole place goes up in fireballs. It will never end, just go around and around forever. You want pessimism? Pick up a newspaper: 1945, 1948, 1967, 1973 . . . They might as well just recycle the same stories every few years, as the publishers of children's comics are rumored to do. Who would notice?

THE ECONOMY: IN HOCK TO THE WORLD

Oh, hush thee, my babe, granny's bought some more shares
Daddy's gone out to play with the bulls and the bears,
Mother's buying on tips, and she simply can't lose,
And baby shall have some expensive new shoes!
—Published in the *Saturday Evening Post*, Summer 1929
(I don't know the author)

Banking is not really about lending money at all, but about
getting paid back.
—Peter Schiff, *The Little Book of Bull Moves*
in Bear Markets (2008)

FAERY GOLD AND THE GOD OF THINGS AS THEY ARE

As I write, in the early days of 2009, the nation is sinking into economic crisis. The word of the hour is "bailout." Our government is desperately pouring money into banks, insurance companies, and automobile companies, in the hope of preventing a cascade of business failures. A cartoon in one of my magazines shows two bearded Saint Peter types on a cloud, watching an asteroid hurtle toward earth. Says one heavenly being to the other: "I suppose they'll be wanting a bailout."

The money being poured is, of course, ours; and it will, of course, never be repaid. Our wealth is being taken away from us. Well, sort of, since we never really had it, anyway.

The principal economic fact of the past thirty years has been the entry of three billion hungry Asians into the world's free workforce, as China abandoned the command economy and South Asia retreated from the worst kind of bureaucratic statism. The Asians were soon very productive, and extraordinarily thrifty. With that kind of competition, it was not possible that the American standard of living could go on improving at the rates of the twentieth century's third quarter—not without some major sleight of hand on the part of U.S. politicians.

The sleight of hand was duly performed. We filled our homes with Asia's products at bargain prices. That left our dollars in Asian banks. The Asians obligingly lent the dollars back to us on the strength of IOUs our government gave them. The precise quantity of dollars we borrowed back was determined by interest rates, which were set at a level high enough to attract the dollars, yet low enough to encourage domestic spending. Very few of these dollars were saved. Some were invested; more were used to buy yet more foreign-made goods, perpetuating the cycle; many more were used to buy and sell our houses to each other at prices that spiraled steadily upward. Trillions were sequestered by federal and state governments, to be used for the creation of more government make-work, or the prosecution of pointless wars in the snake pits of the Levant . . . sorry: Middle East. The IOUs were left for our kids to deal with.

All this made us feel better off, and we gave our politicians due credit. In reality, though, we were no better off at all. Our wealth was faery gold, the kind that melts away into air when the clock strikes midnight. In the fall of 2008, the clock struck.

It's hard to blame the politicians. We get the politicians we deserve. If our decision is that we will turn our faces away from cold reality and live in an opium dream of wishful thinking—of ever-increasing prosperity not supported by thrift and productivity—politicians will oblige.

And we did not in fact blame them. The elections of November 2008 showed, if they showed anything, great satisfaction with our politicians. As I noted in Chapter 3, the "reelected incumbent prevalence" rate for the House of Representatives was 88 percent. Of twenty-nine incumbents running for the U.S. Senate, five were defeated, for an RIP of 83 percent.

In the presidential voting, results were as follows:

Name of Party	Votes Won	Percent of Total
Tax and Spend Party	68,440,793	52.8
Borrow and Spend Party (Also known as "Tax Your Kids and Spend Party")	59,390,576	45.8
Stop Reckless Spending Parties	723,293	0.6
Other parties	Can't be bothered to work out the numbers	

Plainly we, the American people, have no great problem with our politicians. We just want them to spend more—more of that money we don't, in point of fact, actually have. We want them to gin up the production of faery gold.

INFLATION BY ANOTHER NAME

The financial crisis of 2008 was not hard to see coming. Plenty of people *did* see it coming. Investment adviser Peter Schiff, for example, whose book *Crash Proof*, published in February 2007, described the catastrophe of nineteen months later with uncanny accuracy.

Eighty-eight years before that, Rudyard Kipling had given us the essentials in his great poetic tribute to what he called "The Gods of the Copybook Headings":

> *In the Carboniferous Epoch we were promised abundance*
> *for all,*
> *By robbing selected Peter to pay for collective Paul;*

> *But, though we had plenty of money, there was nothing our*
>   *money could buy,*
> *And the Gods of the Copybook Headings said: "If you don't*
>   *work you die."*

In another context, asked about his religious beliefs, Kipling had declared himself a believer in "the God of things as they are." Not for nothing is Kipling a great hero to us in the despised, marginalized, reality-based community.

If real wealth isn't *actually* increasing, the only way to *pretend* it's increasing is by inflation. The government prints more money. With more money going around, everyone feels better off . . . for a while. But then, with nothing extra being produced, prices go up and you're back where you started, only with a depreciated currency.

(Even that may be too much theoretical economics for most citizens to grasp. I was once friendly with a journalist who wrote a financial column for a downmarket London newspaper. He told me that the question he was most often asked by readers was "Since the government controls the printing of money, why doesn't the government just print enough to make everyone rich?" I'm an economics dunce—see below—but at least I know the answer to *that*.)

Plain print-more-money Argentina-style inflation went out of fashion in this country after the dislocations of the 1970s. The sophistication of the modern economy allows more subtle forms of inflation via monetary policy. That's what the great borrowing and house-price boom of the past few years has been about. We didn't produce more, earn more, or save more. We just issued a lot of IOUs: T-bills, mortgage-backed securities, and exotic derivative instruments. This kind of inflation comes due much more slowly than the Argentina kind.

Some of it just did. The rest, our kids will have to pick up.

THE DIVERSITY RECESSION

There was plenty of Diversity gas in the balloon, too, as it soared up away from the real world. How would it be fair—how, in fact, would it not be RACIST—if *this* group could borrow easy money but *that* group couldn't? Where is the justice if professionals and cube-jockey types, Ice People overrepresented among them, could get mortgages but dirty-hands blue-collar and pink-collar workers, with Sun People overrepresented among *them*, couldn't?

The issue of fairness in mortgage lending came up on the radar screens of politicians and judges in the middle 1970s. The related issue of fairness in educational opportunities was coming to a head at about the same time, leading to a high tide of Diversity-by-fiat legislating and judicial ruling. Just about when Bostonians were rioting against forced busing for school integration (April 1976), the federal government was moving to outlaw discriminatory lending to home buyers. The Equal Credit Opportunity Act of 1974, the Home Mortgage Disclosure Act of 1975, and the Community Reinvestment Act (CRA) of 1977 put banks on notice that they had to extend credit to low-income customers and districts, whether it made commercial sense or not.

The business of lending money to home buyers thus became politicized. Politics, as any observer of the modern world knows, is the enemy of economics, everywhere and always. So it was with mortgage lending.

Originally intended to promote fairness in lending, the CRA and its subsequent improvements became a charter for far-left "community action" groups like the Boston-based Neighborhood Assistance Corporation of America (NACA) and the Association of Community Organizations for Reform Now (ACORN) to shake down banks on behalf of low-income borrowers. A typical lawsuit was the one brought in federal court in 1994 by Selma S. Buycks-Roberson, Renee Brooks, and Calvin Roberson "on behalf of themselves and others similarly situated" against Citibank, claiming that the bank had denied mortgages to minority applicants. Calvin Roberson was an ACORN activist. One of the attorneys for the plaintiffs was Barack Obama.

Thus Diversity-whipped, the banks quickly got into line. Mortgage lending had been a pretty rational business until the politicians and activists got their hands on it. Banks had always wanted to lend money—that's what banks are for. (Though Peter Schiff's apothegm, the one I quoted at the head of this chapter, is worth noting in current circumstances.) They had always understood that there would be some level of default on the loans they made, but they tried to minimize that level. They had scrutinized loan applicants for ability to service their loans, and demanded up-front deposits. If any "community" was being underserved from sheer irrational prejudice, entrepreneurs could have moved in and made a bundle lending to that market segment. That's capitalism, bless its sweet rationality.

All that rationality drained away as the nation's political system lost touch with reality in the 1990s. No-deposit, interest-only, and no-recourse loans became commonplace. (In a no-recourse loan, the lender has no recourse against a borrower who defaults. Can't meet those mortgage payments? Put the house keys in an envelope, mail them off to the bank, and move in with your brother's family. Nobody will come after you; the lender has no recourse.)

Even weirder creatures emerged from the mortgage bankers' Island of Doctor Moreau under the Diversity-driven loosened standards of the 1990 and 2000s. There was the "option ARM," for instance, also known as the "Pick-A-Pay" mortgage: "now seen by an array of housing analysts and regulators as the Typhoid Mary of the mortgage industry," observed the *New York Times* (December 24, 2008). (So perhaps I should trade in that Island of Doctor Moreau metaphor for a biological-warfare lab. Does anyone still read H. G. Wells, anyway?) The *Times* explained:

> Pick-A-Pay allowed homeowners to make monthly mortgage payments that were so small they did not cover their interest charges. That meant the total principal owed would actually grow over time, not shrink as is normally the case.
>
> Credit standards went to hell; and the U.S. government was encouraging the process, as part of the political effort to feed us all the illusion that we were getting better off.

The *Times* was not—surprise!—being entirely fair to the Bush administration there. The president addressed the issue out of both sides of his mouth, as he had with the Iraq war, every assertion of grand idealism coming with a little cautionary note of realism attached. Bush was never a complete fantasist. He was always trying to square the fantasy-reality circle. It can't be done, of course.

U.S. foreign policy, Bush told us in that second inaugural speech, had "the ultimate goal of ending tyranny in our world," but—hold your horses—this would be "the concentrated work of generations." So it was with the easy-credit boom, though here there was a time lag between the idealism and the compensating realism.

Home-ownership idealism was built on the notion that everyone should own a house. Alas, as President Bush noted in an October 15, 2002, White House Conference on Minority Homeownership:

> We have a problem here in America because fewer than half of the Hispanics and half the African Americans own the [sic] home. That's a homeownership gap.

Those darn gaps! How to bridge this one?

> A lot of folks can't make a down payment. They may be qualified. They may desire to buy a home, but they don't have the money to make a down payment.

So if we just get rid of that stupid down-payment requirement, Sun People home ownership will soar, right? Right.

> By the end of this decade we'll increase the number of minority home owners by at least 5.5 million families. [Applause.]

A few months later came the follow-through, in a January 19, 2004, press release from the Department of Housing and Urban Development.

> As part of President Bush's ongoing effort to help American families achieve the dream of homeownership, Federal Housing Commissioner John C. Weicher today announced that

HUD is proposing to offer a "zero down payment" mortgage, the most significant initiative by the Federal Housing Administration in over a decade.

There was the idealism. The feeble counter-tug of residual conservative realism came from administration efforts to tighten regulations on Fannie Mae and Freddie Mac, the "government-sponsored enterprises" that were shoveling money into the housing boom. From the *New York Times*, September 11, 2003:

> The Bush administration today recommended the most significant regulatory overhaul in the housing finance industry since the savings and loan crisis a decade ago.
>
> Under the plan, disclosed at a Congressional hearing today, a new agency would be created within the Treasury Department to assume supervision of Fannie Mae and Freddie Mac, the government-sponsored companies that are the two largest players in the mortgage lending industry.

Those halfhearted efforts to slow the runaway locomotive were easily quashed by congressional panjandrums whose pockets had been well stuffed by Fannie and Freddie lobbyists—liberal Democrats like Representative Barney Frank and Senators Chris Dodd and Barack Obama, who by this point had it fixed in their Diversity-addled minds that down payments for home loans were a sinister tool of racist oppression. (The keen complicity of these liberal Democrat politicians in the wealth racket went unremarked by the *New York Times* in their 2008 article—another surprise!)

As with the Iraq war, Bush's idealism wasn't entirely misplaced. People care more about a place they own than about a place they rent. Compare the appearance of a part of town where most people are renters, with a part where most own their homes. By expanding home ownership, down-at-heel neighborhoods could be revitalized, crime reduced, and so on.

And people with houses have a foundation for future wealth. Getting Sun people—non-Asian minorities—to that point would be a laudable goal for government action, if it could be honestly done. The Ice People–Sun People wealth gap in the United States is quite breathtaking. The Pew Hispanic Center trawled through census data in 2004 to get the following figures for median household net worth as of 2002: Hispanic $7,932; non-Hispanic black $5,988; non-Hispanic white $88,651. Now *that's* a gap. (Pew does not break out a figure for Asians. For purposes of highlighting minority distress, the Asian minority, which does rather well, is inconvenient.)

The push to expand home ownership by forcing lenders to extend credit to low-income people who weren't, on rational banking standards, really creditworthy, was bipartisan. It worked, too: The rate of home ownership in the United States climbed from about 64 percent in 1995—a plateau it had held steady at for several years—to 69 percent in 2007. That some large proportion of the extra 5 percent were not creditworthy was a thing no politician could say out loud for fear of violating Diversity protocols.

Intentions here were good. We all know what good intentions pave, though, don't we? Good intentions on the part of an oversized, overambitious government, with all its stupidity and corruption and bureaucratic confusion, with all its hatred of reality and fear of truth, and headed up by a well-meaning but muddle-headed and inarticulate Evangelical-romantic chief executive, can only ever lead to one place.

The political slogan "affordable housing," on every politician's lips for the past twenty years, turned out to mean "finagling the credit markets to get people owning title to houses they can't afford."

But markets are unforgiving things. They don't take kindly to being finagled by politicians, and always have their revenge at last. "Reality," said Philip K. Dick, "is that which, when you stop believing in it, doesn't go away."

The result, as mathematicians say, follows. It's that exercise with the pitchfork again. It's also Kipling again:

> . . . *after this is accomplished, and the brave new world*
>   *begins*

When all men are paid for existing and no man must pay
    for his sins,
As surely as Water will wet us, as surely as Fire will burn,
The Gods of the Copybook Headings with terror and
    slaughter return!

THE COST OF OPTIMISM

Too many Americans—in particular, too many minorities—don't qualify for mortgages? No problem!—just relax the standards! Discourage deposit requirements and the scrutiny of credit histories. Offer no-deposit or Pick-A-Pay loans. Offer teaser loans, with artificially low initial interest rates, the true rate kicking in after two years or so—by which time the house price will have appreciated so much, the buyer can sell at a profit! Who ever heard of house prices not going up?

Or: That unskilled warehouse-shelf-stacker who took out the easy loan, has become a householder, and been embourgeoisified thereby. He is now a member of the middle classes—sober, responsible, thrifty, and earning a good middle-class wage. The home-owning experience has transformed him from Ralph Kramden into Rob Petrie. Heck, before you know it he'll be studying for a law degree at night school! *And voting Republican!* Human nature is infinitely malleable, don't you know? By helping a human being to increase his capital, you increase *human* capital too, see? (I know, I know, but there are people who believe this.)

Here you see the idiot optimism of our political classes in full flood. You also see the tragic consequences that always follow from unbridled optimism. The tragedy here, as with the forced integration of schools, as with the project to democratize barbarous tribal societies where everyone's married to a cousin, is that the people most likely to be hurt in the inevitable fiasco are exactly the ones our smiley-face World Savers set out to help.

That, at least, is what the circumstantial evidence suggests in the case of the home-ownership bubble. Real evidence is strangely hard to come by here, as nobody seems to be tallying home-loan default rates for minorities, in spite of *lending* to minorities being monitored in terrific detail for purposes of Diversity compliance.

We do know that the highly default-prone subprime mortgages were disproportionately issued to non-Asian minorities. In 2006, according to the Joint Center for Political and Economic Studies, "twenty-six percent of mortgages for home purchase by whites were subprime . . . for Hispanics, it was 47 percent and for African Americans, 53 percent." We also know that the states with the biggest increases in home-foreclosure rates are California, Nevada, Florida, and Arizona. If you rank all 50 states by the percentage of the state population that declared itself Hispanic in the 2000 census, those four are ranked 2, 5, 7, and 4 respectively.

I'm not blaming the victims here, I'm blaming the fools who gutted rational banking standards for political and financial profit, and from the dreamy idealism of the cluelessly optimistic. I'm blaming the politicians—which is to say, at one short remove, the electorate. The victims of the housing bust really *are* victims. They were sold faery gold and false hopes by cynics and idiots whose heads are stuffed with an ideology of facile optimism—Wrong but Wromantic.

But don't we have smart people to guard against all this? To scrutinize their databases and spreadsheets so that they can warn us against likely disasters? Don't we have *economists?*

Oh yeah, we have economists.

DISMAL AND DISMALER

Conservatives argue a lot about economics. We all agree that socialism is horrid, that free enterprise is essential in a free society, and that the less government has to do with business, beyond modest and sensible regulation, the better. Beyond those basics, all is rancor. For some conservatives, "free trade" is holy writ; for others, it is an expletive. I have listened to all the arguments a hundred times, like a spectator at a tennis match swiveling his head from side to side, but I still come away with that Omar Khayyam feeling:

> *Myself when young did eagerly frequent*
> *Doctor and Saint, and heard great Argument*
> *About it and about: but evermore*
> *Came out by the same Door as in I went.*

I therefore don't claim any economics expertise; but then, I'm deeply unimpressed with those who do. This goes way back.

My earliest acquaintance with big-time public-affairs economics was back in my first weeks at college in London, when I read a newspaper story about my country's new prime minister, Sir Alec Douglas-Home, who had confessed to being an economic ignoramus. When he had to solve a problem in economics, said Sir Alec, he did so by moving groups of matchsticks around on his desk. These confessions were received with great hilarity by the British intelligentsia of the time, who confidently predicted that such an incompetent would surely wreck the British economy.

Perhaps Sir Alec would indeed have wrecked the economy. We never found out. He served as prime minister for less than a year before his defeat by Harold Wilson in the election of 1964.

Wilson did not merely know economics; he had lectured in the subject at Oxford University, after getting a first-class degree there. If anyone knew economics, it was this guy. Wilson was no matchstick-shuffler, but an intellectual superstar of the dismal science. At age twenty-one he was lecturing in economic history, one of the youngest Oxford dons of the twentieth century.

(Historian Arthur M. Schlesinger Jr. met Wilson in 1962 and recorded the following impression in his journal: "I expected a small, natty young man, and found a small, portly, graying middle-aged man. He is immensely clever, immensely self-satisfied and skates on the edge of pomposity.")

Furthermore, Wilson brought into government as his advisers two more of the same, the Hungarians Nicholas Kaldor and Thomas Balogh. An Oxford don and two Hungarians—how much economics expertise is *that!* No more jiggling around with matchsticks from these guys!

Wilson was in power for nearly eight years, during which time—guess what?—he comprehensively wrecked the British economy. I have regarded economists with a skeptical eye ever since.

It's not that I believe economists are stupid. Of course they're not stupid. You don't get to be an Oxford don without demonstrating considerable smarts. I have no doubt at all that even with the wisdom of my years, if I could be set against the Harold Wilson of 1964 in a debate, I would come out of it looking like a mumbling moron. The same would probably happen if I were set up against Karl Marx, a man of good intellect who educated himself in economics through years of heavy intellectual labor. The fact remains that for all their expertise and diligence and—in Wilson's case, at any rate—academic credentials, the economics they thought they knew was not, in fact, much good.

(I am not quite willing to admit it was no good at all. The lives of my parents and grandparents improved immensely under early managerial socialism. You might say that they would have improved much more under classical liberalism, but how do you know?)

There you have the problem with economic expertise. How can it be tested? The answer seems to be: by wrecking the occasional country. Now, you might say: "Those failed economists were creatures of their time. Planning was all the rage, socialism had not yet been tested to destruction, and they had lost sight of the fundamental principles. Now if they had listened to Hayek . . ."

Sure, okay. But how do I, as a layperson, know that the economists of today are any less creatures of *their* time? How do I know that their theories will not look as daft forty years on as Harold Wilson's managerial socialism does now? I don't, of course, and neither do you, and neither do they. The events of 2008 suggest, at least, that current economic theory needs work; or, if our politicians were ignoring the advice of their economists, that those economists are at fault for not having resigned *en bloc* at the willful ignoring of their advice on the part of their employers.

THE FUTURE OF WORK

Economics may be dismal, but it's not a science. Sciences go forward pretty steadily. A scientific theory, once tested and shown to explain what needs explaining, without contradiction, will not fade in popularity, or be scoffed at for a century at a time while scientists go off and believe in contrary theories.

While I was discussing this with an economist friend, he launched into an explanation of David Ricardo's trade theories. That's great, but I can't help noticing that Ricardo's dates are 1772–1823. Since his time we have, for decades at a stretch, lived under the domination of non-Ricardian economists—mainly socialists of various kinds. Around 1930, pretty much every high-IQ person in the Western world, including most of the economists, was a Marxist. Entire human lifetimes, several hundred million of them, have been lived under non-Ricardian economics.

Now, of course, we are told that those policies were all wrong. But how can a layperson be sure that the economists of today are not all wrong? Some of the things they tell us sound uncannily like what the leaders of the old USSR used to tell their people. "Oh, you may be going through some hardship now, but you are helping to build a radiant future." Perhaps we are, and perhaps we aren't. How can we know?

At my local supermarket, I usually check out at the automated self-checkout gadget. These things started to appear all over the place four or five years ago. I resisted using them at first, partly because I don't like gadgets, partly out of proletarian solidarity with the cashiers, whose jobs were obviously in peril from these things. The convenience of it wore down my resistance, though, and now I use them more often than not.

My economist friend, when I mentioned all that, told me about buggy-whip makers. See, once upon a time people drove buggies, and they needed whips to keep the horses alert, and there were workers who made a living manufacturing buggy whips. Then along came the automobile, and buggy-whip makers were surplus to requirements. "So they got other jobs!" my friend explained triumphantly.

I suppose they did. That, however, was then, and this is now. If low-skill jobs are melting away before my eyes, which they are (and setting aside for the moment the fact that our political class has decided to import eight hundred million unskilled Third Worlders to do more of these vanishing jobs), what are these workers to do? Does the fact that the buggy-whip makers of 1909 got other jobs guarantee that the supermarket cashiers and C++ coders of 2009 will, too? Isn't linear extrapolation of past trends into the future supposed to be the besetting sin of amateur economic know-nothings?

Michael Lind wrote a piece for the *Atlantic Monthly* (January 2004), about America's ability to keep inventing new kinds of middle class. The first middle class (said Lind) consisted of the yeoman farmers of the early Republic, who looked down on what Jefferson called "greasy mechanicals." Then those greasy mechanicals became the inventors, engineers, and factory workers of the industrial boom, and a new middle class was born—people of the machine, who looked down on poor Bartleby the Scrivener scratching away at his ledger book in the countinghouse. As industrial production automated and moved abroad, Bartleby in turn came into his own, and a third middle class of knowledge workers came up: the cube people of our own time, the ones now watching anxiously as their jobs drift off to Bangalore and Beijing.

The assumption here is that like the buggy-whip makers you hear about from economic geeks, like dirt farmers migrating to factory jobs, like the middle-class engineer of 1960, the cube people of today will go do something else, creating a new middle class from some heretofore-despised category of drudges. But . . . what? Which category of despised drudges will be the middle class of tomorrow? Do you have any ideas? I don't. What comes after office work? What are we all going to do? The same thing Bartleby the Scrivener did, perhaps, but collectively and generationally.

What is the next term in the series: farm, factory, office . . . ?

There isn't one.* The evolution of work has come to an end point, and the human race knows this in its bones. Actually, in its reproductive organs: the farmer of 1800 had six or seven kids, the factory worker of 1900 three or four, the cube jockey of 2000 one or two. The superfluous humans of 2100, if there are any, will hold at zero. What would be the point of doing otherwise?

THE ROYAL ROAD TO RICHES

There will, of course, still be rich and poor, but not as there was in the past.

Cai Shen, pronounced "ts-*hie* shern," is the Chinese god of wealth. On the Lunar New Year, traditional-minded Chinese people paste large pictures of Cai Shen to their doors. In these pictures, Cai Shen is dressed in the uniform of an imperial-era bureaucrat.

So it goes in grand centralized imperial-despotic systems, ruled over by a cadre of officials who have proved their aptitude for the work by passing a lot of examinations. Wealth follows power in such systems. The proper and ordinary route to wealth is through the exercise of power.

So it goes in the United States today. This feature of our national life is so much taken for granted, we don't notice it. We read about ex-president Bill Clinton pulling in nearly $52 million in speaking fees for the years 2000–2007; or we read elsewhere of the "contributions" to his presidential library and foundation—organizations over which the ex-president has total control—from foreign potentates (between $15 million and $35 million from Saudi Arabia, between $1 million and $5 million from the sultan of Brunei, etc.); and we smile, and turn the page. Reading of Franklin Raines, former CEO of "government-sponsored enterprise" Fannie Mae, getting millions in sweetheart loans and tens of millions in compensation after con-

---

*When I posed this question in some Internet commentary once, the most popular suggestion in readers' e-mails was "community organizer."

tributing mightily to the easy-credit fiasco, our smiles might be somewhat strained—but hey, it's politics, you know.

Yet these tremendous emoluments are quite a new thing. When Harry Truman left office in 1953, he had no income but his Army pension of $112.56 a month. He had to take out a bank loan while negotiating a deal to write his memoirs. That was the way of things all over the Anglosphere. It was part of the tradition of modest Anglo-Saxon government. When Bob Menzies, Australia's longest-serving prime minister, left office in 1966 after eighteen years in power, having given up a lucrative legal career for politics, he could not afford to buy a house in Melbourne. (Some wealthy supporters eventually put up funds for a house in a respectable suburb.) As late as 1980, I am told, the prime minister of New Zealand had his domestic telephone number listed in the phone book. Farmers used to call him up and grumble about the price of sheep dip.

It all seems like a long time ago. Now government is the royal road to wealth. This is true at every level—look back at Peggy Noonan's observation in Chapter 3 of the booming, glittering Virginia suburbs. We are slipping ever faster toward some postindustrial version of what our grandfathers (and political scientist Karl Wittfogel, in a classic text) called "Oriental Despotism"—an all-embracing paternal state ruled over by an omnicompetent god-king and his remote, sanctified priesthood.

Who today can read Alexis de Tocqueville's famous warning about "democratic despotism" in *Democracy in America* without reflecting that yes, this is pretty much where we are at?

> The sovereign extends his arms over the whole society; he covers its surface with a web of small, complicated, painstaking, uniform rules through which the most original minds and the most vigorous souls are unable to emerge in order to rise above the crowd; it does not break wills but it softens them, bends them, and directs them; it rarely forces men to act, but it constantly opposes itself to men's acting; it does not destroy, it prevents things from coming into being; it does not tyrannize, it hinders, it presses down upon men, it enervates, it extin-

guishes, it stupefies, and it finally reduces each nation to no longer being anything but a herd of timid and industrious animals, whose shepherd is the government.

I have always believed that this sort of regulated, mild, and peaceful servitude . . . could be combined better than one imagines with some of the exterior forms of liberty.

So it can, Al, so it can.

Government wasn't the solution, Reagan told us, it was the problem. That sentiment is as dead as he is. Nobody under thirty believes it, nor even understands it, probably. The government people have won—game, set, and match. We just elected as president a man who, in his autobiography, referred to his scant experience as a private-sector employee as being "behind enemy lines."

Government is the victor; capitalism, the defeated enemy. Capitalism proved too rational for our smiley-face fantasies. If we were to continue Chasing the Dragon through our cherished opium dreams of boundless hope and infinite possibility, capitalism had to be crushed. It has been.

I urge my teenage children, three or four times a week, "Get a government job!" If you have kids, you should do the same. You should, at any rate, if you want them to enjoy one of those big houses with a picture window in the suburbs of northern Virginia. "You have to go farther out to see the foreclosure signs." Two Christmas trees!

It is more or less understood now that private enterprise exists to feed the public-sector behemoth. Every day's news offers fresh evidence. From my *New York Post* this morning (December 28, 2008):

> The city's five pension funds have lost close to 30 percent in the Wall Street crisis this year, threatening to hit taxpayers like an economic tsunami for years to come.

The benefits for New York City workers are *guaranteed by law,* you see. If their own pension-plan investments don't meet the tab, taxpayers must make up the balance. Yes, that would include private-sector taxpayers who have seen their own, *un*guaranteed retirement nest eggs dwindle in the crash. It's only fair! And these people are *public servants*, you know—meek, selfless waiters on those who create the nation's wealth.

The private sector has always been a milch cow for government, of course. Nowadays, though, it is a milch cow for bloated, arrogant, and privileged government that looks on nongovernment types with scorn and contempt.

As with the city, so with the state. Facing a $15 billion budget gap next year, the governor of New York State has *increased* state spending by $1.4 billion, budgeted for nine thousand new state employees, and imposed 137 new taxes on residents! Nothing must subtract from the wealth of government; nothing must retard the growth of government.

Nothing will. Limited government with modest powers? Ha ha ha ha ha! Conservatism? In your dreams!

Thus the United States slips gradually into the managerial state James Burnham warned of. He was a little early with his prediction, but it is coming true at last. We shall strut and fret on the world stage for a little longer as a great power, meddling for a few more years in the everlasting rancors of the Middle East and the irremediable miseries of Africa, till the thud of bombs, the whine of missiles, and the rattle of begging bowls is drowned out at last by the clink-clink of devaluing dollars.

At that point the internationalist pretense will be over. We shall retreat to our natural condition as an Inland Empire, a Middle Kingdom ruled by corrupt, arrogant bureaucrats, who treat us like the peasants of imperial China.

Perhaps we shall paste pictures of these gods of wealth to our doors at "holiday season," before hustling our children off to the examination halls in hopes of their one lifetime shot at security and prosperity—government work.

13

THE AUDACITY OF HOPELESSNESS

Where then shall Hope and Fear their Objects find?
Must dull Suspence corrupt the stagnant Mind?
Must helpless Man, in Ignorance sedate,
Swim darkling down the Current of his Fate?

— FROM "THE VANITY OF HUMAN WISHES,"
BY SAMUEL JOHNSON

Yet, yet a moment, one dim ray of light
Indulge, dread Chaos, and eternal Night!

— FROM "THE DUNCIAD," BOOK IV BY ALEXANDER POPE

IN SUMMARY

So what do we have here? According to me, too many conservatives:

- blithely signed on to the foolish and false Diversity ideology;
- were complicit in, or insufficiently critical of, the expansion and stagnation of federal power;
- have offered only feeble resistance to the decline of our culture;
- will be drowned by a rising tide of feminization;
- are fully invested in the wrongheaded educational theories of our time;
- face the prospect of their fundamental metaphysic being undermined by discoveries in the human sciences. . . .
- . . . and by the ebbing of strong religious conviction;

- were made fools of by George W. Bush's grand world-saving project;
- actually *encouraged* mass Third World immigration—the greatest social-engineering experiment in our history;
- cling to an improbable notion of national exceptionalism as a charm against unwelcome change;
- helped, or did little to hinder, policies of spending and debt that have brought our economy to its knees.

These errors and follies have all been rooted in a misguided optimism. As a consequence of them, we are doomed. We have yielded too much ground to our enemies. Notwithstanding some happy talk (oh, dear) in conservative magazines and blogs, there is no prospect of any real revival of conservatism in the foreseeable future.

I fully expect to pass the rest of my life as an American without ever seeing any major conservative legislation passed by Congress, or any major executive action drawn from conservative principles, or any Supreme Court ruling that will do more than slow the advance of state power by a percentage point or two.

That's to speak of my own lifetime. My children's? Hmm . . . let me work my way around to that.

ENDING ON A CHEERFUL NOTE

How best to end a screed of gloom? The traditional answer has been to do so on an upbeat note. Dr. Johnson, who was an Anglican Christian, actually concluded his magnificent poem, the one from which I took this chapter's first epigraph, by recommending a fatalism that is well-nigh Islamic in its resignation.

> *Still raise for Good the supplicating Voice,*
> *But leave to Heav'n the Measure and the Choice.*
> . . . .
> *Implore [God's] Aid, in his Decisions rest,*
> *Secure whate'er he gives, he gives the best.*

. . . .
Pour forth thy Fervours for a healthful Mind,
Obedient Passions, and a Will resign'd. . . .

Insha'Allah. To be fair to the great moralist, Johnson was a natural depressive, plagued by fears of madness, suicide, and—depending on his precise mood—either hell or blank annihilation. At the time he wrote "The Vanity of Human Wishes" he was struggling with his monumental *Dictionary of the English Language* while trying to support a high-maintenance wife who had gone sexually cold on him and was sinking into hypochondria and alcoholism. It's not surprising that Johnson is one of the great luminaries of the pessimistic persuasion—a gloominary, in fact. (Thanks to my *National Review* ex-colleague Sarah Bramwell for this word.)

Furthermore, Johnson's poem closely follows a model set by Juvenal, one of the ancient Roman authors. Juvenal, writing around A.D. 100, winds up *his* long satirical poem by telling his reader to pray to the pagan Roman gods for

A soul, that can securely death defy,
And count it nature's privilege, to die;
Serene and manly, harden'd to sustain
The load of life, and exercis'd in pain:
Guiltless of hate, and proof against desire . . .

That (it's from Dryden's translation) actually sounds to me more Buddhist than Islamic. Both authors, having described at length—Juvenal goes to 366 lines, Johnson to 368—the absence of anything much to hope for from human life, end on this rather fatalistic, but comparatively upbeat, religious note.

NOT BUYING IT

I find it unconvincing in both cases. Educated Romans were famously irreligious, as that quip of Gibbon's that I quoted in

Chapter 8 illustrates. I wonder how much Juvenal, certainly an educated man, really believed in the rather cheesy Roman pantheon
(which included, at that point, at least four deceased emperors, their
personal foibles and vices perfectly well known to their fellow Romans). We can't actually say for sure, since we know next to nothing
about Juvenal the man; but we can make a reasonable surmise, knowing how the generality of educated imperial Romans thought.

Likewise with Johnson, whose habitual incredulity, according to
his friend Mrs. Thrale, "amounts almost to disease . . . he is a sad
mortal to carry a wonder to." It's hard to see a man of that temper-
ment swallowing revealed religion without mighty misgivings and severe psychic stress. (This opinion is shared by both Jackson Bate and
Jeffrey Meyers, Johnson's two best modern biographers.)

The biblical archetype here is the book of Ecclesiastes, which
takes the same line as Juvenal, who almost certainly did not know Ecclesiastes, and Johnson, who surely did. After twelve chapters of
"vanity, vanity, all is vanity," Ecclesiastes winds up with:

> Fear God, and keep his commandments: for this is the whole
> duty of man. For God shall bring every work into judgment,
> with every secret thing, whether it be good, or whether it
> be evil.

Which, like Johnson's and Juvenal's closings, is uplifting, at least
by comparison with what has gone before.

The impulse to end one's catalog of woe on an upbeat note of
faith has survived into modern times. Tom Wolfe's collection of essays *Hooking Up*, published in 2000, includes an update of his 1996
article on neuroscience, "Sorry, but Your Soul Just Died," which I
quoted at the end of Chapter 7. After twenty pages given over to
the glum news in his title, Wolfe raises for Good the supplicating
Voice:

> I suddenly had a picture of the entire astonishing edifice [of
> modern science] collapsing and modern man plunging head-
> long back into the primordial ooze. He's floundering, sloshing

about, gulping for air, frantically treading ooze, when he feels something huge and smooth swim beneath him and boost him up, like some almighty dolphin. He can't see it, but he's much impressed. He names it God.

Of the four specimens of concluding uplift I have so far quoted, I find Wolfe's the least convincing of all. At least Johnson, Juvenal, and the unknown author of Ecclesiastes didn't have to cope with cognitive science or evolutionary biology.

I very much want to offer you at least one dim ray of light at the end of this long dark tunnel, reader. I'll do my best to supply the traditional closing note of uplift. I'm a conservative: I *like* tradition. If I don't leave you altogether convinced, though, I think I can at least point to some fine literary precedents for that.

TODAY'S JEREMIAHS

Other modern conservative gloominaries, while eschewing frankly religious appeals, also try to close out their messages with something constructive. The ever-reliable Pat Buchanan, in his splendid 2006 jeremiad *State of Emergency*, assures us: "By 2050, America will have become . . . a Balkanized Brazil of 420 million, a Tower of Babel, a replica of the Roman Empire after the Goths and Vandals had passed over." Good grief! He nonetheless goes on to put forth some suggestions to save the situation: better border security, an immigration time-out, ending dual citizenship, and so on.

Pat followed up in 2007 with *Day of Reckoning*: "The American century is over . . . the worst foreign policy disaster of our lifetimes [that would be the Iraq war] . . . We may be looking at what Hobbes called *bellum omnium contra omnes*—the war of all against all." Great stuff! Yet again, at the end come suggested solutions: economic patriotism, an end to the Crusades, putting America first.

Similarly with Mark Steyn's 2006 book *America Alone*. Europe, says Steyn, is a goner, ripe for Islamicization, but the sight of Paris and Rome going up in flames will bring us to our senses in time:

"The advantage for the United States . . . is that Europe is ahead in the line, and its fate may wake up even the most blinkered on this side of the Atlantic." (Can't a blinkered person already be awake, just . . . blinkered? Never mind. Sorry, Mark.) *America Alone* also offers a ten-point program for helping the Islamic world reform itself. Hope! Change!

Further back, here's James Bovard in *Freedom in Chains* (1999): "People must summon the will and resolution to drive politicians out of their own lives . . . If contemporary Americans can cease idolizing the State, a rebirth of the spirit of freedom will begin."

How'd that work out? Let's see: United States Federal State and Local Government Spending for 1999 was $3,053.5 billion on a GDP of $9,201.1 billion—33.2 percent. For 2009 the numbers were $6,090.85 billion on a GDP of $14,258.2 billion—that was 42.7 percent. Early signs for 2010 are that we should easily break 44 percent this year, and European levels in the high 40s to low 50s are visible on the horizon. Oh, well.

Frankly, even the dubiously sincere Ecclesiastes-Juvenal-Johnson-Wolfe Judeo-Pagan-Christian-Islamo-Buddhist-novelist calls to resignation and lustlessness look more realistic to me. Are we in a terminal bind here? Isn't there some way we can Emerson our way out of it? Or must helpless Man, in Ignorance sedate, swim darkling down the Current of his Fate?

Speaking of Buddha:

> *When times are good you don't burn incense;*
> *When times are hard, you hug Buddha's foot.*
>   —CHINESE PROVERBIAL

Certainly we should prepare ourselves for a good long spell of Buddha-foot-hugging. There is, though, as I began this book by saying, a distinction to be made between looking out at the world with calm despair, and finding some inner contentment—even hope, for oneself, one's friends, and one's offspring.

That is a proper, bracing pessimism. How can I direct you to it? With literature. First, meet my heroine.

ANOTHER HAPPY DAY

There are two performance productions with the name *Happy Days*. (And one memoir: conservative pessimist H. L. Mencken's, of his childhood.) One of those performances is a stage play, first produced in 1961, by the Francophile Protestant-Irish playwright Samuel Beckett. The other is a TV sitcom that aired on ABC from 1974 to 1984. Let us compare and contrast.

The principal character in Beckett's play is Winnie: "About fifty, well preserved, blond for preference, plump, arms and shoulders bare, low bodice, big bosom, pearl necklet." In the first of the play's two acts, Winnie is buried up to her waist in a mound of earth. In the second act she is buried up to her *neck*. In both acts a man, Willie, is reclining on the mound behind her, only the back of his head visible to the audience.

Notwithstanding the limits on her freedom imposed by the earth-piles she's embedded in, Winnie remains bright and cheerful. The first act of Beckett's *Happy Days* consists of long monologues about nothing much, delivered by Winnie as she fusses with a parasol and a capacious black shopping bag. Willie interrupts with a few very brief responses. To give you the flavor, here is a sample *in medias res* of Act I. Winnie is three-quarters of the way through a monologue.

> . . . [*Pause. Smile appears, broadens and seems about to culminate in laugh when suddenly replaced by expression of anxiety.*] My hair! [*Pause.*] Did I brush and comb my hair? [*Pause.*] I may have done. [*Pause.*] Normally I do. [*Pause.*] There is so little one *can* do. [*Pause.*] One does it all. [*Pause.*] All one can. [*Pause.*] 'Tis only human. [*Pause.*] Human nature.

Winnie rambles on in this style for several minutes, pausing to rummage in her bag for brush and comb. At last she gives up on fixing her hair.

> Oh well, what does it matter, that is what I always say, I shall simply brush and comb them later on, purely and simply, I

have the whole—[*Pause. Puzzled.*] Them? [*Pause.*] Or it?
[*Pause.*] *Brush and comb it?* [*Pause.*] Sounds improper somehow.

She consults Willie, sitting there silent and still behind the
mound, as to the proper pronoun to use of one's hair. After a long
pause, Willie replies: "It." This monosyllable fills Winnie with joy.

Oh you are going to talk to me today, this is going to be a
happy day! . . . Another happy day.

Human nature, indeed. The second act is almost entirely a monologue by Winnie—now buried up to her *neck* in the earth-pile, remember. Poor Willie has only a single syllable to say in the entire
act. He comes back out from behind the mound, crawling on all
fours, and tries to climb up toward Winnie, but collapses from the
effort.

WILLIE: [*just audible*] Win.
[*Pause. Winnie's eyes front. Happy expression appears, grows.*]

WINNIE: Win! [*Pause.*] Oh this *is* a happy day, this will have
been another happy day! [*Pause.*] After all. [*Pause.*] So far . . .

It sounds like dull stuff, but if well performed, Beckett's *Happy
Days* is a very gripping theatrical experience. Winnie's dogged cheeriness, tinged with anxiety ("So far . . .") as the earth-mound envelops
her, speaks to something in everyone, even though she says nothing
of any substance. Willie's cryptic, even more pointless remarks, and
his failed effort at the end to approach what is left of Winnie, have
peculiar power.

Good cheer in the gathering gloom. Said the playwright himself,
when asked by the *New York Times:* "I'm working with impotence, ignorance . . . My little exploration is the whole zone of being that has
always been set aside by artists as something unusable—as something
by definition incompatible with art."

I'll confess I've never seen a full episode of the TV sitcom *Happy Days*, but judging from recollections of snippets seen in bars, or while passing through living rooms, and from YouTube clips, it's clear that the sitcom *Happy Days* is to the play *Happy Days* as antimatter is to matter. If staged in the same place, they would mutually annihilate in a blaze of gamma rays.

Of the two versions of *Happy Days* on offer here, the one in which the neighborhood dropout slowly morphs into a bourgeois gentleman is Wrong but Wromantic, while the one in which the cheerily chattering heroine disappears slowly beneath a growing pile of dirt, is Right but Repulsive.

I therefore recommend a close study of Beckett's *Happy Days* to the trainee pessimist. Any of Beckett's other works will do almost as well. You might try *Krapp's Last Tape*, in which Krapp, a shabby man of sixty-nine, listens to a tape he made thirty years before, when he was thirty-nine. The taped voice of Krapp-39 mentions that he has been listening to a tape from ten or twelve years earlier, say Krapp-28. Krapp-39 mocks Krapp-28, and Krapp-69, listening, joins in the mockery. Then Krapp-69 mocks Krapp-39 before delivering some random comments on his own withered existence.

> Sat shivering in the park, drowned in dreams and burning to be gone.

It's a great play for putting things into perspective. (John Hurt does a terrific Krapp in the Blue Angels Films production, which is available on DVD.)

Winnie is your real model, though. "One does it all . . . All one can . . . 'Tis only human . . . Human nature . . ." With low to zero expectations, we soldier on, as the earth-pile rises. 'Tis only human. And who knows? By shedding utopian illusions and squarely facing the truth we may yet preserve the legacy of those great eighteenth-century progenitors of ours, who understood that all men have their price; that in politics every man must be supposed a knave; and that the greatest part of men are gross.

THE LUCKIEST GENERATION

Looking back on life in these past few decades, and peering forward, as best one can, into the next few, it seems to me that I have been living in a golden age that will soon end. Born one-quarter of the way from VE Day to VJ Day, and in a robust nation under stable, consensual government, I missed all the greatest horrors of the twentieth century. Unless cursed with an extraordinarily long lifespan, I shall miss the horrors of the twenty-first, too. If the WW2 generation was the greatest, mine has surely been the luckiest.

If I compare my own life with the lives of my parents, and with the prospects for my children, I am struck by my immense good fortune in having been born when and where I was. My parents lived for years in cities over which, every night, armadas of planes flew, dropping bombs. My kids will live in cities under ever-present threat from rogue nukes and bioterror. I have lived my life in cities where the worst hazards I confronted were potholes and tardy restaurant service. Lucky! Lucky!

I was actually born around breakfast time on a Sunday morning, at a nursing home behind Saint Matthew's Church in the small English country town of Northampton. (Annual venue for the nation's biggest ram fair. Really.) With VE Day just four weeks in the past, the church bells were ringing, a thing that had then only recently been repermitted. During World War II, church bells were to signal that the Germans had invaded mainland Britain, and the ringing of them was forbidden for other purposes.

The town's Boy Scout troop was marching up the Kettering Road from Town Centre to the church, with their band a-playing. (This is my father's account of the event.) It was some welcome into the material universe, though my own recollection of it is naturally indistinct.

Subsequent events justified the festive appurtenances. I have gotten through pretty much my entire life without ever having to work very hard, without ever having seen my country invaded, without enduring war or depression, without suffering any horrid illness, without ever going hungry or wanting for anything. What luck! When, as the poet Philip Larkin told us, "Sexual intercourse began / In nineteen sixty-three," I was fit and ready. I bought my first house at age twenty-four and paid for it easily with an undemanding job that occupied me literally and exactly from nine to five, with an hour for lunch, five days a week. (I am not making this up.) Lucky! Lucky! Lucky!

I can't believe my kids—currently sixteen and fourteen—will have that kind of luck. What I hear from friends and neighbors is, you can't get them out of the house. They might go away to college, but they'll come back, likely weighed down with student loan debt, and resume occupancy of their old rooms. There will be no nine-to-five jobs for them to go to after graduation, quite possibly no jobs at all other than in government make-work, which by that time will occupy a Soviet-sized slice of the U.S. economy.

The demographic cratering of the Ice People civilizations will surround them with peevish oldsters and load them down with financial obligations. Their religion will have melted away into a vague welfarized spirituality, though elsewhere different religions may still inspire murder on the grand scale. Even the metaphysical underpinnings of our civilization—volition, responsibility, judgment, reason itself—will have been humbled and shrunk by the neuroscientists.

Nuclear weapons, throughout my lifetime kept safe under guard in just a handful of reasonably well-ordered and rational nations, will be bartered for cash in Third World bazaars and smuggled into American cities ready for the day of judgment. (Perhaps they already have been.) Clever new viruses will mutate, escape from labs, or be released. Britain's Astronomer Royal Sir Martin Rees, in his 2003 book *Our Final Hour*, tells us that

> I staked one thousand dollars on a bet: "That by the year 2020 an instance of bioerror or bioterror will have killed a million people." Of course, I fervently hope to lose this bet. But I honestly do not expect to.

To my kids I should like to say: I am sorry to have brought you into this mess. There were no bells ringing, no bands playing, at either of your births, and it would have been a travesty if there had been. Even the best, most moral, most just, and wisest of us—people like your dad, I mean—live in part by brute biological instinct, and there is no instinct stronger than the one that prompts us to continue the species. So here you are.

It's not all bad, though. Study Samuel Beckett's Winnie. Read the poets—the sturdy, stoic ones like Sam Johnson, Matthew Arnold, and Rudyard Kipling, not the pampered victimological whiners of the Eng. Lit. departments and M.F.A. courses. Brace yourselves to ride out misfortunes, and find happiness in small pastimes and the company of friends. Let your souls be serene and manly, harden'd to sustain / The load of life, and exercis'd in pain.

We are a rugged species, up for anything the universe can throw at us; and as the great gloominaries knew, we will be immeasurably better prepared for nasty surprises if we approach the universe realistically—pessimistically—than if we continue to peer out at our surroundings through a distorting, rose-colored prism of wish-fulfillment fantasy.

And as bad as our situation may look, there are mysterious slow tides moving beneath the surface: things generating their opposites, thesis becoming antithesis. If I stare hard enough at the corpse of American conservatism, I sometimes fancy I see a slight twitch or a passing flush of color. Just my imagination? Who knows?

Uplift-wise, this is the best I can do. It is at least, I believe, up to the standard of great pessimists past.

Oh, I see the conductor has mounted his podium. He is looking at me expectantly, baton poised. Yes, Maestro, I'm through.

L'ENVOI

We're all through. We are doomed. Yet with the right attitude, facing reality without flinching, aware of our fundamental imperfection—the attitude I have tried to express in this book—we can still transmit something of value into the future, while seeking for private contentment in the present as the earth-pile rises. The next few decades look bad, but in there somewhere, for each of us, will be a happy day, another happy day, and then another.

Play us out now, Maestro. That Noël Coward song, please, the one I like. Good night, patient reader, good night.

> *There are bad times just around the corner,*
> *There are dark clouds hurtling through the sky.*
> *And it's no use whining*
> *About a silver lining*
> *For we* know *from experience that they won't roll by.*
> *With a scowl and a frown*
> *We'll keep our spirits down*
> *And prepare for depression and doom and dread.*
> *We're going to unpack our troubles from our old kit bag*
> *And wait until we drop down dead.*

ACKNOWLEDGMENTS

My thanks to Jack Langer for suggesting this book in the first place; then to my agents Glen and Lynn for their support and encouragement; then to Jed Donahue and Julian Pavia, my editors at Crown, for innumerable thoughtful, perceptive criticisms and improvements.

It would be delinquent of me not to acknowledge one further debt. In writing this book, I have borrowed pretty freely from the online writings of my friend Steve Sailer. As well as some ideas, my borrowings include entire phrases—Steve is a master of the memorable phrase. "Invade the world, invite the world, in hock to the world" is one of his coinages. I took "Yale or jail" from Steve, thinking it was his, but he tells me he got it from education reformer John Gardner. I am sure there are other Sailerisms in my text. I have used some of Steve's data, too. He is a great quantitative journalist: I once heard him describe himself as "the only Republican that knows how to use Microsoft Excel" (which may very well be true). In a sane republic, Steve would have some highly paid position advising the government, or a professorship in social science at some prestigious university. In the nation we actually live in, Steve can only be a guerrilla intellectual, emerging from the *maquis* now and then to take a few sniping shots at what George Orwell—Steve's greatest hero, and mine—called "the smelly little orthodoxies which are now contending for our souls."